AA BRITAIN'S BEST

cyc rides 2

46 easy cycle rides in Britain

Produced by AA Publishing

Consultant Editor: David Hancock

Contributors: Jean Atkin, Chris Beeching, David Boys, Brian Curtis,
Steve Day, Stuart Edinborough, Philip Ennis, John Fenna, David
Hancock, Ron Healey, David Hearn, Penny and Bill Howe, Les
Lumsdon, Alan Menzies, Richard Nicholl, Mike Power, Ian Robinson,
Sheila Simpson, Maurice Truby, John Whitehouse

ISBN 0 7495 1761 1

Published by AA Publishing (a trading name of Automobile
Association Developments Limited, whose registered office is Norfolk
House, Priestley Road, Basingstoke, Hampshire RG24 9NY; registered
number 1878835).

The contents of this book are believed correct at the time of printing.
Nevertheless, the publishers cannot be held responsible for any errors
or omissions or for changes in the details given in this book or for the
consequences of any reliance on the information provided by the
same. We have tried to ensure accuracy in this book, but things do
change and we would be grateful if readers would advise us of any
inaccuracies they may encounter.

Colour separation by BTB Colour Reproduction Ltd,
Whitchurch, Hampshire
Bookblock printed in Graficromo, Cordoba, Spain
Bound by Graficromo.

Essential Information for Cyclists

THESE routes have been carefully researched, but despite our best efforts to ensure accuracy, changes may occur at any stage during the lifetime of the book. Please remember that roads are subject to reclassification, resulting in road numbers changing, and that construction of new bypasses may alter road junctions, signposting and traffic priorities. Off-road cycling conditions vary with the changing seasons: routes may become muddy in winter, or overgrown in summer.

All the rides have been devised to incorporate relatively traffic-free country lanes, designated cyclepaths, or good surfaced bridleways and by-ways. Inevitably, main roads have to be crossed or ridden for short stretches, so rules of the road must be observed, including the Highway Code. Ride in single file on narrow or busy roads, keep at least 3ft/m away from other cyclists in wet weather, and take extra care on fast descents. Beware of loose gravel, and look and listen for fast traffic, especially on narrow lanes with blind bends. Always indicate your intentions clearly, and try to anticipate the behaviour of other road users.

Cycling off-road has its own code of conduct. You have no right to cycle on public footpaths, the only 'rights of way' open to cyclists being bridleways and unsurfaced by-ways, but you may meet other vehicles with access on by-ways. Look out for the waymarking arrows: yellow for footpaths, blue for bridleways, red for by-ways. Please give way to both walkers and horseriders, giving adequate warning of your approach. To avoid erosion, keep to the trail.

To guarantee extra safety when cycling, you should equip yourself and your bike adequately. Make sure your bike is in good working order, check your brakes, tyres and wheels and carry any luggage in panniers so that the bike is well balanced. Be seen: wear high visibility clothing and reflective strips, and carry lights at night. It is advisable to wear a safety helmet. Take sufficient food, water, extra clothing (especially a waterproof jacket), and carry essential spares and tools.

The rides, mostly circular trips, have been selected to take you through attractive and varied areas of Britain and Ireland, and to be enjoyable both for experienced and novice cycling families. The approximate distance is always stated. The detailed information box for each route indicates the difficulty of the ride, from 1 (easy) to 3 (challenging). If a route includes steep hills or demanding track cycling, we have highlighted this. Refreshment facilities are listed, but mention in this book does not imply AA inspection or recognition, although establishments may have an AA classification.

The National Grid reference for the start of each ride is given. These numbers relate to the grid squares on the larger scale Ordnance Survey maps (1:50,000), which cyclists may like to use in addition to the maps in this book. If you have to cut the ride short, or decide to make a detour, you will need such a map.

Remember the Country Code; in particular, please close gates behind you and do not discard litter. Guard against all risk of fire.

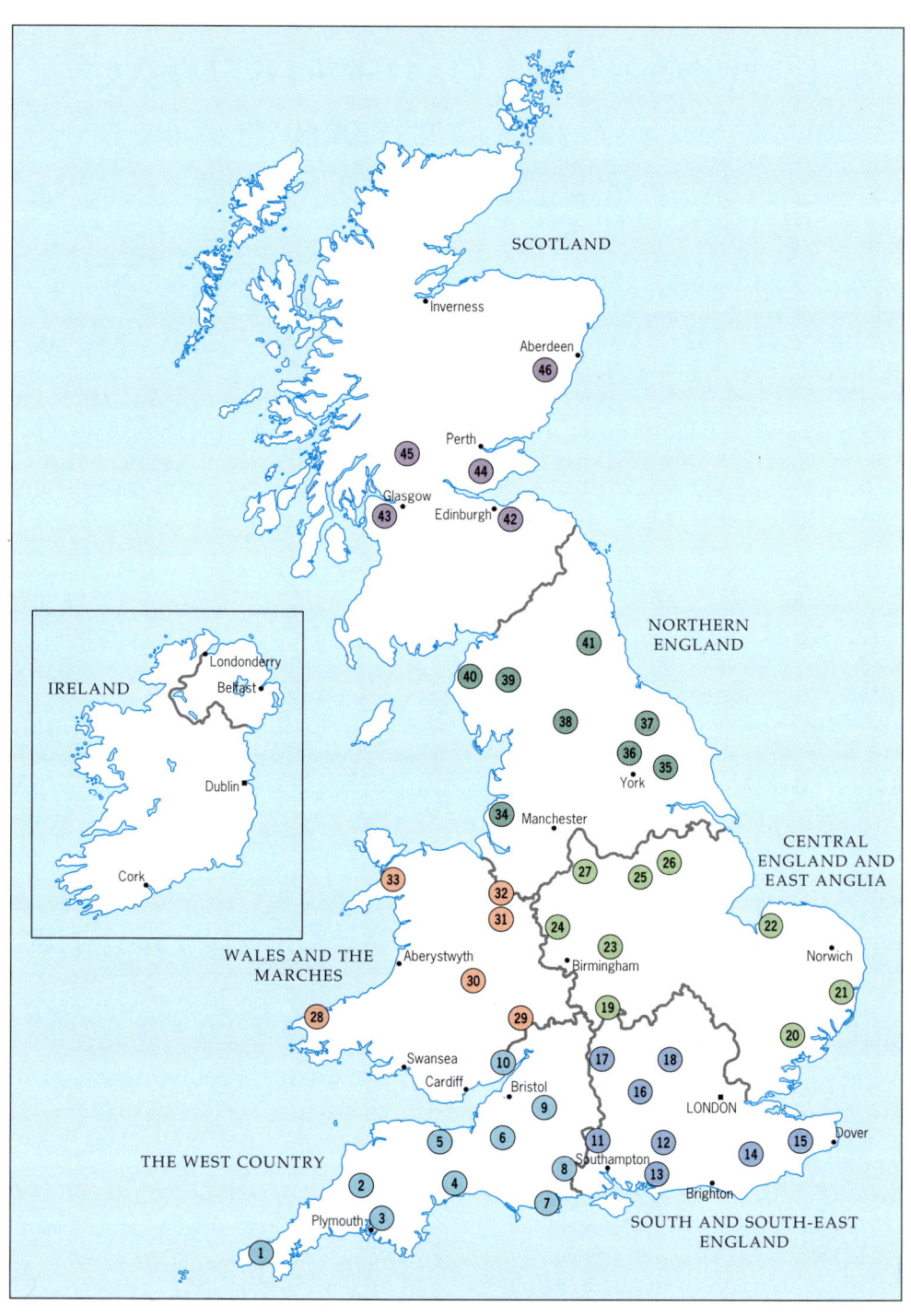

The Rides

The West Country

South and South-east England

Central England and East Anglia

Wales and the Marches

Northern England

Scotland

Introduction

Cycling for Fun

Cycling is a fun activity, a great way to travel and, as a regular form of exercise, it can be an important ingredient of healthy living. It is also an activity in which the whole family can participate.

Choosing a Bike

Walk into any large cycle shop and you will be confronted by a bewildering range of bikes. Most are suitable for local journeys, but if you intend to enjoy a day's ride or a cycling holiday on metalled roads, a touring bike with narrow wheels, drop-handlebars, and multi-gears will be a good choice.

Riders wanting to explore off-road will require a mountain bike designed for rugged terrain as well as for the 'urban jungle'. However, riding them for long distances on the road can be tiring. The lighter hybrid bike, equally at home in the city and most country tracks, is worth considering. Seek advice from your local cycle shop, and if possible, hire a bike before buying to check on its suitability.

Cycling with Children

There are a number of child seats available which fit on the front or rear of a bike and towable two-seat trailers are worth investigating. 'Trailer bicycles', suitable for five- to ten-year-olds, are attached to the rear of the adult's bike, so that an adult has control allowing the children to pedal if they wish. Safety is paramount, and helmets now tend to be the norm rather than the exception.

Cycling can be an enjoyable pastime for all the family

Transporting Bikes

If you are not cycling from home, the most convenient way to transport your bike to the start point is by car on roof-rack cycle carriers or racks that attach to the rear of a vehicle. When fixing be careful not to obscure rear lights, indicators or the number plate on your car. Buy a light board and extra number plate if you intend carrying several bikes on the back of the car.

If you plan to travel to the start by rail check that you can take your bike on the train (especially when using more than one operating company), reserve a space if necessary and label your bike with your name and destination station.

Preparing your Bike

A basic routine includes checking the wheels for broken spokes or excess play in the bearings, and the tyres for punctures, undue wear and the correct tyre pressures. Ensure that the brake blocks are firmly in place and not worn, and that cables are not frayed or

Many trains, especially the newer rolling stock without a separate guard's van, have limited space for cycles

too slack. Lubricate hubs, pedals, gear mechanisms and cables. Make sure you have a pump, a bell, a rear rack to carry panniers and, if venturing off-road, attach mudguards. A set of lights will also be necessary when cycling at night.

Preparing Yourself

Equipping yourself with cycling clothing need not be an expensive exercise. Brightly coloured lycra is popular, but any practical and comfortable casual clothing will do. Jeans or tight trousers can be restrictive and seams may chafe; baggy tracksuit bottoms may become caught in the chain, so ideally wear cycling leggings or tracksuit bottoms made from a stretch material. Fingerless gloves will add to your comfort.

In the summer, wear chamois padded cycling shorts or wear padded underwear under conventional shorts or leggings. For

Pack a basic tool kit: tyre levers, puncture repair kit, a set of Allen keys, an adjustable spanner, and a small screwdriver. Wrap the tools in a rag, which can be used for wiping oily hands. If you can, take a spare inner tube (easier than fixing a puncture), a universal brake/gear cable, and nuts and bolts. Make sure you have a pump and a strong lock with you.

winter cycling, a thermal top, and a windproof and waterproof jacket will keep you dry and warm. Cycling helmets, although not yet required by law, are a wise precaution. Be conspicuous so that other road users can see you clearly; wear light clothing and reflective strips or sashes, especially at night.

Planning a Day's Ride

Take time to plan your day's cycling, to ensure an enjoyable day out for the family. Calculate how long it will take you to reach the start point, including any travelling time. Give some thought to the terrain to be covered; hilly landscapes and off road-sections will slow your progress. Plan for stops along your route, for lunch and to visit places of interest such as historic houses or a picturesque village, and allow for unforeseen stops.

What to Take with You

Pack all you need into waterproof panniers, which will fit either front or rear carrier racks. A handlebar bag is useful for carrying maps and snacks, or fix a map holder on the handlebars.

Take some food, ideally high-energy snacks, such as dried fruit and nuts, cereal bars and fresh fruit and keep your water bottle topped-up during your ride. A first-aid kit, a route card, relevant Ordnance Survey map, and change for telephone calls in case of an emergency will complete your preparations.

One of the joys of cycling is the wonderful scenery

Dedicated Cycle Routes:
The Way Forward

Cycle in almost any country of western Europe and you will find segregated routes built for bicycles, both in towns and the countryside. They may not be part of a nationally planned network, but local and regional initiatives have created facilities for cyclists that leave users visiting from Britain deeply envious; they also beg the question why similarly generous provision for such an environmentally friendly and healthy form of transport has not been made in this country, except in a few enlightened cities like York and Nottingham.

This situation is changing rapidly, however, and many organisations, often in association with local councils, are working towards propelling cycling to the forefront of public awareness. A great many dedicated cycle paths and long-distance trails are being developed all over the country to cater for the increasing number of cyclists.

Since 1979 over 350 miles (563km) of paths have been built, many using disused railway lines or canal paths. They are of benefit to walkers as well as cyclists, and some, like the Cuckoo Trail in Sussex, have been provided with a surface suitable for horse-riders running alongside the cycle route. For any keen cyclist, concern about safety on car-dominated roads is a major deterrent and, if cycling is to make a worthwhile impact on alleviating part of Britain's transport problems,the growing network of routes is particularly welcome. The latent demand is tremendous – there are more bicycles than cars in Britain, but many lie unused for lack of routes on which cyclists of all ages can feel safe from traffic.

The proliferation of cycling clubs in recent years has given a boost to the overall campaign for increased cycle routes. Joining a local group is fun: these varied groups may encompass all forms of cycling and cater for a diversity of enthusiasts' interests, but all help to raise the profile of the bicycle not just as a leisure tool, but as a viable mode of transport in its own right. These organisations also place great importance on the social and environmental impacts of the bicycle and on technical developments, and indeed Britain is at the forefront of design innovations, as shown by the successes of champion racer Chris Boardman.

Cycling is one of the 'greenest' forms of transport and, in this age of increasing environmental awareness, many organisations strongly believe that cycling

Picnic facilities along the Tissington Trail

can play a major role in reducing traffic pollution and congestion. This faith is borne out not only by the experience of cities like Freiburg and Groningen, where over 30 per cent of all journeys are now by bicycle, but by the success of the new routes opening all over Britain. The first was built between Bristol and Bath, and its success has been enormous – over a million journeys a year are now made on the path. Another popular route, the Plym Valley Cycle Way, following the old Great Western Railway and including original viaducts, bridges and tunnels, was a joint venture between Devon County Council and Sustrans, a charity which has pioneered the development of traffic-free routes for cyclists and pedestrians.

Linking the Routes

In 1995 an exciting new proposal to create a 6,500-mile (10,459km) National Cycle Network (NCN) was accepted by the Millennium Commission – the very first national project chosen to mark the millennium. The network will be built in partnership with local authorities, and the target is to have 2,000 miles (3,218km) open

Fremington Quay on the Tarka Trail in Devon

by the millennium with the rest completed by the year 2005. With additions continually being made at the request of local authorities, the final length could be more than 6,500 miles (10,459km). Whatever its eventual length, the National Cycle Network's purpose is to act as an incitement to cycling; greater numbers of cyclists will in turn encourage the provision of more facilities. As part of this objective, the NCN is deliberately routed through many towns and cities, enabling it to pass within two miles (3km) of over 20 million people. This will not only encourage people to cycle to work, to school and to the shops, but will also enable those living around the centres to cycle out into the pleasure of the countryside. Equally, wherever practicable, paths are being routed to pass close to railway stations to encourage the natural synergy between train and bicycle so successfully exploited by other western European countries.

The network will be a series of continuous routes made up of railway, canal, river and special paths, wide promenades and footpaths, forest roads and tracks, town roads that are either traffic-calmed or provided with segregated cycle lanes, and minor country roads. As more and more people rediscover

the pleasures of cycling and its beneficial effects on health, the leisure use of dedicated cycle tracks is likely to account for a rising proportion of journeys and, indeed, some longer routes are already making a significant contribution to local tourist economies: at least 30,000 people are thought to have cycled the Sea to Sea route between Whitehaven/Workington and Sunderland/Newcastle in its first year, 1995. It has transformed the viability of many bed-and-breakfast establishments en route, prompting a University of Sunderland study of its financial impact on the local tourist industry.

Information panel on the Tissington Trail, Derbyshire

Enjoying the Countryside

As leisure cyclists, the very qualities that people look for and appreciate in the countryside – tranquillity, beautiful landscapes, clean air – are threatened by the noise, congestion and pollution generated by motor traffic on the roads.

The contribution that cycle routes can make to relieving pressure in scenic rural areas has been amply demonstrated by the Tissington and High Peak Trails. These were built along closed railway lines by the Peak District National Park in the early 1970s. On sunny summer days the number of cyclists and walkers using these two picturesque routes can be measured in four rather than three figures. People cycle from towns surrounding the National Park or can hire bikes at several points on the trails.

Users of certain routes will quickly notice some distinctive features which were not, perhaps, part of the original landscape – sculptures used to punctuate the paths and act as milestones, gateways, crafted seats, fountains and even lighting.

The value to wildlife of these green areas is always considered when paths are planned and built. Trees are planted where appropriate, and hedges maintained. Hawks and owls in particular find the long stretches useful in their hunt for field voles and other food.

Wildlife abounds along many of the cycle trails

Besides the many sponsored rides and other fund-raising events such as local 'bikeathons', another way of carrying the message around the country, and having a lot of fun in the process, is what looks set to become an annual event – a 'trail-blazing' ride. In 1995 over 800 riders participated either in a section or all of a 1,000-mile (1,609km) ride between Inverness and Dover along what will be the spine route of the NCN. The 1996 ride covers 760 miles (1,223km) between Belfast and Land's End via Dublin, Holyhead, Cardiff and Bristol. The event launches the Wales Green Route between Holyhead and Cardiff in the north and Chepstow in the south, forming the core of a 432-mile (695km) network that incorporates some segregated cycle routes such as the Taff Trail.

Cycling is the only form of transport in Britain with specific targets – doubling cycle use through the implementation of a national cycling strategy. Cycling causes no pollution, it is relatively cheap to provide dedicated space for it, and it is an excellent form of exercise. Cycling's profile is extremely high at the moment, with mountain-biking even making its debut in the Atlanta Olympic Games. But above all cycling is fun – especially when the threat of harm from other traffic is removed.

Useful Addresses

Cyclists Touring Club (CTC)
Cotterell House,
69 Meadrow,
Godalming,
Surrey GU7 3HS
Tel: 01483 417217
Largest cycling club in Britain, providing information and advice on touring, legal and technical matters.

London Cycling Campaign (LCC)/Cycle Campaign Network (CCN)
Tress House,
3 Stamford Street,
London SE1 9NT
Tel: 0171 928 7220
Pressure group that lobbies MPs, organises campaigns and petitions in order to improve cycling conditions in the capital. CCN provides information on local campaigning groups across the country.

Sustrans
35 King Street,
Bristol BS1 4DZ
Tel: 0117 927 7555
Leaflets and/or maps of Sustrans routes are available from the North East office:
Rockwood House, Barn Hill, Stanley, Co Durham DH9 8AN; tel: 01207 281259.

British Cycling Federation (BCF)/British Mountain Biking Federation (BMBF)
National Cycling Centre,
Stuart Street,
Manchester M11 4DQ
Tel: 0161 224 2244
Co-ordinates and promotes track, road and off-road cycle racing.

Audax UK
Ben Steven,
Coniston View,
Redhills Road,
Arnside,
Lancashire LA5 0AN
Organises events for cycle tourists. Series of rides across the country with set distances to be completed within certain time limits, without racing.

Tandem Club
C/o Cycle Touring Club,
Cotterell House,
69 Meadrow,
Godalming,
Surrey GU7 3HS
Tel: 01483 417217
Regional groups organising day rides throughout the year for tandemists. Various weekend and week-long events at home and abroad.

Ancient Monuments, Medieval Churches

This pleasant and varied route weaves its way through quiet Cornish countryside, passing medieval churches, a prehistoric hill fort and the ruins of an Iron-Age village. There are long level stretches with some moderate uphill sections and only one or two short steep sections. The ride is mainly on quiet country lanes, but has a main road start and two quite busy crossings en route.

RIDE 1
CORNWALL
SW475306

INFORMATION

Total Distance
19 miles (30km)

Grade
2

OS Map
Landranger 1:50,000 sheet 203
(Land's End, The Lizard & Isles of Scilly)

Tourist Information
Penzance, tel: 01736 62207

Cycle Shops/Hire
Blewett and Pender, Albert Street, Penzance, tel: 01736 64157
The Cycle Centre, Bread Street, Penzance, tel: 01736 51671
Geoff's Bikes, Victoria Place, Penzance, tel: 01736 63665

Nearest Railway Station
Penzance

Refreshments
There are pubs at Gulval, Crowlas, St Erth, Hayle Causeway, Cripplesease and Nancledra. They all serve food and welcome children.
Places to sample those famous Cornish cream teas include The Wink tea room at Cripplesease.
There are plenty of picnic spots on the right bank of the River Hayle at St Erth

Fields near the Minions, scene of many ancient monuments

START & ROUTE DIRECTIONS

Start

Penzance, on the A30, 24 miles (39km) south-west of Truro, is a lively market town and port facing Mount's Bay. Park at the large pay-and-display harbour car park near the railway station.

Directions

1️⃣ 🚲 Turn left out of the harbour car park then, after a few yards, left again into the one-way system and filter right on to the lane marked 'A30, Redruth'. (This first short section is unavoidably busy with traffic, so take care, especially with youngsters.) Follow the one-way system round to the right, filtering to the left-hand lane, to reach traffic lights. Continue along the A30 out of Penzance for about ¼ mile (0.5km) to a large roundabout. Take the

second exit, signed 'Heliport', then go immediately right, again signed 'Heliport'. In ¼ mile (0.5km) turn left into a quiet lane, signed 'Gulval', which is reached after ¼ mile (0.5km). The Coldstreamer Inn is up to the left. Turn right at Gulval and follow a narrow lane for 2 miles (3km). Turn right at a T-junction, signed 'Crowlas', and pass the Old Inn, soon to reach a junction with the A30. There are shops and the Star Inn down to the left.

2️⃣ 🚲 Taking care, cross the A30 then continue down the lane opposite for 1 mile (1.5km). Turn left, signed 'St Erth', and continue along a pleasant level lane for 3 miles (5km) to reach St Erth. (There are roadside toilets just before St. Erth Bridge.) Directly up the steep hill from the bridge is the Star Inn. From the far side of St Erth Bridge turn left,

signed 'Hayle', and in 1 mile (1.5km), passing a pitch and putt course, reach the B3301.

3️⃣ 🚲 Turn left, signed 'St Ives', and continue along a busy section of road known as Hayle Causeway. It is bounded by Lelant Saltings, the head of Hayle Estuary, on the right and by a wide footpath on the left. After 220 yards (200m) filter right with care and cross the right-hand carriageway on to a side road, signed 'Carbis Bay'. Pass the Old Quay House Inn and continue along the side road for 600 yards (550m) to reach a roundabout. Keep right, signed 'Holiday Route', then at the next roundabout take the first exit left, signed 'Holiday Route'. Pass the Watermill Restaurant on the right and continue steadily uphill (not steep) for 1 mile (1.5km). On a right-hand bend proceed left on to the

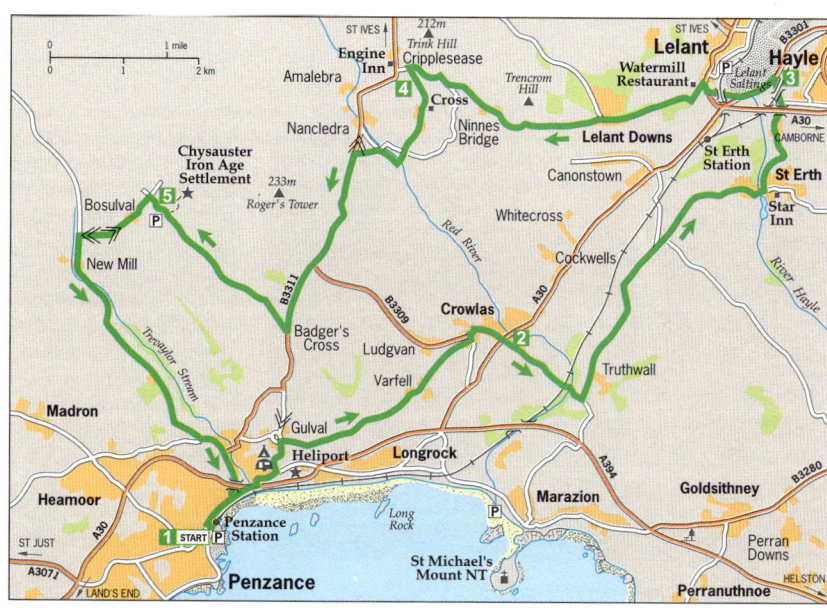

first of two side roads (not signposted). Climb steadily for ½ mile (1km) to reach the National Trust's Trencrom Hill car park, shielded by bushes on the right. Continue along a delightful lane for 1 mile (1.5 km). Pass a junction with a large grassy central triangle, to reach a second junction with a smaller grassy triangle. (The route goes left here, but a short distance straight ahead is a junction with the B3311. About 150 yards (123m) up to the right from this junction, at Cripplesease, is the Engine Inn and opposite the junction is The Wink tea room offering cream teas.)

4️⃣ 🚲 Continue down the narrow lane from the grassy triangle. Pass an old mine engine house on the left and a Cornish cross on the right. Continue straight across at a crossroads and make a steep descent, with care, through twisting bends. Soon, cross a bridge, turn right at a T-junction and continue for 380 yards (350m) to reach a junction with the B3311. Turn left here through a tight corner followed by a brief incline. Continue for 2 miles (8km). On the left there are outstanding views of Mount's Bay and St Michael's Mount. At Badger's Cross turn right, signed 'Chysauster', and continue along a level lane for 1½ miles (2.5km), still following signs to Chysauster. Reach the Chysauster car park (toilets). The ancient Chysauster Iron Age village is up to the right.

The remains of the Iron-Age settlement at Chysauster

5️⃣ 🚲 From Chysauster car park, continue along the lane for 1 mile (1.5km). Watch out for occasional vehicles on the bends. Climb a short steep section, then descend steeply to a T-junction. Turn left, signed 'Penzance'. Go through New Mill and continue for 2 miles (3km), with one short steep section, to reach another T-junction. Go left here, signed 'Penzance', and after 300 yards (270m) join the B3311, keeping right, signed 'Penzance'. In 500 yards (460m) reach a junction with the A30. Turn right here, with care, and soon return to Penzance station and the harbour car park.

PLACES OF INTEREST

Gulval: This charming, flower-filled village is clustered a round a 15th-century church, itself encircled by trees and exotic shrubs. Most of Gulval's fine houses and cottages are Victorian and built of excellent granite. The Coldstreamer Inn is reached up the lane to the left of the church.

St Erth: The River Hayle flows serenely through St Erth. The delightful church, which dates from the 14th century, has been restored over the centuries. A steep little lane leads up to the village centre and to the Star Inn.

The fine 14th-century church at St Erth and the River Hayle

Trencrom Hill: This prominent hill is 550ft (167m) high and has a flat top and vestiges of the embankments that once made it a major hill fort of the Iron Age. There are magnificent views from the top, which is reached on foot by a short but steep climb from a National Trust car park.

Chysauster Iron Age Village: This is an outstanding example of a courtyard house settlement dating from the pre-Roman Iron Age. Substantial foundations of several dwellings, made up of rooms surrounding a central courtyard, survive at this splendidly situated site which is open all year (entrance fee).

WHAT TO LOOK OUT FOR

West Cornwall's characteristic laneside 'hedges', which are stone walls smothered with vegetation, are a riot of colour in spring and summer. Primroses, celandines, wild garlic, pennywort, foxgloves along with polypody fern and mosses and lichens, are just some of the species. Buzzards and kestrels hover above the small inland valleys and, at Hayle Estuary, there are wading birds on the mudflats at low tide, or riding on the water at high tide. Lelant Saltings provides important feeding grounds for migratory and resident birds.

Launceston – A Cornish Farmyard Trail

Passing no fewer than 35 farmyards, this pastoral journey explores little-known agricultural thoroughfares in the lee of the one-time Cornish capital, Launceston – itself a fascinating town. En route you discover mischievous otters, the secrets of glass-blowing, a quaint working steam railway, space-age windmills and at least one picture-postcard village. With Bodmin and Dartmoor constantly in view, a short off-road stretch affords opportunities for likely wildlife sightings in the still forest.

Launceston Station on the Launceston Steam Railway

RIDE 2
CORNWALL
SX329848

INFORMATION

Total distance
29½ miles (47km), with 1mile (1.5km) off-road

Grade
2

OS Maps
Landranger 1:50,000 sheets 190 (Bude) and 201 (Plymouth & Launceston)

Tourist Information
Launceston, tel: 01566 772321

Cycle Shops/Hire
John Towl Cycles, Launceston, tel: 01566 774220

Nearest Railway Station
Plymouth (22miles/35km); Liskeard (12miles/19km). Note: no public transport from Liskeard

Refreshments
Pubs and cafes in Launceston. At Five Lanes the Kings Head welcomes children (open all day). Launceston Steam Railway and Tamar Otter Sanctuary both have comfortable tea rooms; village stores in Canworthy Water and Altarnun. Excellent pasties at the village shop beside the tractor garage in Canworthy Water. Village shops in Altarnun but do not depend on Sunday opening

START & ROUTE DIRECTIONS

Start

Launceston is bypassed off the main A30 trunk route into Cornwall between Okehampton and Bodmin. Ample public parking and amenities near the 13th-century castle make this a good starting point.

Directions

1 🚲 From the castle gate, drop right, downhill, following the A388 Holsworthy and Bude road (St Thomas Road). Continue over the traffic lights (turn right for Launceston Steam Railway) and up St Stephens Hill after the mini-roundabout. At the top of the hill turn left opposite the church, towards Tresmeer, Egloskerry and Canworthy Water. Admire the Bodmin skyline before branching right, signed 'Langore 0.75' after 1¼ miles (1.75km). Turn right at a junction 1½ miles (2.5km) after sleepy Langore, towards North Petherwin. Detour right at the main crossroads at North Petherwin for the Tamar Otter Sanctuary.

2 🚲 Back at the crossroads continue north towards Week St Mary to visit Tamar Glass studio, just past the church. A little further on, turn left on a flat scenic country road, signed 'Canworthy Water 3.75' and continue over three T-junctions following signs to Canworthy Water. The road then climbs gently through Fonston and Warbstow Cross; turn left at the tiny Bethel Methodist Chapel towards Scarsick. A quick descent through a little valley then ascends over a redundant railway bridge (pause to absorb the farmland views). A short climb brings you to a crossroads.

3 🚲 Turn right along the dirt road that becomes a grassy bridleway, climbing

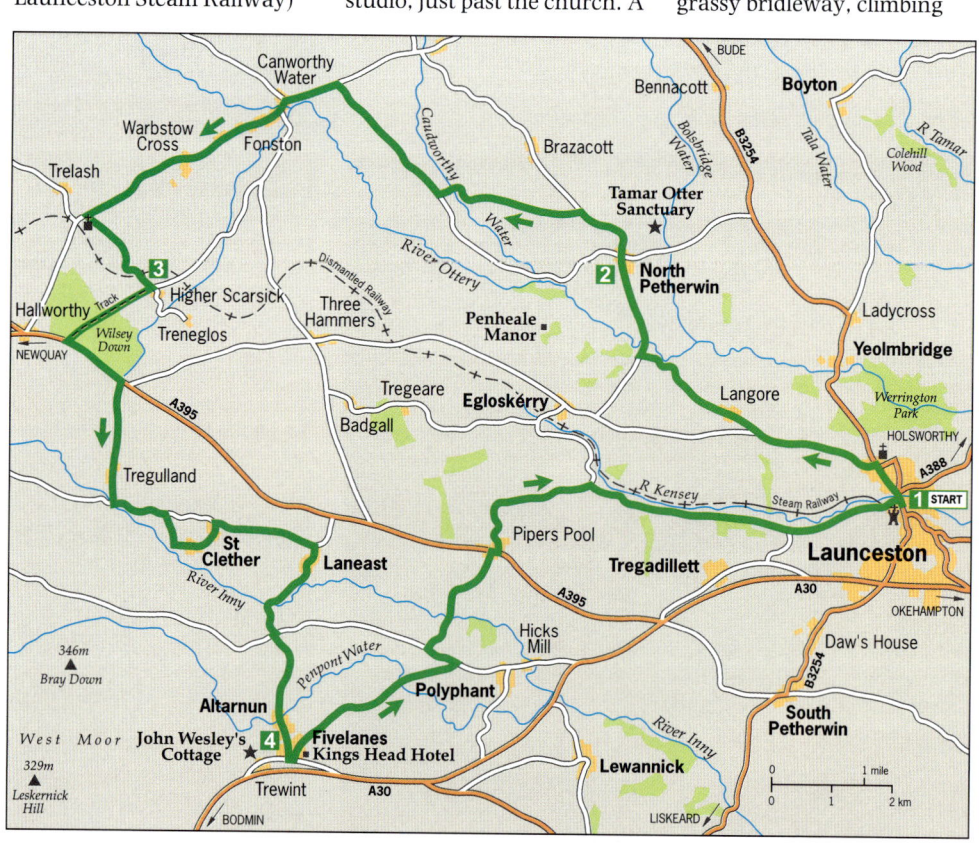

Just one of the inhabitants of the Tamar Otter Sanctuary

towards the pine forest. Cross the forest road continuing straight up the ill-defined grassy trail. It may be better to dismount for the incline and to avoid gorse punctures and uncleared branches on top of Wilsey Down. A silent approach may also be rewarded by fox and deer sightings. Do not deviate although the trail is almost indistinguishable across the timber-strewn plateau; cross a second forest road where a blue waymarker points down through the trees again, soon emerging into a lay-by on the A395 (beware of fast traffic on this road). Proceed left along the main road for ½ mile (1km) then right towards Tregulland. Coast downhill, taking in the nearby wind farm and, across to the right, Brown Willy, Bodmin Moor's

highest point. Turn left at the T-junction then shortly right, through St Clether. Go left at the next T-junction, climbing through the village before turning right to Laneast. A leafy descent precedes a good rest point at the River Inny before the short steep ascent to the T-junction. Turn right, signed 'Camelford', then immediately left to Tresibbett along a quiet road with excellent views of Dartmoor. Fork left at the junction then left again, signed 'Five Lanes', descending to beautifully kept Altarnun – the country of Daphne Du Maurier and Jamaica Inn.

4   Beyond the fork at Five Lanes detour right to John Wesley's cottage. At the

Kings Head Hotel follow signs to Polyphant, passing the primary school. Remain on this road for 2 miles (3km), over a staggered crossroads to a T-junction, signed 'Davidstow and Camelford'. Turn left then soon right, over two T-junctions, signed 'Pipers Pool', to reach the A395. Turn right then quickly left at Sunny Corner Cottage towards Egloskerry; ½ mile (1km) further, branch right (do not miss it) on a bend along a little-used back road, keeping right at the next junction. From here follow Launceston signs back along the Kensey valley. When in Launceston, turn right, back up the hill to the castle and the start point of the ride.

PLACES OF INTEREST

Launceston: Locally pronounced 'Lanson', the town has a trail that takes in the impressive English Heritage castle, once the seat of the Norman Earls of Cornwall. The only walled town in the county, Southgate Arch, the last of four gates, still survives. Narrow streets and Georgian houses enhance Launceston's character, among them Lawrence House (1753), leased from the National Trust as an award-winning local history museum. Lavish carvings on the Church of St Mary Magdalene are also noteworthy.

Launceston Steam Railway: This offers an opportunity to ride in open coaches behind narrow-gauge Victorian steam locomotives along the beautiful Kensey valley – once part of the pre-Beeching, Padstow to Waterloo line. There is also a museum, workshop tours, gift shop and buffet. Restricted service off peak; daily from Whitsun through summer.

Tamar Otter Sanctuary: This centre in North Petherwin is the only place in the West Country breeding British otters and reintroducing them into the wild. Other wildlife includes deer, waterfowl, wallabies and peacocks, and there is also a craft shop, cafe, picnic areas and woodland trail. Open daily, April to October, feeding times 12 noon and 3.30pm (recommended).

Altarnun: This is a very picturesque village with slate and granite cottages and a

Typical of the area is the pretty village of Altarnun

medieval packhorse bridge. The 15th-century church, dedicated to St Nonna (mother of St David, patron Saint of Wales), is sometimes referred to as the 'Cathedral of the Moors'. Of special interest are the 79 carved bench ends depicting local life and Christian symbols.

Wesley's Cottage, Trewint: Isbell cottage was used frequently by John Wesley when on his preaching tours throughout Cornwall. Now restored and open to the public daily, it contains many artefacts relating to Wesley and the Methodist Church.

WHAT TO LOOK OUT FOR

If you are quiet, you may glimpse foxes, deer and buzzards on forested Wilsey Down. Shortly after, technology dominates the landscape in the shape of one of Cornwall's three wind farms. In Altarnun, admire the medieval packhorse bridge and the 6th-century Celtic cross in the churchyard.

Plym Valley – Gateway to Dartmoor

In the space of a few easy miles, this scenic adventure transports you from the coastal estuary of a naval city, across viaducts of the old Great Western Railway, spanning beautiful wooded valleys, to the edge of rugged, stunning Dartmoor. Granite trails and sleepy Devon villages bring the rider to idyllic picnic spots on the banks of Burrator reservoir, and yet more Dartmoor secrets.

Saltram House, the setting for the film Sense and Sensibility

RIDE 3
DEVON
SX522568

INFORMATION

Total distance
28¾ miles (46km), with 13 miles (21km) off-road

Grade
3

OS Maps
Landranger 1:50,000 sheets 201 (Plymouth & Launceston) and 202 (Torbay & South Dartmoor)

Tourist Information
Plymouth, tel: 01752 266030

Cycle Shops/Hire
Saddles & Paddles, Exeter, tel: 01392 424241;
Breakthrough Mountain Sports, Plymouth,
tel: 01752 795419

Nearest Railway Station
Plymouth (2 miles/3km)

Refreshments
Families are welcome in the Burrator Inn, Dousland and the Skylark pub in Clearbrook has a special children's room, but the Royal Oak in Meavy does not allow children under 14. The Plym Valley Railway Cafe is open on Sundays only, but there are plenty of picnic spots along the route, especially at Burrator reservoir

START & ROUTE DIRECTIONS

Start

Follow signs to the Plym Valley Railway Co off the main A38 through Plymouth. Ample parking at the B&Q complex makes this the best starting point for the Plym Valley Cycle Way. Saltram House (NT) and grounds make an interesting 2 mile (3km) southern extension, following the edge of the scenic Plym estuary.

Directions

1️⃣ 🚲 From B&Q follow signs to the start of the trail between the Royal Marines base and the Plym Valley Railway Headquarters. After 1¼ miles (2km) of wooded cycling you reach Plym Bridge, site of the old station. About 300 yards (300m) further on, just before Plym Viaduct, access to Cann Wood offers 6 miles (9km) of off-road bike trails. Cann Quarry historic buildings are accessible below the first of three viaducts, all offering exceptional views. At Bickleigh a short signposted on-road section quickly rejoins the railway path which leads to a fourth viaduct offering distant views of Dartmoor. After the overhead aquaduct, enter Brunel's Shaugh Tunnel (the walls are painted white but a torch is recommended). The trail ends after a further mile (1.5km) with a switchbacked footpath, waymarked with red arrows, bringing you to Clearbrook, just a few metres from the Skylark pub. The Star Inn is down to the left.

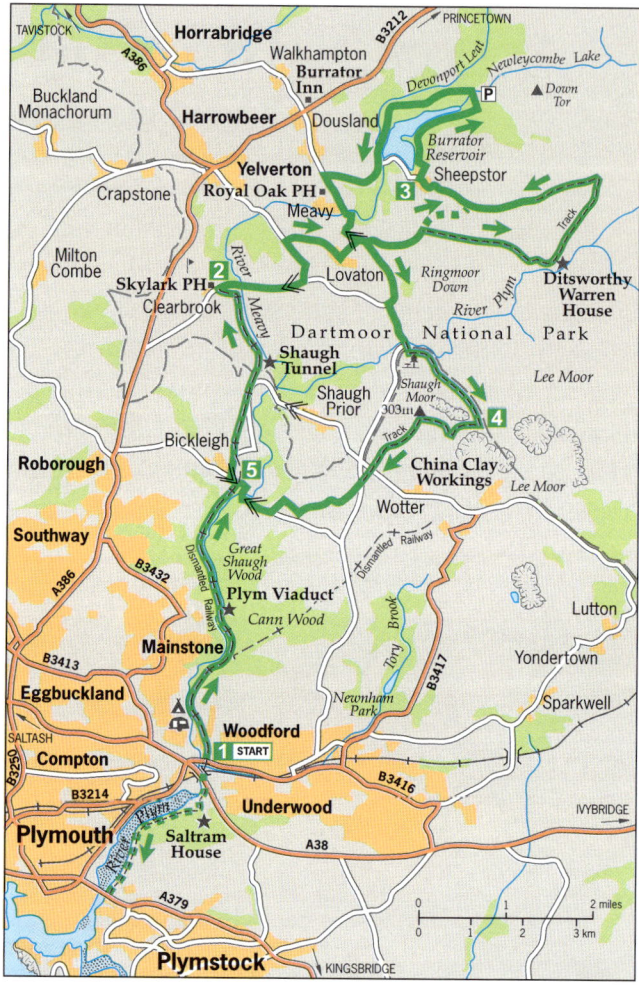

2️⃣ 🚲 Turn right, downhill, through pretty Hoo Meavy, forking right towards Cadover Bridge. At the top of the not unpleasant 875 yard (800m) climb, glance back at the view before heading north towards Meavy. Pass the farmhouse B&B on the left, turn right after ½ mile (1km) towards Lovaton and look left across farming country to the unmistakeable jagged outline of Pew Tor against the skyline. At the T-junction just beyond Lovaton, turn right uphill then immediately left following the Sheepstor sign; Burrator dam can be seen across the valley. After ½ mile (1km), just past the clump of trees and Ringmoor Cottage, go right off the higher road (after the fork), following a bridlepath to a signposted gate in the fence. Note: this slightly strenuous 5 mile (7km) off-road section can be omitted by a ½-mile (1km) detour which leads

Burrator reservoir can be seen in the distance above Sheepstor

straight to Nattor. Follow the wooden waymarker posts for 1½ miles (2.5km) across open Ringmoor Down, wildest Dartmoor, to a second horse gate. Once through, head down towards Ditsworthy Warren House below. After exploring, fork left behind the enclosure on an obvious track (down to the right is the fledgling River Plym). Continue up an ill-defined track to the left edge of the shallow valley passing the very tall standing stones which are off to the right. Over the rise, after about 1 mile (1.5km), take the broad sandy trail sharply back to the left, returning via a rocky descent of about 1¼ miles (2km), past the scout hut and ford. Rejoin the tarmac and turn right to Sheepstor, proceed for ½ mile (1km) following the stream.

3 🚲 Just beyond Sheepstor church, turn right on the perimeter road around Burrator reservoir. At the dam check the water level; bear straight on to the cattle grid ½ mile (1km) away, turning left, signed 'Meavy ¾', or

make a diversion right for ½ mile (1km) to the Burrator Inn. In Meavy keep straight on towards Cadover (turn right for the Royal Oak pub). Avoid the deep ford by using the bridge. A 1:6 hill returns you to Lynch Common junction – follow signs for 1¼ miles (2km) over two junctions to Cadover Bridge. Cross the bridge, turn immediately left up the no through road, climbing for 875 yards (800m) with Trowlesworthy Tors on your left, the quarry on the right.

4 🚲 At Blackaton Cross, turn right through the small car park and on to the bridleway that leads off between the two vast china clay quarries. Stay off the quarry roads. High pressure water extraction work may be visible below. After 300 yards (280m) cross a quarry road and head diagonally right up towards the Saddlesborough Hill triangulation point, which is just visible over the crest, where you will be rewarded with an amazing panorama from Plymouth Sound to Cornwall. Also look

for Brent Tor with its famous church on the top. Follow the descending path which leads directly towards Plymouth Sound, dropping to the right of Hawks Tor rocks to reach the road in ½ mile (1km). Cross the road, with more open ground for a short distance before emerging on tarmac at a cattle grid. Cross it then turn immediately right, continuing to the T-junction at the very end. The road drops right down the hill (beware of the bends and narrow bridge as the road snakes speedily past Bickleigh Cottage at the bottom).

5 🚲 Turn left and dismount for the steep ascent, which is known to the Commandos as 'Heartbreak Hill'! Near the top of the hill rejoin the Plym Valley Cycle Way, returning 3 miles (5km) to the start of the route.

St Michael of the Rock atop Brent Tor

The woodland trail of the Plym Valley Cycle Way

PLACES OF INTEREST

Plymouth: This town of legendary maritime heritage offers much for the visitor, including the picturesque waterfront Barbican and The Hoe, with its old lighthouse, Dome Visitor Centre and spectacular sea views. The City Museum and art galleries are also worth a look, and try a boat trip past the naval dockyard if there is time.

Plym Valley Cycle Way: This is an 8½-mile (13km) Devon County Council and Sustrans project and much of its popular wooded trail follows Brunel's South Devon & Tavistock Railway, built to serve mines and quarries in the area;

some relics are still visible along the gentle route.

Saltram House (NT): Said to be the most impressive house in Devon, this George II mansion, still with its original contents, was the setting for much of the recent Oscar-winning film *Sense and Sensibility*. In the grounds, look for the 19th-century folly, an amphitheatre built across a quarry face.

Ditsworthy Warren House: This abandoned moorland dwelling is historically associated with warrening (rearing rabbits for food and fur). Look for potato caves in the enclosure walls, rabbit warrens, signs of tin mining and one of the largest standing stones on the moor in this notable prehistoric area.

Sheepstor church: Search the churchyard here for the granite tombstones of the white Rajahs of Sarawak; Sheepstor's connections with this distant far-eastern land are described inside the fascinating church.

Burrator reservoir: Supplying Plymouth, this was the first moorland reservoir to be constructed, almost a century ago. With its conifer forests, the whole area resembles a Scottish loch, both for its beauty and its isolated tranquillity. This area affords many woodland and shoreline picnic spots, but swimming is not permitted.

China clay quarries: China clay has been mined on Dartmoor for over 160 years; this open-cast pit was once said to be the largest man-made hole in Western Europe.

Devon Coast and Wooded Coombes – Branscombe to Colyton

RIDE 4
DEVON
SY244898

INFORMATION

Total Distance
16 miles (25.5km), with 1½ miles (2.5km) off-road (avoidable)

Grade
3

OS Map
Landranger 1:50,000 sheet 192 (Exeter & Sidmouth)

Tourist Information
Seaton, tel: 01297 21689

The pretty village of Colyton, on the River Axe

Following the winding coastal lanes through Branscombe with views of the sea, up over the hills to an Iron-Age hillfort before descending to follow the watercourses down to picturesque Colyton, this ride reveals the unspoilt beauty of rural Devon. The wooded coombes are steep, but the hardest climbing is at the start of the ride, so take your time and enjoy the glorious scenery, following quiet lanes lined with wild flowers, often with a bubbling stream alongside.

Cycle Shops/Hire
S Soanes, Colyton, tel: 01297 552308; Mountain Bike Hire, Lyme Bay, tel: 01297 489889

Nearest Railway Station
Axminster (6 miles/9.5km)

Refreshments
Numerous pubs, including Ye Olde Masons Arms, Branscombe, Fountain Head, Street and the Colcombe Castle, Colyton, plus half a dozen tea and coffee shops in Colyton. There is plenty of food and drink available in Seaton and a fine picnic spot at Blackbury Camp

START & ROUTE DIRECTIONS

Start

Seaton is a small seaside resort with a wide shingle beach on the west side of the estuary of the River Axe. It is 2 miles (3km) south of Colyford on the A3052 Exeter–Lyme Regis road, near the junction with the A358 from Axminster. The pay-and-display car park near the Seaton Tramway has ample parking and is clearly signposted.

B3172'. Continue along, then bear left following signs to Beer. The next left, signed 'Seaton Hole', takes you away from the busier road and closer to the coast and views. After ½ mile (1km) turn left up Beer Hill (a steep but short section of the route). At the T-junction turn left along New Road into Beer. Turn right, signed 'Branscombe 3', and continue straight on. Turn right, signed 'Paizen Lane', for an unsurfaced bridleway off-road section. The track climbs and then

2 ⚲ Continue, following signs to Branscombe, down a steep hill into Branscombe (do not turn off left on the way down) past Ye Olde Masons Arms on the right. Bear left and continue along the same lane, with beautiful views, and pass the Old Bakery Tearoom, Branscombe Forge and a church. Continue through Street passing the Fountains Head pub and turn right, signed 'Honiton', and uphill through Bulstone. At a T-junction with the A3052 turn right, signed 'Lyme

Directions

1 ⚲ From the car park follow signs to the Tourist Information Centre on the seafront at Marine Place and take the 2nd exit off the roundabout, signed 'Beer

levels out before meeting the route again in about 1½ miles (2.5km). To avoid Paizen Lane continue, past Beer Quarry Caves on your right, to where Paizen Lane meets the one you are on.

Regis', and immediately left, signed 'Blackbury Camp'. Continue to a T-junction with the B3174 and turn left then next right, signed 'Blackbury Camp'. Continue along the top of the hill into woodland,

Boats on the shingle at Beer

down into Colyton. At the T-junction opposite Soane's cycle shop turn right into Queen Street and continue to explore the centre.

4 🚲 From the Colcombe Castle pub in the middle of Colyton, ride uphill following the B3161 to Colyford and after 50 yards (46m) turn right on the road marked 'Hillhead'. Follow 'Seaton' signs uphill past a picnic site with superb views. Continue, following 'Seaton' signs and at a T-junction with the A3052 turn right, then next left into Harepath Road. Continue, following 'Town Centre' signs. At the T-junction with Fore Street turn right, signed 'Sea Front, Car Parks', and follow signs back to the car park and the starting point.

passing Blackbury Camp Iron-Age hillfort on your right. After ¼ mile (0.5km) turn left, signed 'Southleigh', and continue downhill, through woods with good views, into Southleigh beside a stream.

3 🚲 At a T-junction in Southleigh turn right (no signpost), then take a left turn by the telephone box signed 'Colyton'. Continue for 2 miles (3km) following 'Colyton' signs. Turn left at a T-junction (no signpost)

A welcome stop along the route

PLACES OF INTEREST

Seaton: Seaton lies between two dramatic headlands, behind a mile-long (1.5km) pebble beach. The electric tramway starts from the town and is great fun, following the Axe Valley up to Colyton. There are good views of the countryside and of the waterfowl on the riverbanks from the open-sided trams which sway up the line, with their bells ringing.

Beer: Despite its popularity Beer remains essentially a fishing village. The stone from the quarries above the village has long been used in cathedral and house building. On top of the headland are the popular Pecorama Pleasure Gardens, which include a miniature passenger railway, aviary and children's activity area.

Branscombe: The village clings picturesquely to its narrow lane winding above the sea. The thatched cottages and flowery gardens are charming, and many of the buildings ancient – including a Norman church, an inn (Masons Arms) of 1360 and a forge of 1580.

Blackbury Camp: This Iron-Age hillfort was defended by a single bank and ditch and was built and occupied by cattle farmers. Beautifully situated in woodland above Southleigh, its remains are very atmospheric, and it is a splendid picnicking place for families.

Colyton: Colyton dates back to Saxon times and is packed with history from the following

Flowers decorate a thatched cottage in Branscombe

centuries. It is very small, its winding lanes crammed with cob-walled cottages. The church has a rare octagonal lantern once said to have acted as a beacon for ships sailing up the then navigable River Axe. Inside the church are a Saxon cross and a wonderful family tomb with a reclining, life-size, 17th-century gentleman and his lady wife.

WHAT TO LOOK OUT FOR

The coast and the Axe estuary are home to an abundance of wild birds – curlews, oystercatcher, dunlin, heron, teal, swans and others. The narrow-banked lanes are full of primroses and daffodils in spring, followed by foxgloves and honeysuckle as summer progresses. In the woods around Blackbury Camp look out for squirrels and even deer. A delightful feature of the ride are the little streams which line the lanes, and some small farms with a wide variety of free-ranging farm animals sharing the orchards.

RIDE 5
SOMERSET
ST071435

From Watchet to Williton

This strenuous route has an extremely hilly first half, but the views and the countryside are well worth the effort. With low gears and an unhurried approach the whole route should be rideable. All except the last couple of miles of the return journey to Watchet takes place on very minor roads with little traffic, even in high summer.

INFORMATION

Total Distance
18 miles (29km)

Grade
4

OS Map
Landranger 1: 50,000 sheet 181
(Minehead & Bredon Hills)

Tourist Information
Minehead, tel: 01643 702624;
Bridgwater, tel: 01278 427652

Nearest Railway Station
Watchet

Cycle Shop/Hire
St John Street Bikes, Bridgwater,
tel: 01278 423632

Refreshments
There are many pubs en route: the Notley Arms at Monksilver, the White Horse at Stogumber and the Carew Arms at Crowcombe are all ideal for children, as is Bee World in Stogumber. Watchet also boasts numerous tea shops, cafés and pubs.

The splendid church at Crowcombe

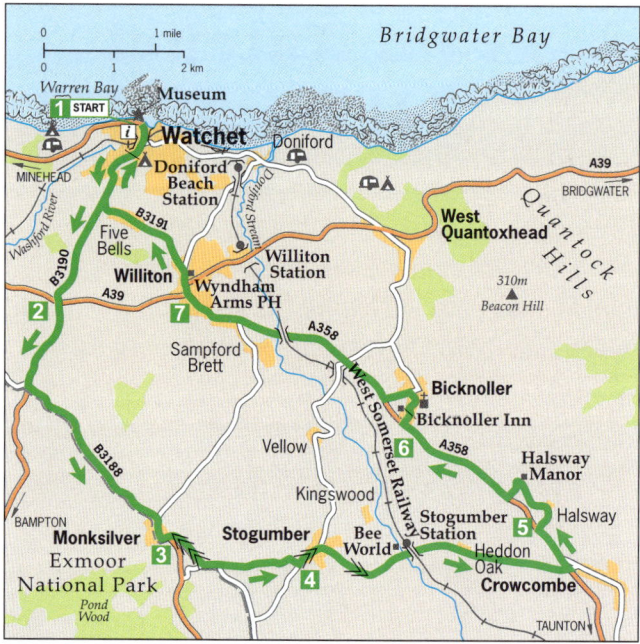

passing the Old Rectory at Nettlecombe. Arrive shortly at Monksilver and continue through the village, following the run of the road.

3 🚲 Shortly after passing a house called 'Brookside', take the left turn off the right-hand bend, following signs for Stogumber. Drop into bottom gear for a sudden sharp rise before the road levels out a little. As a diversion, do not bear left after 'Brookside', but carry on for about ½ mile (1km) to Combe Sydenham Country Park. On leaving the Park, turn left out of the Park and fork immediately right. Continue for ½ mile (1km), rejoining the original route bearing left up through the high banks of hedgerows, still heading for Stogumber.

4 🚲 At the T-junction turn left downhill into Stogumber, taking care on this very steep section. Head into the village then turn right towards Crowcombe. Drop down the

Crowcombe Heathfield, on the the West Somerset Railway. The route stretches for 20 miles (32km) and is the longest preserved railway in Britain

START & ROUTE DIRECTIONS

Start
The route begins from the car park by Watchet station, where there is inexpensive pay-and-display parking as well as toilet facilities. There is also free parking in Watchet, a coastal village on the B3190 between Minehead and Bridgwater.

Directions
1 🚲 From the car park at Watchet station head away from the harbour and up out of the town, crossing over the railway bridge on the B3190. At the T-junction turn right on to the B3190 towards Bampton and Wilton. Climb up the rise and, at the fork, bear right, staying on the B3190. Drop down the other side, taking care when crossing the main road at the junction at the bottom.

2 🚲 Once over the main road, ease up the rise and shortly after the crest, turn left at the crossroads, heading for Monksilver on the B3188. If you need a breather, sit and take in the spectacular views. Enjoy the descent towards Monksilver, but take more care where the lane narrows

The imposing façade of 16th-century Combe Sydenham Hall

rise to reach Bee World and Stogumber station (on the West Somerset Railway, with trains to Watchet). Climb up the rise past the station and follow the road through Heddon Oak to the junction with the main road, over which is Crowcombe. Turn left on to the A358 towards Williton. This is a fast road, although the traffic seems to give cyclists quite a lot of room.

5 ⚲ Continue and after 875 yards (800m) turn right into Halsway. Climb the narrow lane, to pass through Lower Halsway, then Middle Halsway, before reaching spectacular Halsway Manor on the right. Bear left down the main road and turn right heading for Williton.

6 ⚲ After 1 mile (1.5km) turn right into Bicknoller (up Church Lane), past the

bungalows to the Bicknoller Inn and the older part of the village. Bear left past the red-stone church, then left again into Dashwoods Lane back to the main road. Turn right on to the A358 towards Williton. At Williton, slow as you approach the bottom of the hill, and turn left at the white

Toll Cottage into Bridge Street. Follow this over the hump-backed bridge, past the Old School, the church and the Orchard Mill Museum. Leaving the museum, bear left

at the church, turn right on to the A39, heading left at the mini-roundabout.

7 ⚲ Pass the post office and bear left towards Watchet. Continue up the gentle rise before dropping down again towards Watchet. At the next junction, bear right on to the

Boats at anchor in the harbour at Watchet

B3190. Turn left over the railway bridge and return to Watchet town centre.

PLACES OF INTEREST

Watchet: There is much to see here, including the harbour and narrow streets filled with interesting shops. Children especially will like The Puppet Theatre and Tropiquaria, with its exotic collection of snakes and lizards, spiders and free-flying birds. Both are open on weekends and bank holidays (admission fee).

Combe Sydenham Country Park: Where Sir Francis Drake courted Lady Elizabeth Sydenham, the Park is open Sunday to Friday and has a wealth of nature trails and information boards. You can fish for trout, glimpse the shy fallow deer, visit the working medieval corn mill or bakery, or follow the Story Trails.

Bee World: An unusual attraction at Stogumber and a real treat for children, with rare breeds, a bee colony, play area and a good restaurant. There is also a streamside conservation area and nature walks. (Open April to October, admission fee)

West Somerset Railway: Steam and diesel trains run along the scenic route from Bishops Lydeard to Minehead. It will carry bikes with fare-paying passengers (tel: 01643 704996).

Orchard Mill Museum: This centre at Williton has a fine collection of Bakelite and plastic products, an art deco collection, and a shop. The museum also offers B&B accomodation and serves splendid cream teas.

WHAT TO LOOK OUT FOR

The views on this route are quite spectacular, with the sea visible from many of the higher points. The lower sections of the ride tend to be near running water, giving the opportunity to glimpse a huge variety of interesting flora and fauna. The villages themselves are of great interest and most are quiet and unsullied by modern trappings.

The elaborately carved Green Man in Crowcombe church

RIDE 6
SOMERSET
ST503390

Glastonbury and the Somerset Levels

This gentle, 3–4 hour route is almost traffic-free, with plenty of opportunity for picnicking and enjoying the scenery and wildlife havens. Mainly flat or with gentle climbs, there is a short steep climb back into Glastonbury, but this can be walked easily. The area can become busy on bank holidays and fine weekends. Some lanes are quite narrow, so take care with small children when riding alongside the river or canal.

INFORMATION

Total Distance
18 miles (29km)

Grade
1

OS Map
Landranger 1: 50,000 sheet 183
(Yeovil & Frome)

Tourist Information
Glastonbury, tel: 01458 832954;
Wells, tel: 01749 672552

Nearest Railway Station
Somerton (3 miles/5km)

Cycle Shops/Hire
Bikes 'n' Bits, Wells, tel: 01749
670260; City Cycles, Wells, tel: 01749

675096; Pedallers, Glastonbury, tel:
01458 831117; Street Cycle Co, Street,
tel: 01458 847882

Refreshments
Numerous tea shops, cafés and pubs
in Glastonbury, plus the Barton Inn at
Barton St David and the Rose and
Portcullis, Butleigh which caters for
families. Also the Baltonsburgh
Village Stores.

Glastonbury Tor is a famous landmark

Start

The historic market town of Glastonbury, a place of myth and legend, is located on the A39 6 miles (9km) south of Wells. There is plenty of parking in the town centre, mostly pay-and-display but it is reasonably priced.

Directions

1 🚲 From Glastonbury, head up the High Street and turn right at the T-junction at the top to join the A361, following signs for 'Shepton Mallet'. Continue ahead for a few hundred yards to the mini-roundabout, then bear left, keeping on the A361. This road can be busy at times, so take care. Almost opposite is the fascinating Museum of Rural Life.

The Chalice Well is the legendary resting place of the Holy Grail

2 🚲 After 875 yards (800m), just beyond Well House Lane (leading to Glastonbury Tor) turn right into Cinnamon Lane. Take great care; this lane drops steeply and there can be loose gravel around. At the bottom, follow the tight left-hand bend, then enjoy the traffic-free lane. Take the first right and follow the canal for 1 mile (1.5km), when the road leaves the canalside; continue for about another mile (1.5km).

3 🚲 At the end, turn left by the post box, then right, signed 'West Bradley'. To visit the West Pennard Court Barn, turn left here and continue for ¼ mile (0.5km) to find the barn on your right. Retrace your tracks to rejoin the main route. After 100 yards turn right again, still signposted 'West Bradley'. Follow the signs and the run of the road, heading for Parbrook. Swing round the bend at West Bradley House Fruit Farm, ease up the rise past the village church, then turn right towards Hornblotton and Lydford.

4 🚲 Pass the Old School and climb the rise, turning right at the farm at the top, signed 'Baltonsborough and Glastonbury'. Enjoy the easy roll along to Baltonsborough. Go straight past the phone box and down the hill to the junction. The Greyhound pub offers a welcome break, and 100 yards down the road opposite is the village store.

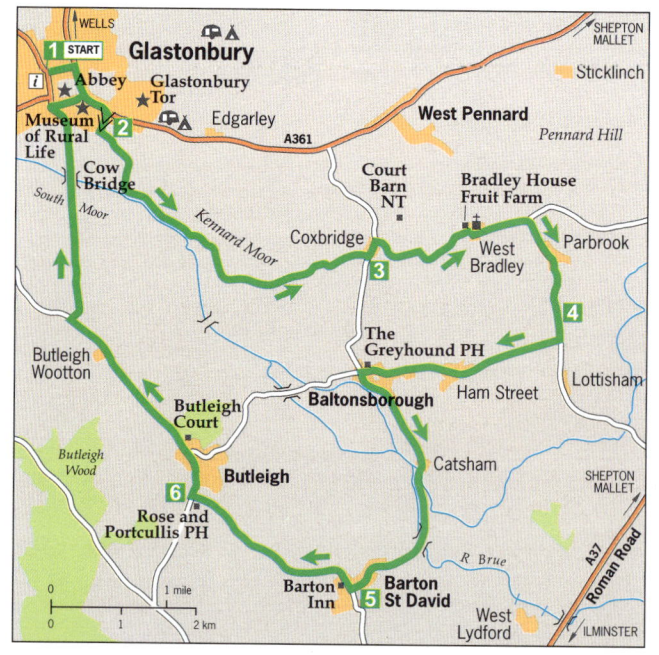

Steps lead down into the Chalice Gardens

Turn left towards Barton St David and follow the well-surfaced lane alongside the river for a while before moving over the river on a tight hump-backed bridge to enter Barton St David.

5 🚲 At the 'major' crossroads (with the phone box opposite) turn right towards Butleigh. Pass the Barton Inn (the converted church), then continue out of the village. Drop down into Butleigh before tackling the ascent through the village to The Rose and Portcullis Inn at the top.

6 🚲 Suitably refreshed, turn right into Sub Road towards Glastonbury. Go past Butleigh Court, then continue for 1½ miles (2.5km) through Butleigh Wootton before turning right at the top of a rise, down across the levels back towards Glastonbury. Cross Cow Bridge, go through the '30' signs, and take the first right into Old Butleigh Road, up the steep ascent. Turn right at the top then, after 220 yards (200m), turn left at the mini-roundabout through the traffic-calming scheme then left again back into Glastonbury High Street to the start point.

The magnificent sight of ancient Wells Cathedral

The sumptuous Long Gallery of the Bishop's Palace in Wells

PLACES OF INTEREST

Glastonbury: This legendary town abounds in interesting places; of particular note are the Abbey and grounds and the Museum of Rural Life near by. Glastonbury sits on the ancient Isle of Avalon, long associated with Joseph of Arimathea, and with King Arthur. Joseph's legend says that as he leaned on a staff here it took root and flowered, a sign which he took to mean he should build a church, the former Abbey. Arthurian legend claims that both Arthur and Queen Guinevere were buried in the Abbey. The Tithe Barn now houses the Somerset Museum of Rural Life.

Glastonbury Tor: Visible from most of this route, the mound supports the only remains of St Michael's Church – the Chalice Well at the foot of the Tor is supposedly the resting place of the Holy Grail.

Wells: Some 6 miles (10km) away is an interesting city famed for its large cathedral, whose Green makes an ideal picnic site. Other attractions here include the Bishop's Palace, Vicar's Close, a street inhabited continuously since the early 1500s, the Wells Cathedral School, and the city's regular Wednesday and Saturday markets.

Street: The main attraction of this town is the 'Clark's Village', a well-designed purpose-built complex of shops selling high-quality 'seconds' and featuring a variety of street entertainments.

WHAT TO LOOK OUT FOR

This route features a wide variety of hedgerow birdlife, as well as opportunities to see kingfishers and heron. There are many old houses, and also some tasteful conversions of barns and churches. Butleigh Court comes as a complete surprise, its castellated features contrasting starkly with other buildings en route. Note also the variety of farming styles, with arable, sheep and dairy farms all within a very small area.

The Isle of Purbeck

The inaptly named Isle of Purbeck is in fact part of the mainland, separated only by a high downland ridge. The Purbeck coast is one of the most dramatic and spectacular in Britain, whilst the stone villages are a delight. The route is fairly demanding in places with some very steep inclines, partly on peaceful country lanes, along bridleways and downland tracks. The terrain is generally good but can be rather bumpy and muddy in places when wet. Allow a good three hours for the ride, not including stops.

INFORMATION

Total Distance
15 miles (24km), with
4 ½ miles (7km)
off-road

Grade
3

OS Map
Landranger 1:50,000 sheet 195
(Bournemouth, Purbeck &
surrounding area)

Tourist Information
Swanage, tel: 01929 422885

Nearest Railway Station
Wareham

Refreshments
There are a variety of pubs, including the Scott Arms in Kingston which welcomes children and has a lovely garden. The Fox Inn, Corfe Castle, one of the oldest inns in Dorset, dating back to 1568, does not allow children inside but there is a large attractive garden. Well-behaved children are welcome inside the Kings Arms, Langton Matravers. The cafe in Kimmeridge is open all day, as are tea rooms in Corfe

Set on a high mound overlooking the attractive stone village of Corfe Castle are the striking remains of the medieval castle

START & ROUTE DIRECTIONS

Start

From the A351 Wareham to Swanage road, pass through the village of Corfe Castle then turn immediately right on to the B3069. Bear left at Kingston soon to turn right when you reach the signpost to Worth Matravers. Just before the village there is car park on the right owned by The National Trust. Funds raised by a 'trust the motorist' collection box at the entrance contribute to the upkeep of the facilities.

Directions

1️⃣ 🚲 From the car park turn left and cycle back along the lane, turning left at the road junction with the B3069. Continue into Kingston passing The Scott Arms on your right and head uphill. Follow this peaceful lane for about 1 mile (1.5km) then turn left through the gateway, signposted 'Encombe House and Lower Encombe', and bear right following the signed bridle-way up and across the downs to the gate at the top. Pass through and continue beside the wood until you reach the viewpoint on Swyre Head. Looking east you can see St Aldhelm's Head, to the west Kimmeridge Bay and Encombe House in the valley. Cycle back to the small gate in the wall and follow the route across Smedmore Hill passing through a number of gates before descending a rather bumpy gravel track towards Kimmeridge; enter the lane and turn right. While here it is well worth a detour through Kimmeridge to the bay, a popular spot for divers. The folly on the clifftop (Clavell's Tower) was built in 1831 by the Reverend John Richards.

2️⃣ 🚲 After cycling uphill enjoy a long coast down this peaceful lane towards Bradle Farm. Follow the lane to the left through the valley, cycling up between high flower-filled banks to the road. Keep straight ahead at the crossroads, signed 'Stoborough'. After a fairly demanding climb and passing the last of the houses in Cocknowle, pass through the gate on the right and join the ridge path leading to Knowle Hill, signposted 'Corfe Castle 1¾ miles' (2.75km). The ridge affords lovely views across

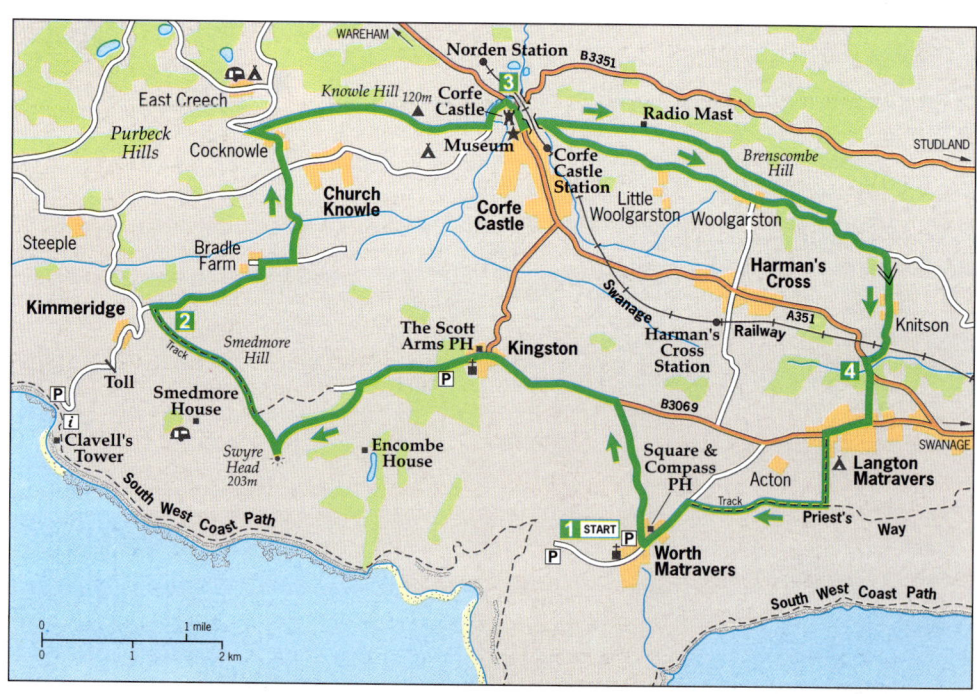

The Flying Scotsman *on the restored Swanage Railway*

Poole Harbour. Follow the well-ridden path through a couple of gates, after which the track descends to a wooden gate. Your route ahead is downhill on a firm grass track eventually reaching the road at Corfe.

3 Turn left, then right at the main road and continue carefully for a short distance around the foot of the castle, taking the second left up and under the railway bridge. A short detour to the right takes you into the centre of Corfe and the entrance to the castle. Either stay on this peaceful country lane for about 2½ miles (4km) turning right when you reach the T-junction towards Knitson or,

for a more challenging and scenic ride, join the signed bridleway on the left leading to Brenscombe Hill. Fork right at the radio mast then follow the track for about 2½ miles (4km), keeping close to the hedge. The route is periodically signposted 'Ulwell'. After a gentle descent, eventually reach two gates on the right hidden slightly in the dip, signed 'Underhill Road ¼'. Reach the lane and turn left, then fork right at the T-junction towards Knitson.

4 On reaching the main A351, turn left, carefully riding the short distance along this often busy road, crossing over on the bend;

cycle up the lane to Langton Matravers. Turn right and, after passing the last of the village houses, turn left on to the wide gravel track. Keep straight at the cottages, pass through the gate into the field and follow the grass track to the gate at the top, turning right on to Priest's Way. At the end of the track pass through the gate into the field; proceed across to the far gate, enter the lane and turn left back to Worth Matravers. Before leaving take time to explore the little village, then, after 220 yards (200m), turn left at the mini-roundabout, go through the traffic-calming scheme then turn left again back into the High Street in Glastonbury to return to the start point of the ride.

Corfe Castle's parish church stands opposite the village houses

PLACES OF INTEREST

Worth Matravers: Local stone-built cottages surround the small duck pond and green in this delightful Purbeck village. The attractive *Square & Compass,* one of the last remaining unspoilt inns in Dorset, is set on a high ridge with views towards Winspit and the sea.

Smedmore House: The Smedmore Estate is administered from the family seat at Kimmeridge; the owners still live in the house, which is open to the public at certain times of the year.

Swyre Head: This site of an ancient tumulus makes a wonderful viewpoint.

Corfe Castle: Its ruins are now owned by the National Trust but the castle was once the residence of the Bankes family. In 1646 the castle was gallantly defended by Mary Bankes against the Parliamentarians under Cromwell but was eventually captured and partly demolished, with much of the stone used to rebuild damaged houses in the village. The castle is open all year but times can vary with the season.

Swanage Railway: Closed by Beeching in the 1960s, this attractive line has been re-opened with the support of enthusiastic volunteers and now runs from Norden to Swanage. It is hoped one day that the line will run all the way to Wareham and link with the national network. For details of the talking timetable tel: 01929 424276.

WHAT TO LOOK OUT FOR

Wildlife is plentiful in the Purbeck Hills especially in early summer when vast areas are given over to wild flowers, notably garlic-smelling ransoms, bluebells and primroses, while later in the year the heathland turns purple. The cry of seabirds abounds along the coastal strip as they squabble for nesting sites along the cliffs. Listen out, too, for the whistle of the Swanage steam train leaving Corfe Castle, stirring childhood memories for some.

Wiltshire and Hampshire

RIDE 8
WILTSHIRE/HAMPSHIRE
SU176215

INFORMATION

Total Distance
25 miles (40km), with 7 miles (11km) off-road

Grade
2

OS Maps
Landranger 1:50,000 sheet 184 (Salisbury & The Plain); Pathfinder 1:25,000 sheet 1262 (Salisbury [South] & Broad Chalke)

Tourist Information
Salisbury, tel: 01722 334956

Cycle Shop/Hire
Hayball & Co Cycles, Salisbury, tel: 01722 411378

Nearest Railway Station
Salisbury (6 miles/10km)

Refreshments
There are five pubs and a cafe in Downton, pubs in Woodgreen, Rockbourne and Coombe Bissett, a pub and tea rooms in Breamore and a cafe at Rockbourne Roman Villa. Throughout the ride there are many picnic spots, including the banks of the Avon and the ancient Moot in

A circular, varied ride, interesting to both the naturalist and historian, over a mixture of country roads, tracks and byways, exploring the Wiltshire/Hampshire border. Cycle along the Avon valley, savouring part of the New Forest, enjoying a stately home and a Roman villa, delighting in Wiltshire's clear chalk streams, riding across its wide open downland and visiting one of its finest nature reserves.

Downton, Castle Hill, almost anywhere in the New Forest, the River Avon again at Breamore Mill, the green at Breamore, the Roman villa at

Rockbourne, high on the downs above Stratford Tony, by the River Ebble in the village itself and on Coombe Bissett Nature Reserve

The handsome manor house of Breamore

START & ROUTE DIRECTIONS

Start

The village of Downton is set on the B3080, 6 miles (10km) south of Salisbury just off the A338. There is parking along the wide main road (The Borough), near the Co-op.

Directions

1 🚲 Head east and, after ⅔ mile (1km) turn right down Moot Lane (note The Moot on the right). Continue through the outskirts, holding your nose by the sewage works. After 3 miles (5km), turn right, signposted 'Woodgreen', and shortly turn left after the Horse & Groom, signposted 'Godshill'. Keep left, climbing the narrow country lane, turning right for Castle Hill. Take a breather at the viewpoint, then continue for 1½ miles (2.5km), turning left at the T-junction to return to Woodgreen, initially up a steep twisting hill, levelling out on a broad woodland ride

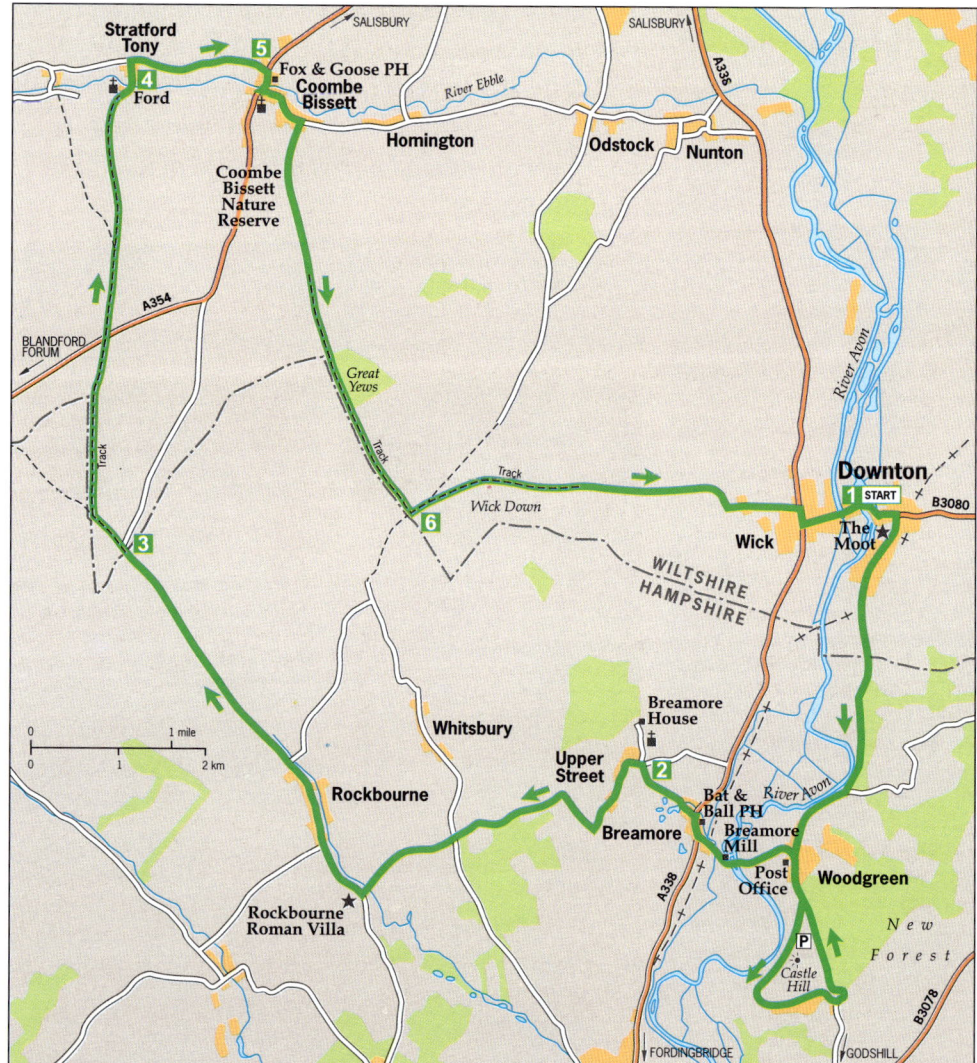

The River Avon flows beneath Castle Hill

and then down the sharp drop into the village. Bear left for Breamore at the Post Office and cross the two bridges over the River Avon, noting Breamore Mill on the right. Turn right after the bridge. At the A338 turn right, crossing the road with care, and after 109 yards (100m) turn left just after the Bat & Ball in Breamore. Follow the Breamore House signs to the crossroads.

2 🚲 Go straight over to visit the house, otherwise turn left, heading for Whitsbury. The road here runs through open country but then enters pleasant mixed woodland. After 1½ miles (2.5km) continue on the same road, now signposted 'Rockbourne', turning right after a further ½ mile (1km). Rockbourne Roman Villa is immediately on the left, followed by charming Rockbourne, then a long straight road.

3 🚲 After 2½ miles (4km), at a sharp right-hand bend, take the track straight ahead,

shortly turning right at a junction. Gently ascend the well-surfaced track, enjoying the fine views to the east. After 1½ miles (2.5km) go through the farm gate (close it after you) and then carefully cross the busy A354 to take the track opposite. Take the right fork by Throop Bungalow (avoiding the permanent patch of mud), then enjoy the long, easy ride as the hedges open out to give stunning views over the downland. After ¾ mile (1km) take the right fork and begin the ever-steepening descent towards Stratford Tony, with the track now becoming a deep, sunken lane.

4 🚲 At the River Ebble you can try riding through the ford, but prudence dictates walking 55 yards (50m) left up the path, crossing by the public footbridge (not the private footbridge). Rejoin the road opposite the ford and cycle to the T-junction, turning right for Coombe Bissett.

5 🚲 Once at the village, after 1 mile (1.5km) turn right on to the A354, crossing with care, and just after the Fox & Goose turn left, signposted 'Homington'. Shortly turn right up the steep Pennings Drove where you soon find Coombe Bissett Nature Reserve on the right – a splendid place to stop, picnic and enjoy the view. Continue up the Drove which starts to level out, and after 1 mile (1.5km) the tarmac ends. Take the grassy track to the left, trundling downhill for ¾ mile (1km) where it starts to rise again past the bulk of Great Yews wood (private) on the left. At the end of Great Yews go straight ahead.

6 🚲 After 1 mile (1.5km) turn sharp left then take the right fork. Continue along the straight grass/earth track over Wick Down to meet a tarmac road. From here it is a long freewheel down Wick Down road to the A338. Cross at the traffic lights and you are back in Downton.

Intricate mosaics at Rockbourne Roman Villa

PLACES OF INTEREST

Downton: A charming village with old cottages, a converted mill, and the historically important Moot (site of a Norman castle).

Castle Hill: Part of the New Forest, the view here, high above the Avon valley is splendid. Down below, the sinuous curve of the Avon winds past, and in the distance is Breamore Mill, where the Avon rushes through the mill-race of this converted building.

Breamore: The 16th-century Breamore House is open to visitors and has a fascinating museum of country life. Adjacent is Breamore church, over a thousand years old, and the huge green in the nearby village is surrounded by attractive and varied cottages and houses.

Rockbourne Roman Villa: Discovered in 1942, mosaics, baths and hypocausts testify to the luxurious life led by its Roman inhabitants.

Stratford Tony: In this classic Wiltshire chalk-stream village, a few lovely houses stand beside the trickling River Ebble. The ford is an ancient crossing-point, there is an old Roman road here, and on a hill is the squat 13th-century church.

Coombe Bissett: By the 17th-century bridge is a beautiful converted barn, complete with a veranda on stilts in the river. Opposite, a large Norman church stands high on a grassy mound and the village has many examples of flint-built cottages.

Coombe Bissett Nature Reserve: This is Wiltshire Wildlife Trust's finest chalk downland reserve. Famed for its burnt orchids, many rare and beautiful plants can be seen throughout the year. In summer literally clouds of chalkhill and Adonis blue butterflies dance before you – this is downland as it used to be, before modern agriculture arrived.

WHAT TO LOOK OUT FOR

This route is a naturalist's delight. Birds, butterflies and deer share the deciduous woodland and acid heaths of the New Forest with its sturdy ponies. In autumn the fungi-hunter will find over 500 species. The country lanes abound with snowdrops, primroses and celandines, followed by bluebells, wood anemones, cranesbill and lords and ladies. The downland is a favourite haunt of buzzards and red kites have even been seen here. The nature reserve has early gentian in spring, masses of orchids in summer followed by devil's-bit scabious and autumn gentian, not to mention over 30 species of butterfly. Be sure to take your time, binoculars and reference books.

RIDE 9
WILTSHIRE
ST862615

Holt and Lacock

INFORMATION

Total Distance
13¾ miles (22km)

Grade
2

OS Map
Landranger 1: 50,000 sheet 173
(Swindon & Devizes)

Tourist Information
Chippenham, tel: 01249 657733;
Bradford-on-Avon, tel: 01225 875797

Nearest Railway Stations
Bradford-on-Avon (4 miles/6.5km);
Trowbridge (4 miles/6.5km);
Melksham (3 miles/5km)

Cycle Shops/Hire
Lock Inn Cottage, Bradford-on-Avon,
tel: 01225 868068

Refreshments
There are many tea shops, cafés and
pubs in Lacock and Bradford-on-Avon,
plus the Roebuck at Westrop, the
Forrester's at Atworth, the Bell at
Broughton Gifford and the Harp and
Crown at Gastard.

This moderate and mostly flat route links three National Trust properties and the area covered can become busy on bank holidays and fine weekends. Some lanes are quite narrow, so take care if riding with small children.

A stone-built cottage in the pretty village of Lacock

START & ROUTE DIRECTIONS

Start

The National Trust village of Holt lies on the B3107 close to the River Avon. The start point is the The Courts (NT), located some 3 miles (4.5km) north of Trowbridge, on the B3107.

Directions

1 🚲 Leave The Courts, turning left on to the main road. After 410 yards (375m) turn right into Leigh Road opposite the Tollgate pub and enjoy the flat lane as it meanders between tall hedgerows. Shortly turn right, signed 'Holt Manor'. Ride through the grounds past the manor house and old gateway, and turn right at the end. Shortly pass Great Chalfield Manor on your left. Follow the road sharp right through the long avenue and up the slight ascent.

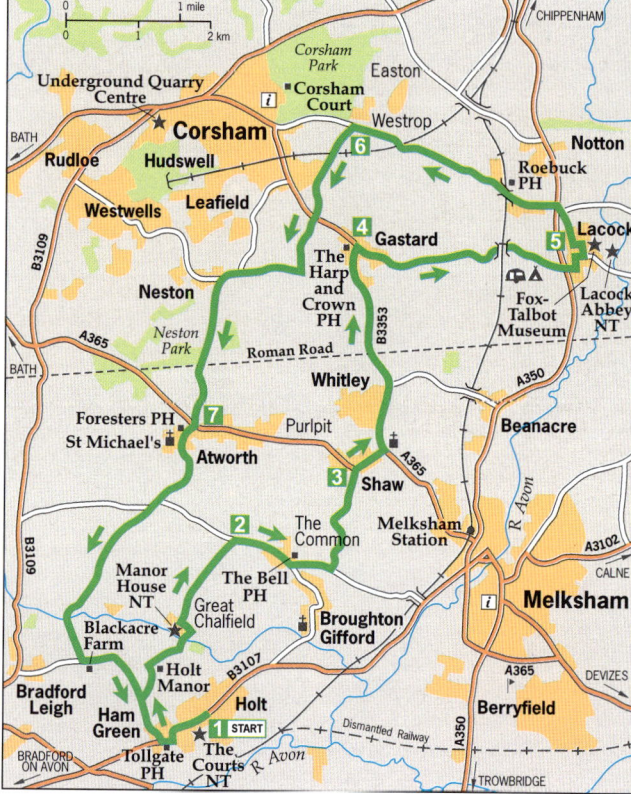

2 🚲 Turn right at the junction and head down towards Brougton Gifford. After The Bell on the common, bear left, signed 'Melksham', then take the next left, signed 'Norrington Common and Shaw', into a delightful lane.

3 🚲 When you reach Shaw, turn right on to the main road and soon turn left on to the B3353 heading past the church, towards Corsham. Once out of Whitley, pass under the pylons and continue up a steady climb. Approaching Gastard, pass

through the '30' signs and freewheel down the other side.

4 🚲 Just on the left-hand bend, turn right into Plains End opposite the Harp and Crown. Continue to the end of the lane to the junction with the A350. Almost opposite is a gap through the fence. Dismount, cross the road and walk through this gap. Remount, continue to the end of the road, turn left then left again into Lacock.

5 🚲 Head north out of the car park into the centre of Lacock. Go straight through the village, passing the main

Barge trips on the canal at Bradford-on-Avon

A solitary fisherman on the lush banks of the River Avon

street on your right, down the dip and up the ascent to meet the A350 after ¼ mile (0.5km). At the junction use the cycle crossing and turn right, then left into the lane almost opposite. Continue past the houses and into open country. Follow the road over the railway bridge and left, following the lane past the Roebuck pub.

6 🚲 Take the next turn left into Ladbrook Lane towards Neston and continue over the railway bridge. At the end, go straight over into Monk's Lane. Take great care here as visibility is poor, so listen as well as look. Follow Monk's Lane up past the Depot and curve right at the top into Neston. After 5½ miles (9km) turn left towards Atworth – a gentle descent with good views and wooded sections, but take care on the bend near the bottom.

7 🚲 At the junction with the A365 turn left, then right on to Bradford Road. Bear left at the Forester's pub, go down the hill, straight through the crossroads, then bear left, signposted 'Holt 3'. Go straight past the 'Little Chalfield' sign then bear left down the dip, over the stream and up the other side. Turn left at the end, continue past Blackacre Farm and Leigh house, then follow the road round to the right. At the end, turn left opposite the Tollgate pub and retrace your tracks to The Courts, taking extra care when turning right back into The Courts.

The courtyard of the Abbey at Lacock

The magnificent packhorse bridge at Lacock

PLACES OF INTEREST

The Courts: This is where local weavers once came to settle their disputes and, although the house is not open, the gardens are and feature a long herbaceous border, lily pond and small lake.

Great Chalfield Manor: This moated Tudor manor (although the gatehouse is much earlier) features many fascinating artefacts. The Great Hall contains three masks set into the wall through which the women could secretly observe the goings-on in the room.

Lacock: This National Trust site has a wealth of interesting buildings and exhibitions. Lacock Abbey dates from 1232 and the house now on the site surrounds and incorporates much of the original buildings. Originally a medieval nunnery, the buildings survived the Dissolution of the Monasteries in 1539 and the Great Hall was rebuilt in Gothic style in the 18th century by Fox-Talbot's great-grandfather. A 'barn' near by houses the fascinating Fox-Talbot Museum of Photography.

Bradford-on-Avon: Originally a thriving textile centre, the town still has many interesting buildings, including a huge tithe barn, and the gaol, originally a chapel but later used to lock up the local drunks, situated on the old bridge. The town's oldest building, the tiny Saxon Church of St Lawrence, was originally built by St Aldhelm in about AD 700 as part of a monastery, which was later destroyed by the Danes.

WHAT TO LOOK OUT FOR

The route runs through some unspoiled countryside offering a haven to many species of wildlife. If conditions are quiet you may well chance upon badgers or foxes, and some fields have large populations of rabbits. Most of the woodland is very old and well established, harbouring many types of native British birds, including finches, woodpeckers and thrushes.

Forest of Dean – Ancient Forests and Woods

The route covers some of the most beautiful and unspoiled countryside in Britain. Although quite hilly, the climbs tend to be long rather than steep and the views from the hilltops are quite spectacular. Some lanes are quite narrow, so take care if riding with small children, and beware the longer descents; you can reach quite a speed.

RIDE 10
GLOUCESTERSHIRE
SO577108

INFORMATION

Total Distance
17½ miles (27km)

Grade
4

OS Map
Landranger 1:50,000 sheet 162
Gloucester & Forest of Dean area

Tourist Information
Coleford, tel: 01594 836307;
Lydney, tel: 01595 855895;
Cinderford, tel: 01595 823284

Nearest Railway Stations
Lydney(7 miles/11km); Chepstow
(15½/25km); Gloucester
(18½ miles/30km)

Cycle Shop/Hire
Pedalabikeaway, tel: 01594 860065;
the Crown Inn, Coalway, tel: 01594
836620/844927

Refreshments

Many tea shops, cafés and pubs in
Cinderford and Coleford, plus picnic
sites en route and pubs at other
centres: Rising Sun at Broadwell
(children's garden); Speech House
Hotel at Beechenhurst; White Hart Inn
at Cinderford; Rising Sun at Ruspidge;
Woodman at Parkend; Beechenhurst
Lodge picnic site

This former mill now houses the fascinating Dean Heritage Centre

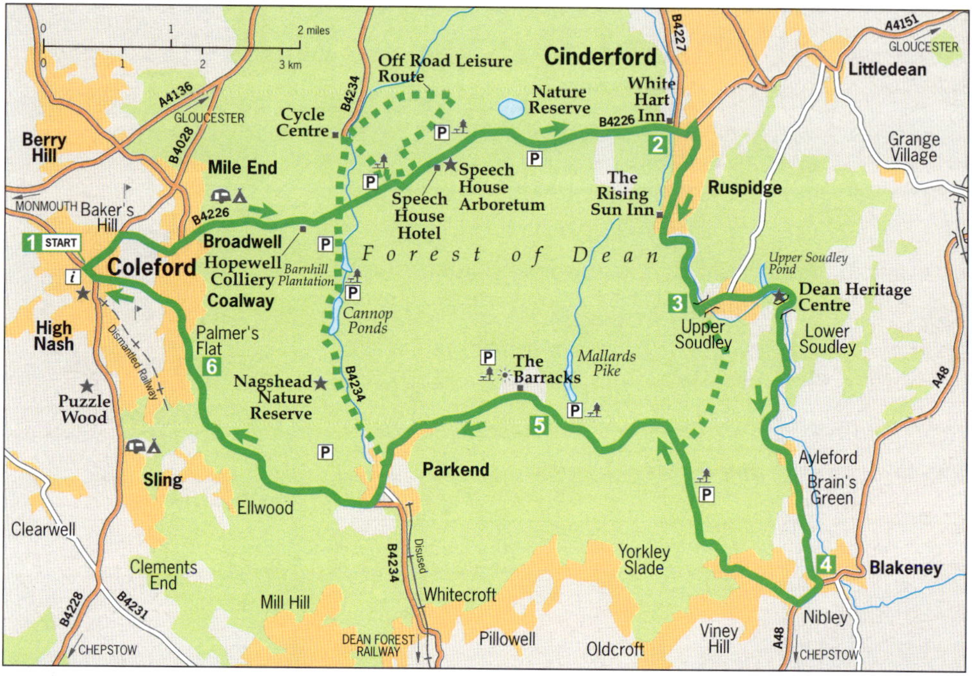

Map labels:

Cinderford · Littledean · GLOUCESTER · B4151 · B4227 · Off Road Leisure Route · Nature Reserve · White Hart Inn · B4226 Inn · Cycle Centre · B4234 · Mile End · Speech House · Speech House Arboretum · The Rising Sun Inn · Ruspidge · Grange Village · Berry Hill · A4136 · GLOUCESTER · B4028 · MONMOUTH · Baker's Hill · B4226 · Broadwell · Speech House Hotel · *Forest of Dean* · Upper Soudley Pond · Dean Heritage Centre · START · Coleford · Hopewell Colliery · Barnhill Plantation · Coalway · Cannop Ponds · Upper Soudley · Lower Soudley · A48 · High Nash · Dommeller Railway · Palmer's Flat · Mallards Pike · The Barracks · Puzzle Wood · Nagshead Nature Reserve · B4234 · Ayleford · Brain's Green · Sling · Parkend · Ellwood · Yorkley Slade · Blakeney · Clearwell · Clements End · B4228 · B4231 · Mill Hill · B4234 · Disused · Whitecroft · Nibley · Viney Hill · A48 · CHEPSTOW · DEAN FOREST RAILWAY · Pillowell · Oldcroft · CHEPSTOW

Scale: 0 1 2 miles / 0 1 2 3 km

START & ROUTE DIRECTIONS

Start

The small town of Coleford is situated on the B4028 and B4228 Chepstow road, 1 mile (1.5km) off the A4136 east of Monmouth. The ride starts from the Gateway supermarket car park near the centre of town.

Directions

1 ⬧ From the car park drop downhill to the traffic lights by the King's Head in Grove Road and turn right on to the B4028 towards Cinderford. After a mile (1.5km) turn right into Baker's Hill on to the B4226, signposted 'Cinderford'. It is a short gentle climb into Broadwell and past the Rising Sun Inn. Head straight through the village and out into the Forest of Dean. There is a long descent past Hopewell Colliery. Continue straight on past the Pygmy Pinetum on the corner and up the longest climb of the route past Beechenhurst Lodge picnic site and on to the Speech House Hotel. From here the road rolls gently before a long easy descent into lower Cinderford.

For a short cut, at the crossroads turn right heading south on the B4234 past Barn Hill Plantation. Gently climb up to Parkend, then turn right to rejoin the main route.

The calm setting of the Forest of Dean is ideal for a day out

2 🚲 Climb up the rise, turning right at the White Hart Inn into Ruspidge. (For Cinderford town centre and its Friday market, turn left after the White Hart and follow this road for about ¾ mile (1km), then retrace your tracks to rejoin the route at the White Hart.) Follow the road down enjoying the freewheel, and pass the Rising Sun Inn to shortly leave the built-up area and re-enter the

The laundry room inside the miner's cottage musem

forest. Keep an eye open for sheep straying over the road.

3 🚲 Follow the road around to the left and over the bridge into Upper Soudley. The large lake on the left is Upper Soudley Pond, with many nature trails and information boards on this fascinating site. On the right is the Dean Heritage Centre. The road swings over the river and bears left heading along the opposite bank. Climb the road to the top before rolling down the other side. At Brain's

Green is small general store on the common, before rolling on down to the A48.
Short cut: Ignoring the initial left turn, instead turn right and follow the road gently uphill. After about 1 mile (0.5km) follow the main run of the road gently right, and descend to the main road. Turn right and rejoin the main route.

4 🚲 Turn right on to the A48 for about 1 mile (0.5km) then right again, signposted 'Parkend and Coleford'. Past the remaining arches of the viaduct the road starts to climb gently again. The area is now heavily wooded and there are many picnic tables alongside the stream. Head past the small road joining from the right and carry on towards Coleford.

5 🚲 Head on past the turning for Mallards Pike Lake, and past terraces of houses called The Barracks – an interesting mix of stone and red brick under slate or tiled roofs. Follow the road through Parkend towards Coleford.
Freewheel down through the houses to the bottom where there is a left turn to the Dean Forest Railway. Carry straight on past the Woodman pub and Nagshead Nature Reserve. Start to climb up past The Folly Cottage before levelling out.
Ease up the rise to Palmer's Flat and past the Crown Inn at Coalway before dropping down into Coleford, turning right on to the B4228 and back towards the town centre and the starting point.

PLACES OF INTEREST

Coleford: The town was once the 'capital' of the Forest of Dean; the market hall dates from the 17th century and the town's Charter derives from Charles II, since the Manor sheltered Charles I after the battle of Edgehill.

Speech House and Arboretum: Formerly the inn where the Forester's Court was held 10 times a year, this is now a hotel with good refreshment facilities situated high up in the forest.

Dean Heritage Centre: An old mill, but now converted to house craft workshops, a café, an agricultural display, forester's cottage, a beam engine, wash house, mine and museum. There is also much to interest children, including a bee-hive and ants' nests, as well as occasional special events.

WHAT TO LOOK OUT FOR

Unspoiled countryside here offers a haven to many types of wildlife and native British birds. 'Nooks and crannies' formed as the route winds its way after following the general route of streams and rivers offer wonderful habitats for riverside creatures as well as water-loving flora and fauna.
There is a wealth of interest in the area, ranging from disused and dismantled railway lines to old industrial sites, water courses, activity centres and some beautiful cottages and villages.

Nature and woodland trails also start and finish here.

Dean Forest Railway: The line has stations at Norchard, St. Mary's Halt and Lydney Town. Steam locomotives, coaches, wagons and railway equipment are on show, and special events and other attractions are held mainly during the summer at weekends. Open April to October, the line will carry bikes with advance warning, tel: 01594 845840.

Puzzle Wood: Iron-age workings here date back to before Roman times. There are refreshments, tea rooms and rare breeds livestock exhibits.

Nagshead Nature Reserve: Open from mid-April to the end of August, there are woodlands, bluebells, pied flycatchers, butterflies, dragonflies, autumn colour and nature trails.

Norchard Station on the Dean Forest Railway

Chalk Stream, Downland and Thatch

From peaceful traffic-free pedalling along the old 'Sprat and Winkle' railway line, close to the River Test – Hampshire's famous trout stream – to gently undulating and scenic country lanes, this interesting and varied ride delves into the delights of the Test Valley. Allow plenty of time to enjoy serene river views, picture-postcard thatched villages, an ancient hillfort and a former 12th-century Augustinian priory (NT) along the way.

RIDE 11
HAMPSHIRE
SU345304

INFORMATION

Total Distance
25 miles (40km), with 8 miles (13km) off-road; shorter route 20 miles (32km)

Grade
2

OS Maps
Landranger 1:50,000 sheet 185 (Winchester & Basingstoke)

Tourist Information
Romsey, tel: 01794 512987

Cycle Shops/Hire
Abbey Cycles, Romsey, tel: 01794 515328; Cycle World, Romsey, tel: 01794 513344

Refreshments
Depending on your start time, the

John of Gaunt pub (opposite the car park) is well worth patronising for good-value home-cooked food. For light lunches and teas along the way stop off at the delightful Squirrels Holt or Lilley Tea Rooms in Stockbridge (also pubs), Longstock Gardens (when open), Mottisfont post office tea rooms and at Mottisfont Abbey (NT). Pubs on the route include the idyllically positioned Mayfly at Testcombe (open all day), the Peat Spade in Longstock and the friendly Tally Ho! in Broughton (excellent ales)

The famous sight of the trigonometry point at Danebury Ring

START & ROUTE DIRECTIONS

Start

Horsebridge is a tiny hamlet beside the River Test, situated off the A3057 between Romsey and Stockbridge, 4 miles (6km) north of Romsey. Park free at the Test Way car park opposite the John of Gaunt pub.

Directions

1 🚲 Turn left out of the car park, cross the River Test and turn right to join the waymarked Test Way. This section of the long-distance trail follows a former railway route north for 3 miles (5km) to Stockbridge, affording delightful views across the lush river valley from the level and well-gravelled old track bed. On reaching tarmac and the edge of Stockbridge, proceed ahead to a roundabout and turn left if you wish to explore this attractive little town. Otherwise, continue ahead along the A30, soon to bear left at the next roundabout to join the A3057, signposted 'Andover'.

2 🚲 In 100 yards (90m) bear left on to a gravel track and follow the arrowed Test Way along a further stretch of old railway line, parallel with the main road. After 2½ miles (4km), pass beneath the A3057 and immediately bear right to join that road to reach the Mayfly pub across the river, if in need of refreshment. Continue along the old track bed for ½ mile (0.5km) to the A3057, turn left and then right, signed

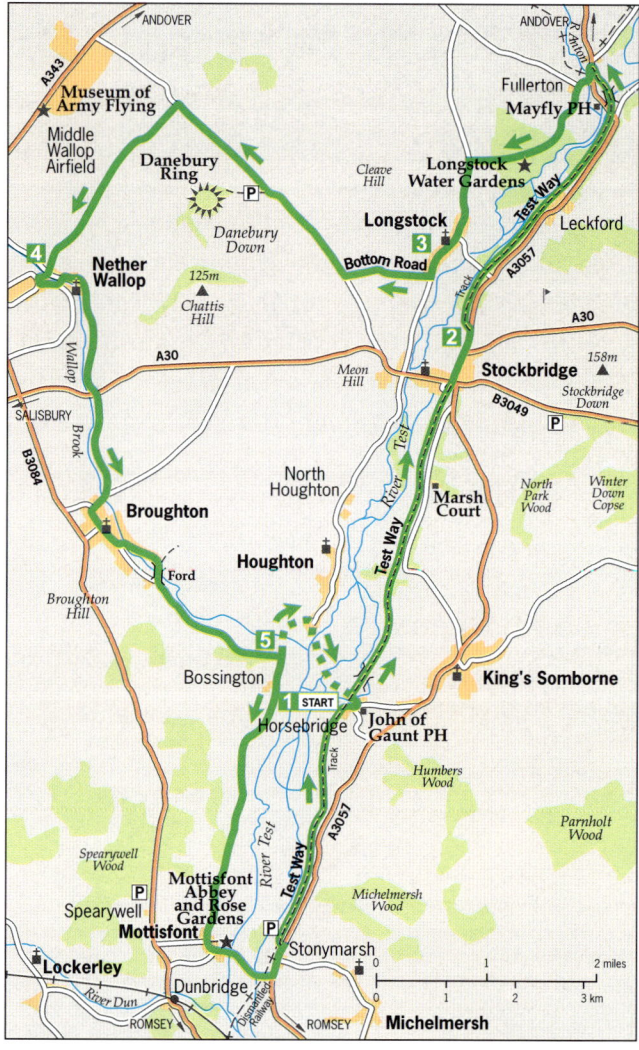

'Longstock'. Cross the River Anton, pass picturesque Fullerton Mill, then keep left at the next junction, soon to ascend gently past Longstock Water Gardens with fine valley views to a T-junction. Turn left and descend into Longstock.

3 🚲 Cycle through the village, then turn right up

Bottom Road on its southern fringe and steadily climb out of the river valley on a narrow lane to reach a T-junction (unsigned) opposite farm buildings. Turn right and follow an undulating downland road for 1 mile (1.5km) to reach the entrance to Danebury Hillfort. Remain on this gently rolling open road with good views for a

further 1 mile (1.5km) towards Middle Wallop Airfield and take the first left (unsigned) on to a narrow lane. Keep to this peaceful route for 2 miles (3km) and descend into the Wallop Valley and Nether Wallop.

④ 🚲 Cross straight over the valley road into the charming village centre, bearing left just before the Five Bells pub along a pretty thatched cottage-lined street, soon to pass the lane arrowed to the church. Turn right at the valley road and continue for 1 mile (1.5km) to the busy A30. Taking great care, cross straight over, signed 'Broughton', and enter the

village in a further 1 mile (1.5km). At a T-junction opposite the Greyhound pub, turn left, signposted 'Houghton'. Pass the church and shortly bear left along Rookery Lane. Where it ends at a crossing of tracks, turn right and soon cross a small bridge beside a ford on the Wallop Brook. Turn left along the valley road and cycle for 1½ miles (2.5km) to return to the Test Valley and a T-junction at Bossington.

⑤ 🚲 For a shorter route, omitting Mottisfont Abbey, turn left and keep to the road through Houghton and across the river valley back to Horsebridge. For the main

The small and pretty riverside town of Stockbridge

route, turn right and follow a splendid undulating lane, affording some of the best Test Valley views, for 3 miles (5km) to Mottisfont. Proceed through the village to reach the main entrance to Mottisfont Abbey and Rose Gardens. Keep to the lane and shortly cross the River Test to reach the A3057. Turn left, then in 200yds (180m) bear left through a car park to rejoin the Test Way. Head north along the former railway line for 2 miles (3 km) back to Horsebridge, then bear right beyond the old railway station to the car park.

PLACES OF INTEREST

Test Way: This trail traverses Hampshire from north to south from Inkpen Beacon to Totton, a distance of 46 miles (74km), mainly following the Test Valley and with 10 miles (16km) along the disused Test Valley railway.

Stockbridge: This attractive one-street town, popular with anglers, as the famous Chalk Stream, is one of the most sought after game fishing rivers in the world. Stretching across the idyllic Test Valley, the town has numerous specialist shops and tea rooms.

Longstock: With charming thatched cottages strung out along a narrow lane, complete with working farms at either end, a good pub and a 19th-century church displaying medieval tiles and a beautiful chancel arch, Longstock is the quintessential Hampshire village. The unique wooded Water Gardens have been created with a mosaic of ponds and streams close to the Test.

Danebury Hillfort: This important Iron-Age hillfort, comprising a double bank and ditch and an inner rampart covered with beech trees, commands extensive Hampshire views. Excavations have revealed a pattern of streets, shrines and over 100,000 fragments of pottery.

Nether Wallop: As delightful as it sounds, this village follows the course of the Wallop Brook for over a mile (1.5km), and boasts a wealth of beautiful old cottages and a hilltop church

Mottisfont Abbey sits elegantly in its well-kept grounds

containing a remarkable set of well-preserved 11th-century wall paintings. The village, and particularly the shop and neighbouring cottages, feature in the Miss Marple television mysteries.

Broughton: This is a well-kept village of thatched timbered houses and fine farmhouses surrounded by thatch-topped walls. In the churchyard stands a splendid circular dovecote, built of brick in 1684 and once housing 482 pairs of pigeons, the young birds providing a constant supply of meat. It is one of the few dovecotes in England with a potence open to the public.

Mottisfont Abbey (NT): Set picturesquely beside the River Test, Mottisfont Abbey is an 18th-century house adapted from a 12th-century Augustinian priory. It contains a drawing room decorated by Rex Whistler and the cellarium of the old priory, but the real attractions are the magnificent trees and the famous walled rose garden – well worth visiting in June for the heady perfume.

WHAT TO LOOK OUT FOR

Wild flowers abound along the unspoilt former railway track, with colouful violets, primroses, daffodils and bluebells lining the route. The bordering thickets are a haven to nightingales and warblers, while on the adjacent river and in the meadows you may see little grebes, swans, herons, kestrels and, if you are lucky, the flashing blue of the kingfisher. Note the grand white building (Marsh Court) on the hill as you approach Stockbridge, which was designed by Sir Edwin Lutyens. Where the route ventures close to the River Test look out for the curious little thatched fishing huts that grace the well-tended riverbanks and islands of this celebrated trout-fishing river.

Surrey – Heath and Woodlands

This is a delightful ride along quiet Surrey lanes and tracks, taking in several areas of classic heathland around both Frensham Great and Little Ponds. Various parts of the route follow rivers and streams which, apart from the Ponds themselves, add another dimension to a ride already rich in flora and fauna.

RIDE 12
SURREY
SU843403

INFORMATION

Total Distance
16½ miles (26.5km), with
8 miles (13km) off-road

Grade
2

OS Map
Landranger 1:50,000 sheet 186
(Aldershot & Guildford)

Tourist Information
Farnham, tel: 01252 715109

Cycle Shop/Hire
Cycle Scene, Aldershot,
tel: 012252 25640

Nearest Railway Stations
Farnham (4 miles/6.5km),
Bentley (5 miles/8km)

Refreshments
There are a variety of pubs, restaurants and cafés en route, including: The Pride of the Valley Hotel and Restaurant, a free house with garden suitable for families; Mariners Hotel and The Holly Bush pub, an excellent country inn with special children's menu. A picnic area at the start is excellent in summer and has a kiosk and stalls

Sailing boats on Frensham Great Pond

START & ROUTE DIRECTIONS

Start

Frensham Great Pond lies just off the A287 Farnham–Hindhead road.

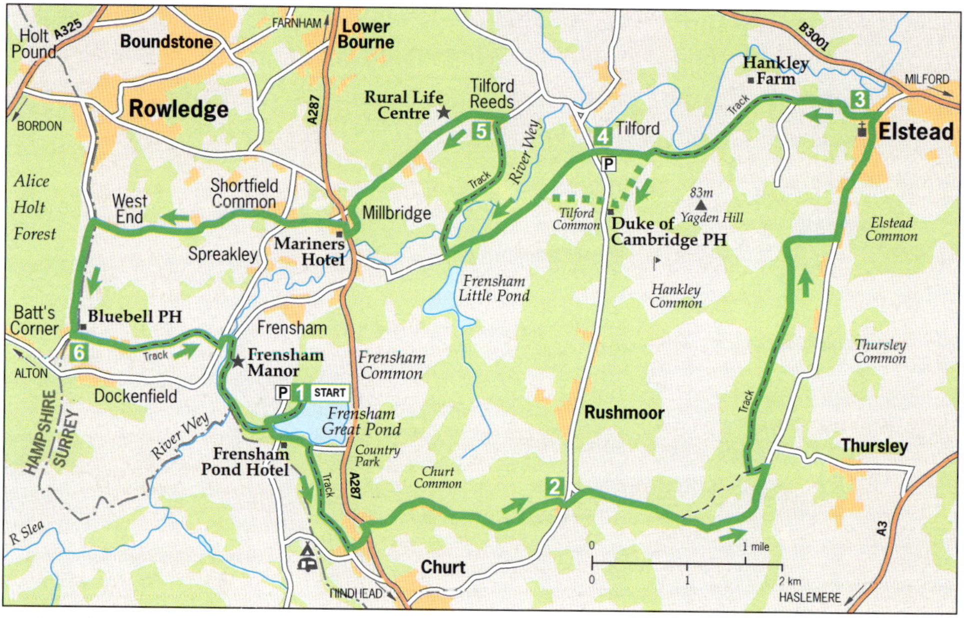

Churt, the left again at a T-junction and first right towards Tilford and Thursley.

② 🚲 Continue past the Pride of the Valley pub and go straight over the crossroads

(1.5km) turn left again into Westbrook Lane by St James's church.

③ 🚲 Pass a farmyard to a triangle and bear right along a bridleway past Hankley

Park in the car park about ¾ mile (1km) along on the left. Parking and toilet facilities are available between 9.00 and 6.00 all year round.

Directions

① 🚲 From the car park facing the water, turn right, follow the edge of the water to the road and turn left. Bear left at Frensham Pond Hotel, then soon turn right on to a bridleway. Once past Coppice Cottage, fork left uphill (quite steep for a very short distance – you may wish to walk this section). Bear right, then, on reaching a drive, turn left. At the road turn left towards

towards Thursley and Elstead. After 2 miles (3km) turn left on to a bridleway, signed 'Houndown'. Go over the bridge, bear right and carry on across the road past Chailey Wood and past a cemetery to a T- junction. Turn left and after 1 mile

Farm on the right, following blue marker arrows. At Stockbridge Pond bear right following red arrows to Tilford. (If you are in need of refreshment bear left across

The watermill in the village of Elstead

Thursley Common is just one of the scenic spots in the area

Hankley Common golf course to the car park, turn right and The Duke of Cambridge pub is on the left. Leaving the pub, go straight across the road on to the bridleway, then left at the end to rejoin the main route.)

4 🚲 At Tilford go straight across the road on to the byway, fork left following the red marker arrows and turn right at the public conveniences. To visit Frensham Little Pond carry straight along the byway for about 150 yards (140m), turn right and the car park is on the left. Following the bridleway marked '513', bear right past Keeper's Cottage across the bridge, through the farmyard and bear right along a bridleway. Bear left through the woods to the end and turn left.

5 🚲 Pass the Rural Life Centre on your right and continue to the main road, opposite the Mariners Hotel. Turn right and first left into 'Wirecut'. Turn left past The Holly Bush pub then right, signposted 'Broomfields and West End' and bear left into West End Lane past West End House and converted oast houses. Turn left at a T-junction and then second left past The Bluebell pub.

6 🚲 Carry straight on to a bridleway to reach the road. Turn left, first right over the river and right again through the gates of The Old Mill House. A bridleway is straight ahead up the hill. Follow this along the river bank, keeping left, to the end, where you turn left and then first right to take you back to Frensham Great Pond and the car park from where you started.

PLACES OF INTEREST

Frensham Common, Great and Little Ponds: The 1000 acres (405ha) covering these areas are owned by the National Trust and are replete with a wealth of flora and fauna. The common has a line of large prehistoric barrows, and most of the area is now a country park. From the Great Pond there are a selection of self-guided walks ranging from 25 minutes to 2½ hours. Frensham Pond Hotel, overlooking the Great Pond, was originally built in the 15th century as a private residence, and now provides a unique blend of country house charm with 20th-century facilities for those looking for a luxury break.

Rural Life Centre, Tilford: This extensive museum complex contains one of the biggest private collections of village and rural life artefacts in the country, and illustrates many aspects of farming over the past 100 years. The Centre is open from April to September and has ample car parking with café and picnic areas, and plenty to interest all age groups.

Frensham: The focal point of this village is St Mary the Virgin Church, a most interesting building, referred to in 'The Annals of Waverly Abbey', and dating back to 1239. The church has a Norman font and, beneath the tower, is a great copper cauldron over 400 years old, which according to tradition belonged to a local witch.

WHAT TO LOOK OUT FOR

This area abounds with wildlife, especially around Frensham Common and Great Pond, where mammals include roe deer, foxes and badgers, along with approximately 200 species of birds. Nesting by the ponds in the summer are many pairs of reed warblers and great crested grebes, whilst in winter among the wildfowl visible are pochard, goldeneye and tufted duck. The Great Pond is also a sanctuary for rare species such as the Dartford warbler, the woodlark, the silverstudded blue butterfly and the sand lizard. The Common is also one of only two sites in the country with a native population of all six British reptiles.

Relaxing on the shore of Frensham Little Pond

Sussex Wood and Downland

RIDE 13
SUSSEX
SU896186

INFORMATION

Total distance
Option 1: 17.5 miles (28km),
with 11 miles (17.5km) off-road;
option 2: 11 miles (17.5km),
with 7 miles (11.5km) off-road

Grade
3/2

OS Map
Landranger 1:50,000 sheet 197
(Chichester & the Downs)

Tourist Information
Midhurst, tel: 01730 817322;
Petworth, tel: 01798 343523

Nearest Railway Station
Haslemere 11 miles (17.5km)

Cycle Shop/Hire
Weald Cycles, Midhurst,
tel: 01730 815656

Refreshments
There are a number of good picnic
spots and a wealth of good pubs,
including The Three Moles at Selham,
Sussex Pub of the Year 1994, but
children are not allowed. The
Foresters Arms at Graffham, a 17th-
century freehouse with real ales, a

This is an attractive and varied ride following woodland trails and country lanes through the heart of the Cowdray estate, taking in both Duncton and Graffham Commons. The ride provides two options: Option 1, which utilises more off-road sections, is a longer and more testing ride. Option 2 is more for the casual holiday cyclist, having many attractive stop-offs. Those choosing Option 1 may wish to carry some refreshment as one longish section, whilst providing many attractive picnic spots, has no really suitable pubs for cyclists.

good restaurant and large garden, welcomes cyclists, walkers and children. The Hollist Arms, Lodsworth, another attractive freehouse, offers a similar welcome. The Horse Guards Inn, Tillington is more of a restaurant

than a pub, except in the garden during nice weather, and has excellent food. The Unicorn, Heyshott, also welcomes children and offers full restaurant facilities, and lunches and bar snacks

The majestic ruins of Cowdray House

Start

The tour begins at Heyshott Green, a village signposted on the left 2 miles (3km) south of Midhurst off the A286 Chichester road. There is ample parking on the edge of the quiet lanes that cross the green at the centre of the village.

Directions

1 ᨯᨯ Take the clearly marked gravel bridleway leading north opposite the pond in the centre of the village. At the fork, keep to the right-hand bridleway. After about 100 yards (100m) the bridleway bears to the right. At the crossways the bridleway kinks to the left, then straightens up alongside the main track. It is best to cycle on the bridleway itself rather than on the main track which is very sandy. At the junction, bear right, go straight across the fire break and over the disused railway bridge. At the road, turn right passing Todham stables on your left. At the triangle take the left-hand fork for Lodsworth and continue over the hump-backed bridge and across the river. Then go straight across the A272 on to the bridleway (you may wish to walk your bike across this busy road). Reaching the road at the top, turn right. After a couple of hundred yards, cut left on to the bridleway. At the junction of bridleways, keep right, soon rejoining the road to Lodsworth by Heath End Farm. When you reach the

centre of the village by the chestnut tree and with the Hollist Arms on your left, choose Option 1 (long) or Option 2 (short).

Option 1

2 ᨯᨯ Go left by the Hollist Arms towards Lodsworth Common and Haslemere for 1 mile (1.5km), passing the turning to Leggatt Hill with the river on your right. Turn right into River Park Farm, signed 'private road and bridleway', then left on to the bridleway. Follow this, bearing left on the main track up the hill and go through the gate into the yard. Bear left past the lake on your left, pass the old pumphouse on your

right, cross the bridge to the road and turn right. Continue past Old Mill Farm on your right to the T-junction, then turn right. Follow the Petworth Park wall on your left through Pheasant Copse. Pass the sign for River Common and head uphill, passing a tower on your left. Continue through Upperton, bearing left towards Tillington. Proceed past the cricket ground on your right, enjoying views of the South Downs. Cycle through Tillington, pass the Horse Guards pub on your right and the church on your left.

3 ᨯᨯ At the junction with the A272, turn left and

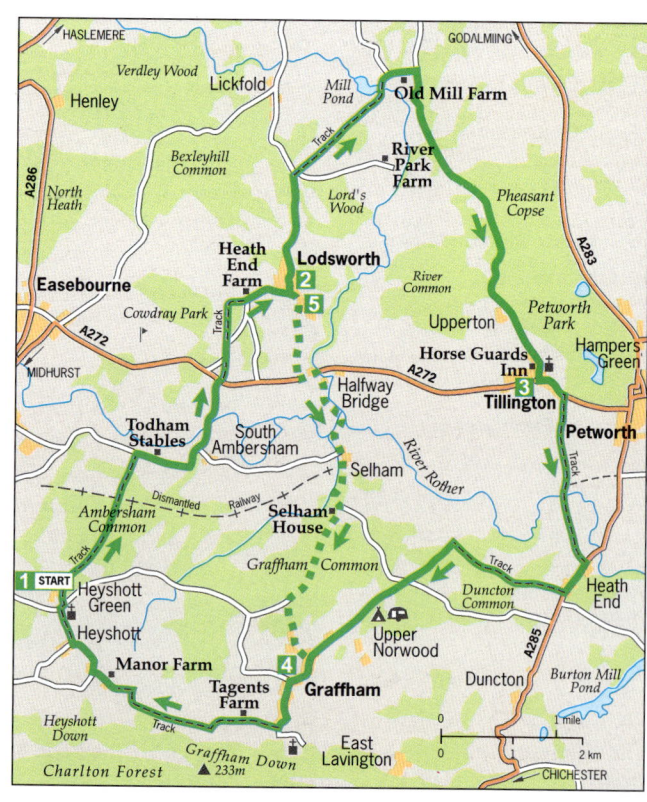

proceed for about 600 yards (550m) before turning right just past the Almshouses on to the bridleway. Follow this all the way down the hill, straight across the crossroads to the end and turn right past the farmyard, over the river bridge and along the track. On reaching the A285 Petworth to Chichester road, turn right uphill, then immediately right, past the BP garage on to a bridleway. At the bottom, bear left and then take the right-hand track (a bridleway) along the edge of the wood to the top. At the top, watch out for a bridleway which kinks left and immediately right; it is signposted. At the road, turn left then, at the junction, go straight across, following signs to Graffham, eventually passing the village shop and post office and the Foresters Arms on your left.

4 Carry on, following the sign to the church. Turn right along the bridleway to Tagents Farm. Follow the track around to the left and right along the bridleway at the foot of the downs. Pass the footpath to Hayland Farm and, on joining the track, turn left through Manor Farm to the road. Turn left then immediately right, past the Unicorn Inn and Heyshott church back to the green and your starting point.

Steam threshing at the Weald and Downland Museum

Option 2

5 At the Hollist Arms turn right, following the road to Halfway Bridge. At the junction with the A272 turn left for 400 yards (370m) by the Halfway Bridge pub, and then turn right for Selham. Continue over the river, and cycle through Selham, passing the Three Moles pub on the left. Bear right past Selham House, then cycle across Graffham Common, following signs for Graffham. At the end, turn right on to the main route by the Foresters Arms and proceed as for stage 4.

Elegant Petworth House houses a fine art collection

PLACES OF INTEREST

Cowdray Ruins: This great Tudor mansion, built between 1520 and 1542, was destroyed by fire, although the main kitchen is intact. The ruins are open from April to September afternoons, except Wednesday and Thursday. Adjacent Cowdray Park is the venue for polo matches in summer, mainly on weekends and bank holidays. For fixtures tel: 01730 813257.

Petworth House and Park (NT): All that remains of the 13th-century building, rebuilt in the 17th century, is the chapel, but the state rooms and galleries here contain one of the finest art collections in England, with works by Gainsborough, Van Dyck and, notably, Turner. The walled grounds and house are open to the public from the end of March to September, except Monday and Friday.

Graffham and Duncton Commons: These areas harbour an extensive range of wildlife and plantlife, especially primroses and, later, bluebells – a riot of colour in season.

WHAT TO LOOK OUT FOR

A wide variety of flora and fauna can be seen along this most scenic route, including primroses and bluebells. The ride affords magnificent views of the South Downs, as well as the pleasures of Petworth Deer Park.

Bewl Water and the High Weald

RIDE 14
KENT
TQ676337

INFORMATION

Total Distance
19 miles (30.5km), including
5 miles (8km) off-road

Grade
2

OS Map
Landranger 1: 50,000 sheet 188
(Maidstone & Weald of Kent)

Tourist Information
Royal Tunbridge Wells,
tel: 01892 534660

Cycle Hire
Bewl Bike Hire, Bewl Water,
tel: 01860 386144

Nearest Railway Station
Wadhurst (4 miles/6.5km)

Refreshments
Many pubs along the route, including
Elephants Head at Hook Green, with
family garden, The Swan at
Lamberhurst Down and the Globe
and Rainbow at Kilndown, also with
family garden. Kiosk facilities at Bewl
Water Visitor Centre, Bayham Old
Abbey and Bedgebury Pinetum. Tea
rooms/restaurant at Lamberhurst
Vineyards. There are picnic spots at
Scotney Castle, Bayham Abbey ruins
and at Bedgebury Pinetum

The High Weald presents a countryside of patchwork fields, hedges and woodlands, with steep-sided valleys giving dramatic views of rolling slopes. This ride takes in the romantic historic sights of Bayham Old Abbey and Scotney Castle. Bedgebury Forest and Pinetum give you an opportunity to get away from the roads and enjoy the quietness and beauty amongst exotic trees. But take great care when cycling along the short section of the A21.

Bedgebury Pinetum houses the national collection of conifers

START & ROUTE DIRECTIONS

Start

Bewl Water lies 15 miles (24km) south-east of Royal Tunbridge Wells in the heart of the Kent and Sussex High Weald. The ride starts from the visitor centre car park, accessed from the A21 2 miles (3km) south of Lamberhurst.

Directions

1 ☙ Follow the 'Exit' signs out of the car park. When you rejoin the lane turn left past a low barrier and follow the narrow lane, designated as 'restricted access'. After a long gradual descent for 2 miles (3km) past Bartley Mill fishery and cross a bridged stream.

2 ☙ Turn right for a short climb to the B2169, then right again, signposted 'Lamberhurst'. Continue for 1 mile (1.5km) past the turning for Bayham Abbey Lake and take the next drive on the left, signposted 'Bayham Old Abbey Ruins'. Return via the same drive back to the B2169 and turn left towards Lamberhurst.
Proceed through Hook Green, past the Elephant's Head, continuing for 1½ miles (2.5km) beside vineyards to meet the A21. Opposite is the driveway to Scotney Castle (NT), which is well worth a visit, but take care crossing the busy A21.

3 ☙ Return via the same driveway back to the A21 from the castle car park and turn left. Climb the long gradual ascent for 1½ miles (2km), turn left again for Kilndown and enter the village to view the old Christ Church. Continue for 110 yards (100m) and turn right at the Globe and Rainbow Inn. The road soon bends sharply left and then meanders for 2 miles (3km) to Bedgebury Cross. At the

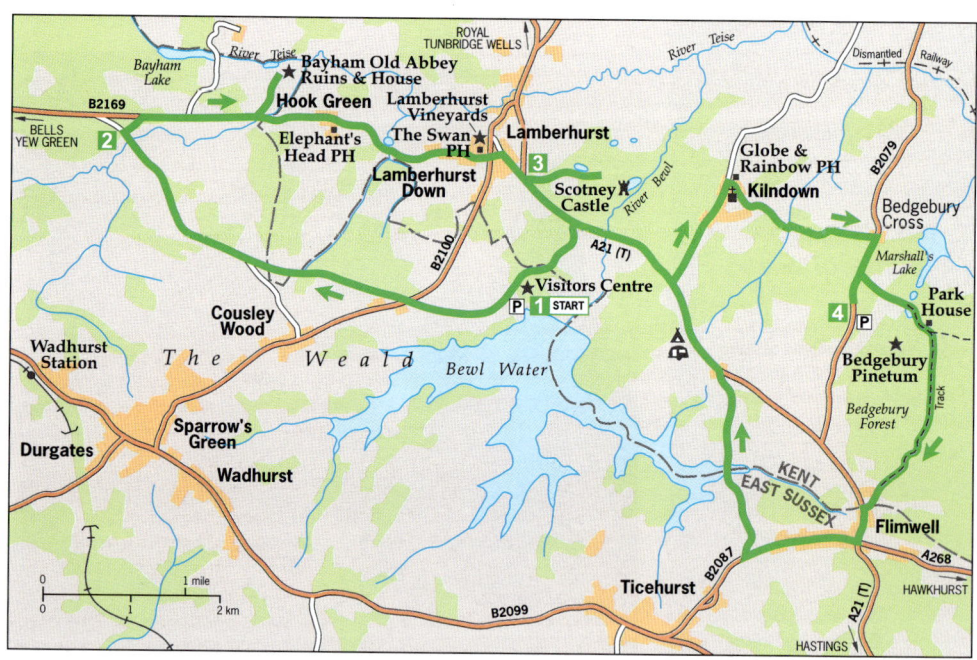

short climb do not miss the view over Bewl Water on the left. After 1 mile (1.5km) keep right when the lane feeds into another from the left. Follow Lamberhurst Down. At The Swan pub turn left for the entrance to Lamberhurst Vineyards, or continue straight across the crossroads T-junction with the B2079 turn right and continue for 1 mile (1.5km) to the car park entrance of Bedgebury Pinetum.

The evocative ruins of 13th-century Bayham Abbey

4 Leaving the Pinetum car park turn right and retrace your tracks for 400 yards (350m). Turn right on to the next driveway, marked 'Private Road'. Follow this bridleway downhill to the lake at the bottom, stopping for a few moments to take in the tranquil mood of Marshall's Lake. Proceed uphill until the drive turns into a rough track, continuing past Park House on the right and the Forestry Commission buildings on the left. Take the right fork of the bridleway (not straight on) and follow blue waymarkers. The track continues around the perimeter of the Pinetum, overlooking the wealth of shapes and colours of the tree collection. As you enter a dense pine plantation the track forks; keep left and continue for a short distance up to open terrain. Keep right and follow the blue arrows. Continue on the main track over a ramp to rejoin a tarmac drive leading to the A21 opposite Godfrey's Diner. Turn left and then right at the traffic lights on to the B2087, signposted 'Ticehurst'. Continue for 1½ miles (2km) and turn right into Rosemary Lane, which becomes a causeway across one leg of Bewl Water, a good viewpoint and stop-off. At the end of the road turn left back on to the A21 and continue for about 2 miles (3.5km) to the entrance road on the left, signposted 'Bewl Water'. Now follow the lane back to the visitor centre car park. From here the road continues along a 2-mile (3.5km) descent into Wye. For the final part of the journey, follow the 'P' signs past the church to return to the car park and starting point.

PLACES OF INTEREST

Bewl Water: This is a large flooded valley providing many associated watersports – fishing, sailing and windsurfing among others. It also has good nature trails around the perimeter, providing access for birdwatchers and walkers. Close to the main car park is a visitor's centre with a restaurant, information desk and a playground.

Bayham Old Abbey Ruins and House: Situated in the picturesque wooded valley of the River Teise, this impressive abbey was built in the 13th century by Premonstratensian monks from France. In the 18th century the remaining ruins that survived the Reformation were landscaped to provide a romantic view from Bayham Old Abbey House.

Lamberhurst Vineyards: Established in 1972, there are

WHAT TO LOOK OUT FOR

Bewl Water provides a haven for wintering wildfowl, especially large numbers of tufted duck and pochard during hard weather. Passage migrants during spring and autumn include waders such as greenshank and sandpipers. Late autumn is a good time to see ospreys 'stocking up' on their return flight to Africa. Hawfinches are a speciality at Bedgebury Pinetum; they are best identified by their call as they tend to keep to the tree-tops, making them elusive. In spring the hedgerows abound with primroses, lady's smock, celandines and, later, bluebells. During autumn the pinetum has a rich variety of rare and beautiful fungi.

guided tours of the vineyards, winery and cellars to see the fascinating wine-making process, from vine to glass. The tour finishes with a chance to taste the wines seen in production.

Scotney Castle: A National Trust estate with the ruins of a moated 14th-century castle surrounded by picturesque landscaped gardens, this is well worth a visit. Rhododendrons,

azaleas, water lilies and wisteria all flower in profusion.

Bedgebury Pinetum: The National Conifer Collection was started by the Forestry Commission and Kew Gardens during the 1920s and now provides a beautiful landscape in which to wander amongst exotic trees with a rich variety of shapes and colours.

Scotney Castle gardens

The North Downs Way and the Stour Valley

This ride explores the undulating ridges and dry valleys of the North Downs Way between the pretty and historic villages of Wye and Chilham. It follows the Stour Valley overlooking the neolithic long barrow of Jullieberrie's Grave, returning to enjoy superb views from the chalk downland of the Devil's Kneading Trough on the Wye Downs.

RIDE 15
KENT
TR052467

INFORMATION

Total Distance
22 miles (35km), with 5 miles (8km) off-road

Grade
2–3

OS Map
Landranger 1:50,000 sheet 189 (Ashford & Romney Marsh)

Tourist Information
Ashford, tel: 01233 629165

Cycle Shops/Hire
Trev's Cycle Centre, Ashford, tel: 01233 641310;
Ken James Ltd, Ashford, tel: 01233 634334

Nearest Railway Station
Wye (½ mile/1km)

Refreshments
The Tickled Trout pub next to the railway station has an attractive family garden on the river's edge. At Chilham there is The White Horse and The Woolpack Inn, and The Compasses at Sole Street offers a children's room and picnic area. There are also tea rooms and restaurants at Wye and Chilham

The flower-decked White Horse pub in Chilham

START & ROUTE DIRECTIONS

Start

Wye lies 5 miles (8km) north-east of Ashford alongside the Great Stour river, 1½ miles (2.5km) off the A28. The free village car park is 220 yards (200m) west of the central Church of St Martin and St Gregory.

Directions

1 🚲 From the car park turn left through the estate to the end of the road. Turn right and pass The Tickled Trout pub and go over the railway. Turn right again into Bramble Lane and after 1 mile (1.5km) go straight across the A28 into White Hill, signposted 'Challock'. After a slight climb for ½ mile (1km) turn right along a farm track to Soakham Farm, and follow the red waymarkers, labelled 'North Downs Way'.

2 🚲 The track passes through the farm and continues beyond double gates. As the track narrows it bends left then right and climbs very steeply. It is advisable to walk the short distance to the ridge top and savour the superb views and wild flowers. At the top the track enters a coppice woodland. After 110 yards (100m) reach a fork and keep right following the red waymarkers. Continue through the woodland, straight across the crossing of ways and keep left at the next fork. Follow the top of the ridge, overlooking the valley towards Chilham. As you join the larger spruce plantation keep right, following the red waymarkers for 1½ miles (2.5km). On reaching a barred gate turn right and descend the ridge with caution because of loose stones. Bear left at the bottom and exit through another gate to rejoin the tarmac lane. Keep straight on through Mountain Street to Chilham. At a sharp right bend, fork left up School Hill to the village square. At the top on the left is the entrance to Chilham Castle.

3 🚲 Across the square, facing The White Horse pub, turn right into the High Street and continue past the Woolpack Inn. Keep left and then turn right to join the A28. Turn right on to the main road and shortly turn left on to a rough track. Cross the railway bridge and turn left to follow the red waymarkers labelled 'Stour Valley Walk'. In 545 yards (500m) take the next sharp right bend where the view overlooks the site of Julliberrie's Grave. (A footpath to the left leads to the site.) The cycle route continues to the right, meandering and undulating alongside the ridge for about 1½ miles (2.5km) when the track joins the Mystole Road. After ¾ mile (1.2km) turn right and follow the slow climb from Thruxted up into

The lush, green valley of the Devil's Kneading Trough

Denge Wood. Continue to a crossroads and turn right for The Compasses inn at Sole Street, or continue on towards Waltham. At the next T-junction turn left into the village, then right at the Lord Nelson pub into Church Lane, following signs to St Bartholomew's Church.

4 🚲 Descend a steep hill for ¾ mile (1.2km), bear left to a T-junction and turn right, signposted 'Hastingleigh and Ashford'. Continue for ¾ mile (1.2km), turning right at Dean Farm, and soon fork left to Elmstead. Climb the short, sharp hill to the top and then turn right, signed 'Wye'. The views from the next bend makes the climb worthwhile. Continue down the steep hill,

taking care at the sharp right bend. Proceed straight across the next crossroads to Hastingleigh. Keep right past The Bowl inn and, after 1 mile (1.5km), the road runs alongside the ridge of the Wye Downs. Pause at the Devil's Kneading Trough (access

opposite the car park) to explore the chalkland.

5 🚲 The road continues along a 2-mile (3km) descent into Wye. Follow the 'P' signs past the church to return to the car park and starting point.

The beautiful Adonis blue butterfly, a welcome midsummer sight

PLACES OF INTEREST

Wye: This is a very old settlement, commanding the river gap of the Great Stour through the North Downs. Today it is a centre renowned for agricultural learning and research. The main street is dominated by the Church of St Martin and St Gregory, built in the late 12th century. Wye's 'Crown', to the east of the town on the North Downs Way, was cut into the chalk hillside to record the Coronation of Edward VII in 1902.

WHAT TO LOOK OUT FOR

The Chalk downlands offer a superb habitat for specialist plants, with orchids abundant in early summer. Dropworts, salad burnet, common centaury, bellflowers and harebells appear during the height of mid-summer, along with chalkhill and Adonis blue butterflies. The woodlands in April and May are alive with cuckoos, chiff-chaff, willow warblers and blackcaps announcing their arrival.

Chilham and Chilham Castle: Lying across the Great Stour at the end of a steep-sided ridge, Chilham is recognised as one of the prettiest villages in Kent. Its village square of half-timbered houses and historical St Mary's Church are popular tourist attractions. At the western edge is Chilham Castle, a Jacobean mansion of 1616. The gardens, designed by 'Capability' Brown in 1771, are well worth a visit. At the foot of the ridge lies a large heronry which is known to date back at least 800 years.

Julliberrie's Grave: This neolithic long-barrow, some 5,000 years old, later became the burial place of a tribune of Julius Caesar's army.

St Bartholomew's Church, Waltham: This simple 13th-century church is ringed with old yew trees in the churchyard. The walls are of flint and brick and the present building originated in Norman times but contains work of the Early English, Decorated and Perpendicular periods.

Devil's Kneading Trough, Wye Downs: A valley formed by ice some 10,000 years ago, this natural formation is part of the Wye and Crundale Downs Nature Reserve. It is rich with flowers of chalk downland, especially orchids. Views of the English Channel can be seen on clear days.

Wye Downs, including Wheatfield, the Pilgrim's Way and Broad Down

Through the Thames and Pang Valleys

Incorporating peaceful lanes, good surfaced bridleways and wide downland tracks, this varied ride explores some beautiful rolling countryside. Cycle through unspoiled Berkshire villages, visit a fine Elizabethan mansion, and savour the splendid views of the Chiltern Hills from the Ridgeway. Generally easy pedalling through the valleys, but with some long, steady climbs.

RIDE 16
OXFORDSHIRE/BERKSHIRE
SU600807

INFORMATION

Total Distance
30 miles (48km), with
3½ miles (5.5km) off-road

Grade
3

OS Maps
Landranger 1:50,000 sheets 175
(Reading & Windsor) and 174
(Newbury & Wantage)

Tourist Information
Wallingford, tel: 01491 826972;
Reading, tel: 01734 566226

Cycle Shop/Hire
Berkshire Cycle Company, Reading,
tel: 01734 661799; A W Cycles,
Reading, tel: 01734 420300; Mountain
High (Shop), Pangbourne,
tel: 01734 841851

Nearest Railway Station
Goring-on-Thames

Refreshments
There are plenty of places to eat and drink along the way. For welcoming tea/coffee or light lunch stops try Goring Heath Post Office (good garden), Mapledurham House/Watermill (if visiting), Duck's Ditty (not Sundays) in Pangbourne, the Royal Oak at Yattendon (good food) and the Riverside Tea Rooms in Goring. Basildon House (NT) also has a decent café if exploring after the ride. Pubs worth visiting include the Bull in Stanford Dingley, the Pot Kiln at Frilsham (splendid location) and the unspoilt Bell at Aldworth – all welcome children. Take a picnic and sit beside the Thames at Pangbourne or Streatley, or relax in Mapledurham Country Park

A river launch glides along the tranquil Thames at Pangbourne

START & ROUTE DIRECTIONS

Start

Goring-on-Thames is an attractive village beside the Thames on the B4009, ⅓ mile (0.5km) off the A329 between Reading and Wallingford. Pay-and-display car park (free Sundays) and toilets are in the centre, signed along Manor Road off the High Street opposite the Miller of Mansfield pub.

Directions

1️⃣ 🚲 Walk your bike along the footpath beside the toilets to the High Street (B4009) and turn right, soon to cross the railway to reach a

T-junction. Turn right on to the B4526, signed 'Reading', then where the B-road is arrowed right, keep straight ahead into Gatehampton Lane past the railway station. Leaving the village, pass an access drive to Gatehampton Nurseries on your right and begin to ascend a narrow metalled lane, signed 'not suitable for motors'. Keep to the tarmac road, climbing steadily out of the Thames Valley, with splendid views, to reach Upper Gatehampton Farm at the top. Pass beside a metal gate and follow this traffic-free lane to the B471.

2️⃣ 🚲 Cross straight over, signed 'Goring Heath', pass

the Rising Sun pub, then keep left at the next junction (grass triangle) and soon reach a T-junction. Turn right towards Mapledurham and pass Goring Heath Post Office (teas). Remain on this level stretch of road for 1½ miles (2.5km) and turn right on to a single-track lane, signed 'Mapledurham'. Soon descend for ½ mile (1km) to Mapledurham House, Watermill and Country Park beside the Thames. Return along the lane and take the arrowed bridleway left at a whitewashed cottage, arrowed 'Whitchurch' (good valley views). Pass through the gates, join a wide gravel track and soon pass Hardwick

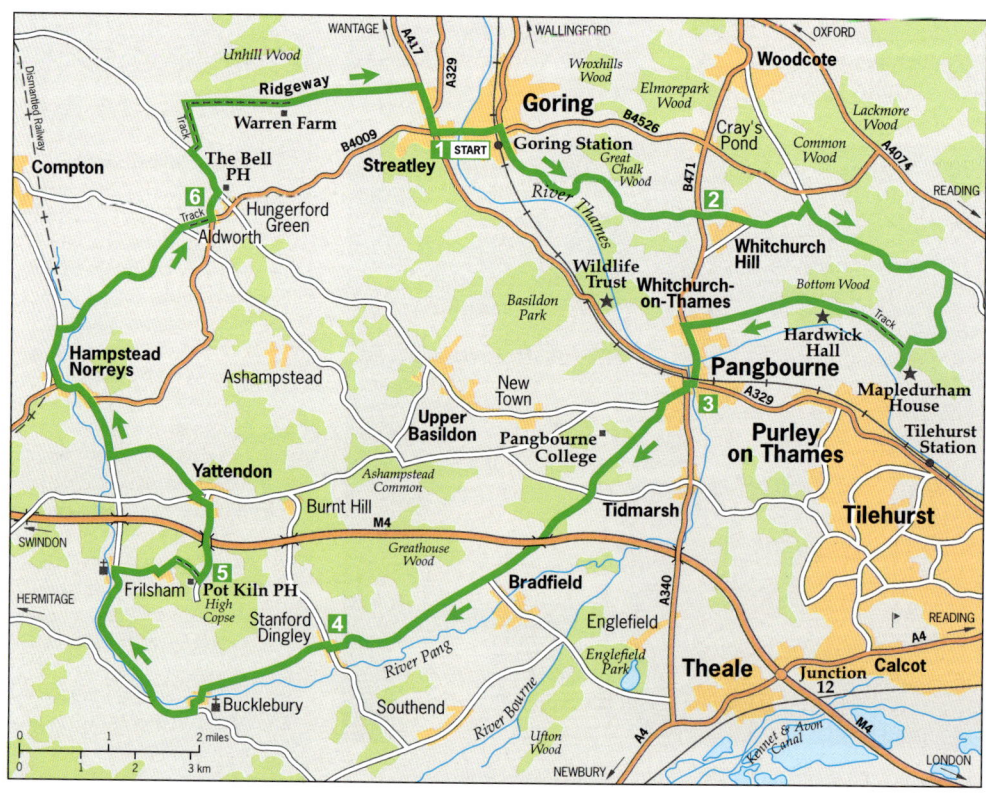

The town of Whitchurch has links with author Kenneth Grahame of Wind in the Willows *fame*

House (Toad Hall in *Wind in the Willows*); follow its metalled drive to a lane. Keep ahead, passing Bozedown Vineyard (weekend tastings) and soon enter Whitchurch. At the T-junction with the B471 turn left downhill into the village and cross the Thames via a toll-bridge (free to cycles) into Pangbourne.

3 ⛷ Bear right at the roundabout in the village centre, then left at the next roundabout on to the A340 (Basingstoke). Almost immediately turn right by the church into Pangbourne Hill, signposted 'Upper Basildon'. Gradually climb for ¼ mile (0.5km) then turn left along Bere Court Road, signed

'Pangbourne College'. Follow this delightful narrow lane for 1 mile (1.5km) to a crossroads and go straight on towards Bradfield (Dark Lane). Shortly, pass beneath the M4, then proceed across the next crossroads, signposted 'Stanford Dingley'. To explore Bradfield turn left. With views left across the Pang Valley, keep to this gently undulating lane for 2 miles (3km) to a T-junction and turn left if you wish to visit Stanford Dingley (fine church and pubs).

4 ⛷ Your main route heads right, then immediately left, signed 'Bucklebury', through this valley on a narrow road. Turn left at the next T-junction into Bucklebury, crossing the River Pang to a T-junction near the church. Turn right towards the Hermitage, pass Briff Lane, then turn right (Frilsham) and cross a footbridge beside a ford. Immediately bear left at a fork of lanes and follow the river for 1½ miles (2.5km) to reach Frilsham church, beside Frilsham Mill, its millstream and a manor house. Turn right just past the church and climb steadily into Frilsham village. Pass the playing field on your left, then take the arrowed bridleway right and gently descend on a good gravel track to reach a lane beside the Pot Kiln pub.

5 ⛷ Turn left and follow the lane across the M4 into Yattendon, taking second right into the village centre. Bear left, then right by the Royal Oak for Hampstead Norreys and shortly descend

back into the Pang Valley to a T-junction. Turn right into Hampstead Norreys, bearing left along the B4009 through the village. Turn left along Water Street at the small roundabout beyond the church, signed 'Compton'. Leave the village, keeping right at a T-junction, then in ¼ mile (0.5km) turn right (unsigned) beside an isolated house (Uplands). Climb out of the valley on a quiet lane to reach a T-junction opposite the drive to Pibworth House. Turn right, then immediately left along a waymarked, narrow-hedged bridleway leading to Aldworth.

6 ⛷ On reaching a lane turn left uphill, passing the parish church into the village centre. Keep left (The Bell and old-fashioned shop to your right) and follow the metalled lane out of the village on to open downland. Disregard the byway left and soon take the arrowed byway right, a wide stony track that undulates with fine Thames Valley and Chiltern views to a T-junction with the Ridgeway. Turn right and start a long, easy descent off Thurle Down, the sometimes rough track gives way to tarmac at Warren Farm. Proceed for 1½ miles (2.5km), turn right along the A417. At the junction with the A329 (traffic lights), turn right then left at the following crossroads and descend through Streatley. Cross the Thames back into Goring, passing the Miller of Mansfield pub to locate the footpath back to the car park beside the newsagents and your starting point.

PLACES OF INTEREST

Goring-on-Thames: This attractive Thames-side village enjoys a glorious setting between the Chiltern Hills and the Berkshire Downs. There has been a settlement here since prehistoric times, as the ancient Icknield Way and Ridgeway converged on a ford across the River Thames here. It is an ideal place from which to enjoy a pleasant stroll along the Thames Path.

Mapledurham: This secluded village beside the Thames has charming 17th- and 19th-century red-brick buildings and a delightful 14th-century church clustered around an Elizabethan mansion. The house featured in the TV series *The Forsyte Saga*, and both the house and the nearby watermill – the last corn and grist mill on the Thames – were used for the setting of the film *The Eagle Has Landed*. The house and watermill are open summer weekends and bank holidays; the country park has a picnic area and tea room.

Pangbourne: This pleasant town on the confluence of the Thames and Pang rivers was home to Kenneth Grahame, author of *The Wind in the Willows*, and, strolling along the riverbank, you can imagine his characters rowing up the river. The Swan Hotel is featured in Jerome K Jerome's *Three Men in a Boat*. Near by, and well worth a visit, is Basildon Park, an imposing 18th-century house owned by the National Trust (open), and Beale Park, where colourful exotic birds can be seen in an attractive riverside setting.

Stanford Dingley: Straddling the River Pang, this picturesque village boasts some fine old cottages, two decent pubs and one of the oldest churches in Berkshire. Mainly dating from 1200, it is an enlargement of a smaller church that existed before 1066 and houses a Norman font and fragments of 13th century wall-paintings.

Aldworth: This unspoiled downland village with a fine

An immaculately kept cottage in Goring-on-Thames

church is famous for its remarkable monuments thought to date from the 14th century known locally as the Aldworth Giants. Opposite the Bell Inn stands the now disused village well, which at 327 feet is one of the deepest in the country.

The Ridgeway: This ancient trail, reputedly the oldest highway in Britain, once linked East Anglia and Dorset. Now a national walking trail, it explores the Chilterns and Berkshire Downs between Ivinghoe Beacon in Buckinghamshire and Avebury in Wiltshire.

WHAT TO LOOK OUT FOR

Stretches of woodland flanking many of the tiny lanes abound with bluebells, wild garlic and other colourful flowers in spring and the call of the cuckoo is never far away. Bucklebury churchyard is pretty as a picture in spring, with a profusion of flowers lining its stone path. Look carefully for the carvings – a cross with a seated figure and a man with a wheel – on the south-east buttress of the church and note the fine stained-glass window which, unusually, shows a clean-shaven Christ looking up to Heaven. Pangbourne features one of England's few surviving privately owned toll-bridges, the right to toll having existed since 1792, when the ferry was replaced by the bridge. Also in Pangbourne look out for the old village lock-up behind Church Cottage in Pangbourne Hill.

RIDE 17
OXFORDSHIRE
SP252122

Burford and the Windrush Valley

This route links two Cotswold towns which have very different and distinctive characters. The Windrush Valley is the link between them; it is a haven of beauty and wildlife with some of the most picturesque villages in England along its length. The route itself is mainly flat, but there are one or two climbs which require low gears and a steady approach.

INFORMATION

Total Distance
19¼ miles (31km)

Grade
2

OS Maps
Landranger 1:50,000 sheets 163
(Cheltenham & Cirencester) and
164 (Oxford & surrounding area)

Tourist Information
Burford, tel: 01993 823558;
Witney, tel: 01993 775802)

Nearest Railway Station
Shipton-under-Wychwood
(4 miles/6.5km)

Cycle Shops/Hire
Giles Sports, Toys and Cycles,

Carterton, tel: 01993 842396;
Halfords, Abingdon, tel: 01235 521965

Refreshments
Many tea shops, cafés and pubs in
Burford and Witney and pubs along
the route, with many picnic
opportunities along the Windrush
Valley

The enormous church in Burford dates from Norman times

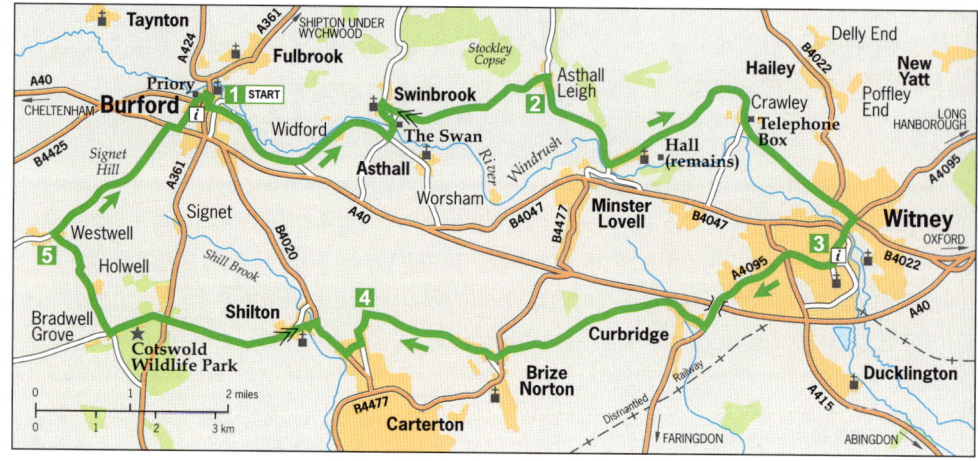

START & ROUTE DIRECTIONS

Start
Burford is a classic Cotswold town, just off the A40 between Oxford and Cheltenham road, on the A361 Chipping Norton road. There are plenty of car parks and on-street parking. The route starts from the bottom of the High Street in Burford.

Directions
1 🚲 Head up the High Street towards Lechlade on the A361. Turn left into Swan Lane after about 220 yards (200m) from the bottom of the High Street. At the crossroads go straight over, and at the end bear right almost opposite a house called The Mill. After a mile (1.5km) bear left, then at the crossroads turn left for Swinbrook and Shipton.

2 🚲 Cross over the bridge into Swinbrook past the Swan pub and follow the road up through the village. Drop down the rise and turn very

sharp right just after the church, taking the small gravelled lane up away from the village through the small ford, then turning left up the rise. Follow this road (with its views over the neighbouring village of Asthall) to the T-Junction at Asthall Leigh.

Witney was once famous for its two mills

Minster Lovell Hall's residents have suffered great misfortune

3 ▓ Turn right towards Minster Lovell and Witney, pass the converted church and drop back into the valley. Follow signs for Minster Lovell, and when you reach the village take the left turn before you cross the river. (If you wish to explore this delightful village cross over the river and turn right on the opposite bank. The village is ½ mile (1km) up the hill.) Retrace your tracks to rejoin the main route. Follow the road past the remains of Lovell's Hall and follow the main run of the road to Crawley. Keep right through Crawley, past the phone box and keep following signs for Witney. As you come into Witney bear right at the mini-roundabout, go over the river bridge and head for the town centre.

4 ▓ Go up the main street, and at the junction by the Tourist Information Centre turn right. Carry on to the large roundabout, turning left on to the A4095. Follow this road to Curbridge. Turn right into Curbridge, following the road towards Brize Norton. Swing around the Z-bends as you approach Brize Norton, turning left at the mini-roundabout, then turn immediately right. Continue, heading for Carterton and Shilton. After a mile (0.5km) the road turns sharp left, 220 yards (200m) later turn right, then right again towards Shilton.

Turn left in to Shilton, go past the Rose and Crown, up the hill, and enjoy the freewheel and the long stretch to the main road.

5 ▓ Take care crossing the main road (the traffic moves quite fast here) and go past the Cotswold Wildlife Park, heading for Holwell. At Bradwell Grove turn sharp right then head up into Holwell, past the small village church.

Drop down into the valley and roll into Westwell. Turn right as you enter Westwell (signposted 'Burford') go up the gentle rise, past Freedlands Farm and over Signet Hill, to the A40. Turn right, and soon left into Tanners Lane.

Head down the lane, turn left at the bottom and right at the Lamb Inn into Priory Lane, following the lane round the tight bends, past the 'School' sign and back into Burford High Street.

PLACES OF INTEREST

Burford: The town has a wealth of architectural interest, including the Bear Inn, Grammar School and Crown Inn, all of which date from the 15th century. Other buildings (such as The Bull) were given a later Georgian façade. The Priory is an Elizabethan house, once owned by William Lenthall, former Speaker to the Long Parliament. The church is one of the largest in Oxfordshire, with a Norman west door, though most of the rest dates from the 15th century.

Minister Lovell: One of the loveliest villages in the Windrush valley, this was home to the ill-fated Lovell family, whose members seem to have perished by a variety of misfortune. The church contains 15th-century glass but is now mainly 19th century in style.

Witney: According to the Domesday Book, Witney was blessed with two mills, and it has a worldwide reputation for blanket making. Its location makes it ideal, with the clear water of the Windrush combined with the wool from local sheep. There is much of architectural interest, including a church with many Norman features but a 15th-century spire some 156 feet (48m) tall.

Cotswold Wildlife Centre: The centre could be a stop for a welcome break before the last leg of the ride back to Burford. Visitors will find refreshments and picnic tables as well as a wide variety of wildlife exhibits designed for both adults and children. There are nature trails to explore, the fun of feeding some young animals and many information boards which explain the work of the centre. There is also a souvenir shop.

The old village post office in Minster Lovell

RIDE 18
BUCKINGHAMSHIRE/ HERTFORDSHIRE
SP993082

Hill and Vale

INFORMATION

Total distance
27 miles (43km), with 2 miles (3km) off-road and a diversion of 2 miles (5km)

Grade
3

OS Maps
Landranger 1:50,000 sheets 165 (Aylesbury and Leighton Buzzard) and 166 (Luton and Hertford)

Tourist Information
Berkhamsted Library,
tel: 01442 877638

Cycle Shop (no Hire)
Dees, Berkhamsted, tel: 01442 877447

This ride includes the magnificent beechwoods of Ashridge Park, the wide views over the Vale of Aylesbury from Ivinghoe Beacon and some pleasant lanes and villages, concluding with the well-surfaced and interesting towpath of the Grand Union Canal. There are some steady climbs to attain the viewpoints, but much of the route is flat or gently undulating with one sharp descent. The whole area is easy to reach from London, so, if possible, try to visit away from weekends.

Nearest Railway Station
Berkhamsted

Refreshments
Pennyfarthing Hotel/Restaurant, Berkhamsted. Way In, Post Office, Berkhamsted. Town Farm Tea Rooms,

Aldbury. Cafe, Ashridge Monument. The many good pubs along the way include The Bridgwater Arms, Little Gaddesden, The Stag, Mentmore, The Old Swan, Cheddington, The Duke of Wellington, Cheddington Wharf, and The Valiant Trooper, Aldbury

The remains of 11th-century Berkhamsted Castle

Start

Berkhamsted is situated off the A41 south-east of Tring. Start from either Berkhamsted railway station, the nearby station car park or by the Castle (there is more parking in St John's Lane, off High Street)

Directions

1️⃣ 🚲 Head north up Brownlow Road with Berkhamsted Castle on your right. Following cycle way signs, turn left uphill towards Ashridge. At the junction at the top of the hill by the war memorial, turn left towards Ashridge and at the bottom of the descent go straight on past the sign 'Private Road to Ashridge Management College' to the gentle climb

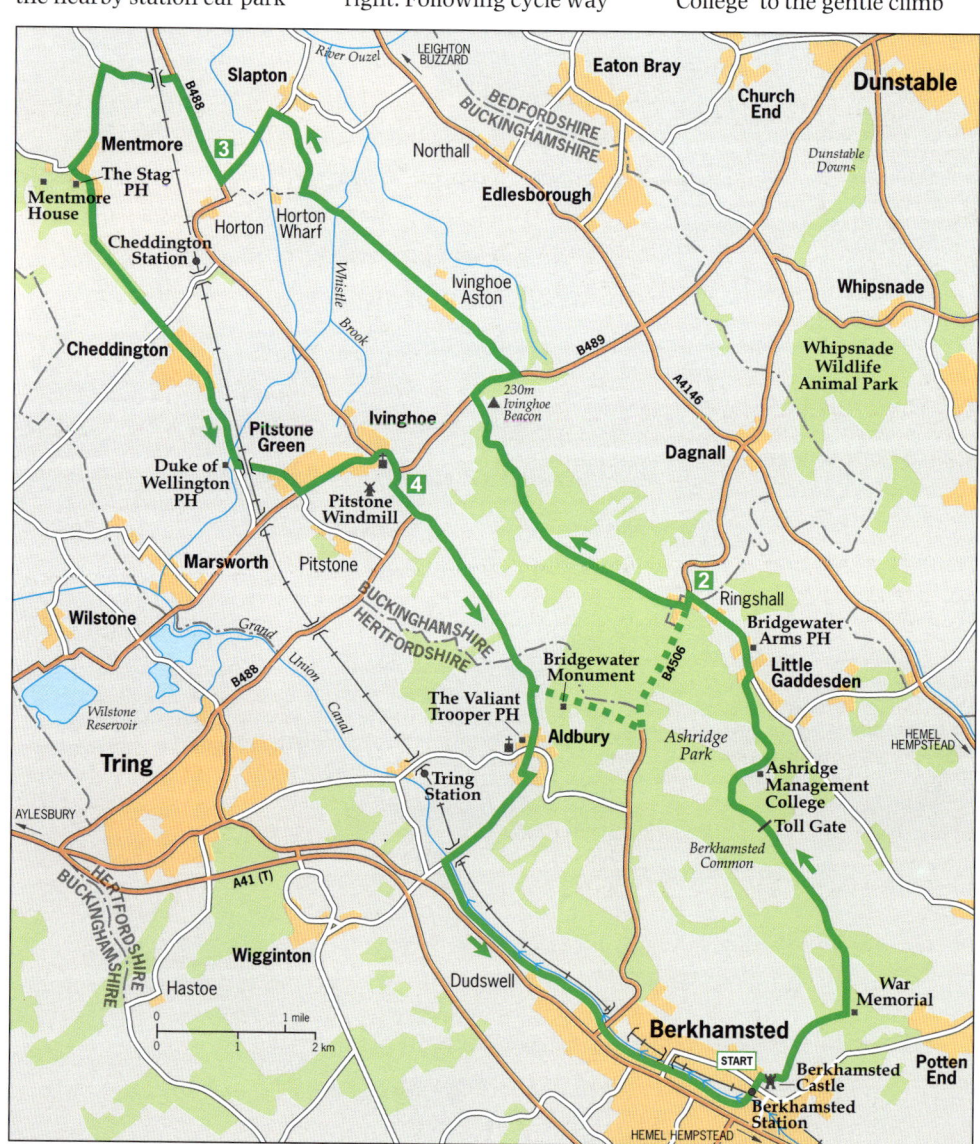

The granite Monument is the main focal point of Ashridge Estate

through the woods to the magnificent mansion, once home of the Dukes of Bridgewater (beware the large sleeping policemen). After the toll gate (no charge to cyclists) descend and climb to leave the grounds at Little Gaddesden. Turn left to Ringshall.

2 🚲 By the Deerleap Swimming Pool turn left on the B4506 and immediately right, signed to Marsworth and Ivinghoe. (Otherwise detour 'out and home' to the Bridgewater Monument along the B4506 for 2 miles (3km) then turn right. As the trees of Ashridge Common thin out, enjoy grand views from the Chiltern edge north to the Whipsnade lion chalk carving. As the road approaches the descent it bends sharply left and the track straight on leads to the summit of Ivinghoe Beacon, well worth the short walk entailed. Carefully descend to

the B489, turn right, descend again and in ½ mile (1km) turn left, signed 'Ivinghoe Aston'. On the right is the deep valley, Incombe Hole, a geological reminder of the extent of the last Ice Age. Continue for 3 miles (5km) to the outskirts of Slapton, where you turn left towards Horton and the B488.

3 🚲 Turn right on the B488 and in 1 mile (1.5km) take the next left under the railway bridge that was the site of the Great Train Robbery, then left again, signed 'Mentmore', once home of Lord Rosebery. From the pretty green there are more wide views north. Turn left and enjoy the descent to the avenue. The house will appear on your right. Continue over mini-roundabouts through Cheddington and after crossing the hump-backed

bridge over the canal, turn left by the Duke of Wellington pub to Pitstone Green and left again at the roundabout to follow the B486 through Ivinghoe to bear right on the B488 past Pitstone windmill (well worth a visit).

4 🚲 Continue uphill, straight on where the major road bends right, on the narrow lane signed 'weight limit 7.5 tons'. Look back from the top of the hill at the last wide view and descend to Aldbury, straight over the crossroads and along the winding lane to the canal bridge. Turn left and walk down to the grassy towpath which can easily be ridden to the next bridge. Here turn left on the bankside road to Dudswell, then cross to the south side of the canal and turn left again on the semi-surfaced towpath all the way back to Berkhamsted.

PLACES OF INTEREST

Elaborate bench-ends in Ivinghoe church

Berkhamsted Castle: Pleasing but fragmentary remains of the moated motte and bailey 11th-century castle, with its later links with the Black Prince, make for a relaxing stroll.

Ashridge Park: The home of the Duke of Bridgewater, who from 1765 pioneered the building of canals in Britain by the engineer, James Brindley. The Grand Union Canal, which opened up trade between the Midlands and London, was built between 1793 and 1805 and with it the reservoirs around Marsworth, now nature reserves of great importance. There are a number of information boards along the canal. This visit may whet the appetite for more exploration on the area's towpaths and reservoirs, where many different varieties of duck may be seen, as well as coots, moorhens, herons and the occasional kingfisher. The park also contains fallow and muntjac deer and the edible dormouse or glis-glis.

Ivinghoe: The handsome church by the village green has 15th-century poppyhead bench-ends and an hourglass on the pulpit to remind the preacher to stop! On the wall outside is a fire hook to remove burning thatch. Ford End watermill is thought to date back well before 1798 and gives milling demonstrations occasionally. Near by is Pitstone postmill, dated 1627.

Aldbury: This is a most photogenic village, with pretty cottages grouped round the pond, a tree with a circular seat by the stocks, a shop and a typical church.

WHAT TO LOOK OUT FOR

The beechwoods of the Chilterns in spring are a poem in pale green with bluebell fringes. In autumn the gold covers the trees and the ground beneath. These are the best times to explore them. In winter there may be more bird activity by the canal, but there is always something of interest along the waterside, with narrow boats traversing the locks. There is a nature reserve as you approach Ivinghoe Beacon.

Warwickshire Lanes

RIDE 19
WARWICKSHIRE
SP396519

INFORMATION

Total Distance
20miles (32.5km), with ½ mile (0.5km)
off-road

Grade
2

OS Map
Landranger 1:50,000 sheet 151
(Stratford-upon-Avon)

Tourist Information
Leamington Spa, tel: 01926 311470;
Warwick, tel: 01926 492212

Cycle Shops
John Atkins Cycles, Leamington Spa,
tel: 01926 430211; Kelvin Cycles,
Leamington Spa, tel: 01926 423309;
C H Smith Cycles, Leamington Spa, tel:
01926 425742; Warwick Cycle Centre,
Warwick, tel: 01295 410358; Wirdman
Cycles, Warwick, tel: 01295 492886

Nearest Railway Station
Leamington Spa (9 miles/14km),
Warwick (10 miles/16km)

Refreshments
Excellent café at Bishop's Bowls lakes,
but the track to it is unsurfaced.
Lunches and a play area at The Great
Western pub, Bishop's Itchington and
at the Shakespeare Inn, Harbury.
Lunches at The Malt Shovel, Bishop's
Itchington and at The Crown, The Dog
Inn and The Gamecock, Harbury

The route starts and finishes at the Burton Dassett Country Park with its excellent views, following an undulating route along quiet lanes, gated roads, a short stretch of 'B' road and a bridleway around a field. Some of the finest Warwickshire countryside may be seen along the way. A walk to the unique Chesterton Windmill is a must and gives the opportunity to see more fine views on the way.

Chesterton Windmill, dates originally from the 17th century

START & ROUTE DIRECTIONS

Start

Burton Dassett Country Park lies midway between Banbury and Leamington Spa, 3 miles (5km) south-east of junction 12 of the M40 motorway. There is an official car park on the hills.

Directions

[1] ◱ From the Beacon, head west and take great care on the very steep descent. Turn right before the motorway, signposted 'Northend', then right again at the Red Lion. Follow the lane through Northend as far as the T-junction.

[2] ◱ Turn right, signed 'Fenny Compton', then shortly left, signed 'Knightcote'. After ¾ mile (1km) turn right (not signed). Follow a gated road for 3 miles (5km) into Bishop's Itchington, passing Holmes House, where the surface is slightly rough, going under a railway bridge (can be muddy in wet weather) and crossing the railway. There is now a steep descent to the river which is followed by a steep climb away from it.

[3] ◱ At the T-junction turn left into Poplar Road, bear left at the post office then right into Chapel Street. Opposite the church turn right on to the B4451 (not signposted). Continue along the B4451 up a short, sharp climb, away from Bishop's Itchington and past Bishop's Bowls Lakes. Turn left on to the B4452, opposite the Great Western

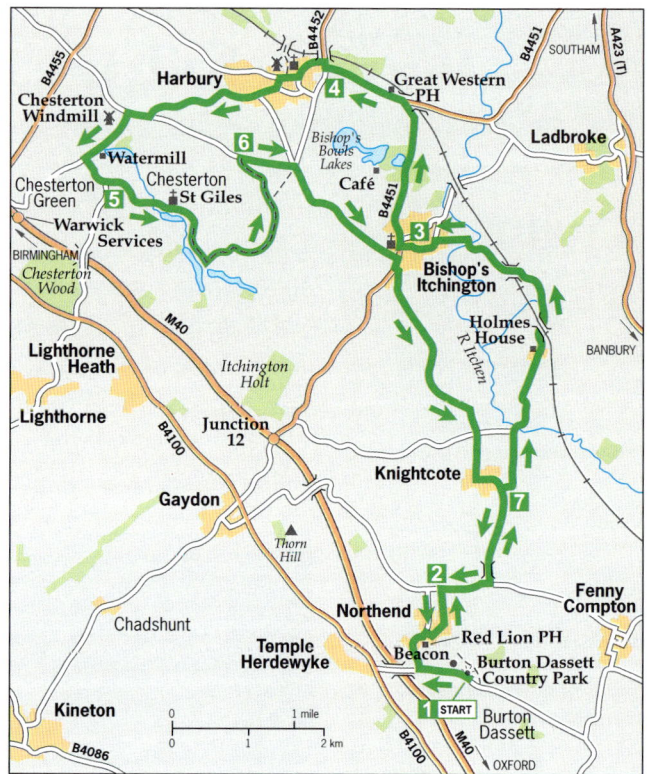

pub, just over 1 mile (1.5km) from Bishop's Itchington. After a further ¾ mile (1km) turn right, signposted 'Harbury'.

[4] ◱ In Harbury turn immediately left into Hall Lane, soon bear left into Crown Street and then turn right into Church Street, passing the church on the right. Go straight on at the crossroads, left into Chapel Street, then right into Park Lane at the T-junction to leave Harbury. After 1¼ miles (2km) turn right at a fork, signposted 'Warwick', and shortly left, signposted 'Chesterton'. The windmill is on your right. Go downhill for

just over ½ mile (1km), passing a watermill on the left, before turning left, signed 'Chesterton'. Go straight on at a 'no through road' sign, signposted 'Chesterton Church'.

[5] ◱ On reaching the church, continue through the gate (the surface is now classified as a bridleway) and pass the ponds on the right. Fork left and negotiate a short, sharp climb. Bear left at the farm buildings, then left again at a junction in 220 yards (200m). After a further ¼ mile (0.5km) the tarmac bears right and becomes a footpath, and there is a private drive straight on.

*Harbury church serves a large
and bustling community*

B4451 and then turn
immediately left, signed
'Knightcote'. After 2 miles
(3km) go straight on at the
crossroads into Knightcote.
A short distance later note,
on the left, the junction on
the gated road in stage 2 of
the ride.

7 ➊ In 1 mile (1.5km) turn
right at a T-junction,
signposted 'Northend' and in
a further 660 yards (600m)
turn left into Top Street.
Continue through Northend
turning left at the Red Lion.
Turn left again, signposted
'Burton Hills', and climb
steeply back to the
starting point.

*Burton Dassett offers fine
moorland and a country park*

Instead, turn left through the
white gates on to a bridleway
and continue along the edge
of the field for ½ mile (1km).
The private drive is now
beyond the hedge on the right
of the bridleway.

6 ➊ Go through the gates
and turn sharp right on to the
lane. At the 5-way junction
continue straight on,
signposted 'Bishop's
Itchington'. After 1¼ miles
(2km) turn right on to the

PLACES OF INTEREST

Burton Dassett: Ghost sightings on the hills have been attributed to vapour rising from the natural spring there. The fine church in the villlage is part-Norman.

Michael. Bishop's Bowls Lakes, to the north, are popular for a variety of watersports, wildlife and plant life.

Harbury: A large sprawling village with five pubs and several shops, many modern

with tales related by locals and others of ghostly sightings. One of these tells of Roman soldiers and their horses marching along the nearby Fosse Way.

Chesterton: Despite the recent opening of the nearby

Bishop's Itchington: This large village features the impressive Church of St

developments have tended to dominate the older buildings, but the past manifests itself

The sprawling village of Harbury

motorway, Chesterton still exudes an air of peace and tranquillity. It is notable for its windmill. In 1632, whilst Governor of Warwick Castle, Sir Edward Peyto, the Parliamentarian famed for his defence of the Royalists, built the stone arched windmill. Originally, it may have been an observatory. It has now been fully restored and is cared for by the Warwickshire Country Council. The isolated Church of St Giles dates mostly from the 14th and 15th centuries. It is usually open and is well worth visiting for its ancient features.

WHAT TO LOOK OUT FOR

Birdlife along the route (mainly at Bishop's Bowls Lakes) includes that gem of birds, the kingfisher, and also Britain's smallest bird, the goldcrest. Great-crested grebe, mute swans and Canada geese may also be seen around the water. Robins, tits, greenfinches, chaffinches and bullfinches are visible at the feeders near the cafe, and it is quite normal to glimpse stoats in the area.
Amongst the wealth of plants growing here are bee orchids, yellow wort, cowslips and mare's tail. The ponds along the bridleway beyond Chesterton church are also visited by waterfowl, so take a break there and see what you can identify.

Constable Country

A hilly ride using ancient winding byways through the beautiful countryside that inspired world famous artists. With trees forming green tunnels, secretive lanes lead up short, stiff climbs to unfenced open roads with magnificent views of the Stour, Brett and Box valleys. Designed in a lop-sided figure-of-eight, this is a ride to be savoured at leisure.

INFORMATION

Total Distance
20 miles (32.5km)

Grade
3

OS Maps
Landranger 1:50,000 sheets 155 (Bury St Edmunds & Sudbury) and 168 (Colchester & The Blackwater)

Tourist Information
Hadleigh, tel: 01473 822922

Cycle Shop/Hire
Ipswich, tel: 01473 259853

Nearest Railway Station
Manningtree (2miles/3km)

Refreshments
The Red Lion Inn, East Bergholt, has a family dining-room and a beer garden.

Both The Carriers Arms and The Bee Hive serve food. There are tea rooms at both East Bergholt and Flatford, and picnic benches in the car park at Flatford. The Cock at Polstead caters for cyclists; it has a beer garden and children's play area (groups are advised to contact them in advance, tel: 01206 263150).
There are many places to picnic all along the route and churchyards usually have seats

John Constable spent much of his youth at Flatford Mill

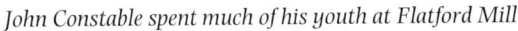

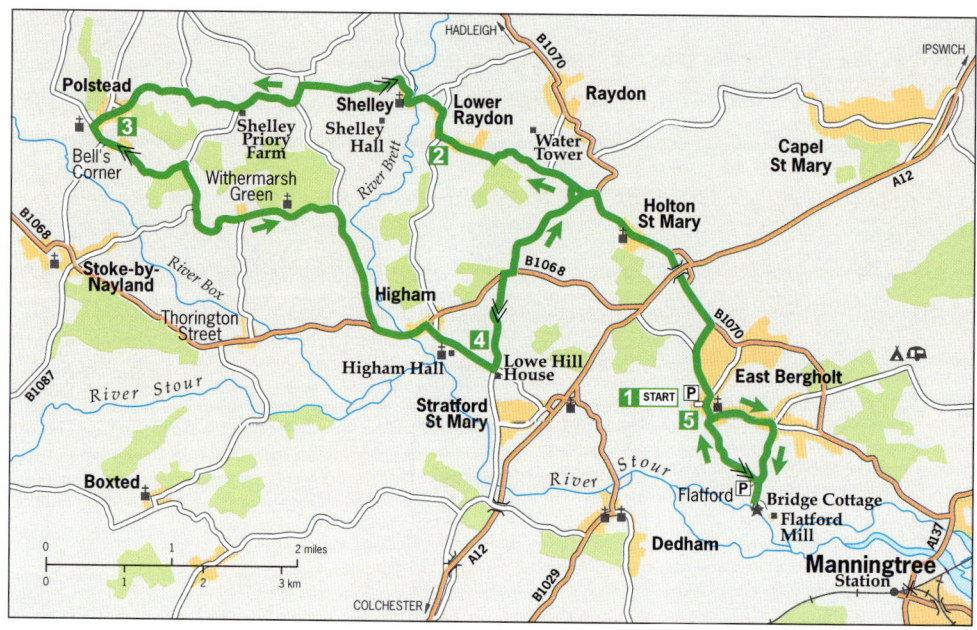

Start

East Bergholt is a large village near the Suffolk/Essex border above the River Stour, south of the A12 Ipswich to Colchester road. There is a free car park and toilets on Gaston Street.

Directions

1 🚲 Turn left out of the car park to begin the long loop of this ride, first noting the 16th-century timbered house on the left. Turn left into Hadleigh Road, signed 'Ipswich', and right, still in Hadleigh Road, at the fork of Ipswich and Colchester routes. Then turn left at a T-junction on to the B1070 for 1¾ miles (3km). This is an access road to the A12 (with a wide grass verge and pavement) so take care. Pass

under the A12 and continue through Holton St Mary. Beyond the village turn left on a right-hand bend, signed 'Higham and Shelley', then fork right, signed 'Raydon and Shelley'. Turn left at the next junction still following signs for Shelley. Go down a gentle slope with a water tower, the first of several along the route, visible on the skyline. The lanes become extremely narrow, often with high banks, though it is generally quiet enough to hear approaching vehicles. Climb past a golf course with views across the Brett valley, typical black, clapboard barns, and a nursery called Windy Brow. The lane now drops down to Lower Raydon.

2 🚲 At a T-junction turn right, signed 'Hadleigh', then left for Shelley. Cross the river with Shelley church ahead and the Hall on the hillside to

the left. The lane swings right past Chapel House, a magnificent example of local architecture and colouring. Take the first left, signed 'Polstead', and climb steeply, with an ancient knarled hedge on the left, its roots sheltering a large rabbit warren. This is a good hill to walk, with fine views across the valley. Turn left at the T-junction. It is now high, fairly level going all the way to Polstead. Turn right at the next junction and continue along unfenced narrow lanes with passing places, through arable farmland. Watch for grit on the road. Turn right, again signed 'Polstead', beside a modern barn conversion and with Shelly Priory Farm on your left. Follow the lane left at the next junction and continue into Polstead.

3 🚲 From Polstead Green bear left and cycle through

the village to a T-junction beside the pond. Turn left here, signed 'Stoke by Nayland', and soon left again at Bell's Corner, signed 'Shelley'. The extremely narrow sunken lane climbs steeply out of the Box valley – another good hill to walk. Turn right, signed 'Stoke by Nayland', continuing along the top of the wood. On the bend take the lane ahead for Withermarsh Green, past the round threshing shed on the left, and two thatched cottages on Withermarsh Green. In ¼ mile (0.5km) there is a small Catholic church on the left and the lane descends with glorious views of the Brett valley. Turn right at a T-junction, continue with the River Brett on the left, then turn left on to B1068 for Higham. Cross the Brett and continue through the village

to a green. Turn right, signed 'Stratford St Mary'. Almost immediately on the left is a cottage called Geldhall, dated 1550, and on the right the timber and plaster vicarage and a stony drive leading to Higham Hall and St Mary's Church. From the churchyard of this lovely flint building the meeting of the Stour and Brett can be seen across the meadows.

4 🚲 Continue past the vicarage for a mile (1.5km) and turn left into very narrow lane, signed 'Green Lane', which crosses the valley then climbs steeply (possibly another short walk) through more rabbit warrens soon to reach the B1068. Turn right and first left, signed 'Holton', and in 1 mile (1.5km) bear right, signed 'East Bergholt', then right again on to the

B1070, signed 'Ipswich'. Go through Holton St Mary, under the A12 and in another ½ mile (1km) turn right into Hadleigh Road, East Bergholt. Bear left at the next junction, right on to Gaston Road and right into car park.

5 🚲 The second loop of this ride is only 2½ miles (4km), but allow plenty of time. Turning right out of the car park, go through the village passing the church on the left. Follow the one-way system signs left for Flatford, then take the first right, watching out for walkers on these narrow lanes. Pass the car park and continue to Bridge Cottage, Flatford. Retrace the route uphill; follow a lane to the left back to East Bergholt.

The tranquil scene of a solitary swan at Polstead

PLACES OF INTEREST

East Bergholt: This large, yet peaceful village features a magnificent stone and flint church with a unique timber bell-cage in the churchyard and an unusual, unfinished tower. John Constable's birthplace is marked by a plaque on the original railings of East Bergholt House. His father, a wealthy miller, owned Flatford Mill and Willy Lott's cottage.

Flatford: A place of pilgrimage for art lovers – Bridge Cottage (NT) stands beside the River Stour and houses a collection of Constable's paintings. It has a tea garden, shop and information centre, and offers guided walks. The Granary Museum is along the lane and

Colourful gardens in East Bergholt

there are boats for hire at the bridge. Cross the river to the footpath and walk left to see Flatford Mill, and Willy Lott's cottage.

Shelley: Although comprising only a handful of houses, a church and small river, this village is so typically English and beautiful. The little church has five bells, three dating from the 1600s.

Polstead: The village takes its name (Pool-stead) from the large pond close to church and Hall, between which a gospel oak stood for over a thousand years marking the spot where missionaries preached. This peaceful village, some of whose residents sailed on the *Mayflower*, is probably best known for the Red Barn murder of 1827.

WHAT TO LOOK OUT FOR

Britain's ancient hedgerows are a haven for wildlife, they are also a record of local history. Amongst their roots you may see stoats or even foxes hunting in the rabbit warrens, and badgers also make their homes here. Look at the art of the old craftsmen who 'layed' them years ago to make a dense barrier against stock. Count the variety of species which will help you to assess their age (one species represents roughly 100 years). Look for primroses, harebell and cranesbill round their roots and count the wide variety of birds nesting in the wild tangle of their branches. Churchyards like that in Shelley village are also miniature nature reserves.

RIDE 21
SUFFOLK
TM509761

Heath and Marsh

In an area of great natural beauty, gentle undulating country lanes and heathland tracks invite exploration. Nature reserves and historic villages battling with the sea for survival create a paradise for nature lovers, artists and photographers alike.

INFORMATION

Total Distance
23½ miles (38km), with
8½ miles (13.5km) off-road

Grade
2

OS Map
Landranger 1:50,000 sheet 156
(Saxmundham & Aldeburgh)

Tourist Information
Southwold, tel: 01502

724729/722366;
Hadleigh, tel: 01473 822922

Cycle Shop/Hire
Byways Bicycles, Darsham (holidays),
tel: 01728 668764; Suffolk Cycle
Breaks, Needham Market (holidays),
tel: 01449 721555

Nearest Railway Stations
Darsham (2 miles/3km),
Halesworth (9 miles/14.5km)

Refreshments

The Harbour Inn caters for families in
Southwold, where there are also
various tea shops, take-aways, and
restaurants. The White Horse,
Westleton serves food (beer garden)
and there are benches beside the
village pond. There is a café on the
beach at Dunwich, where The Ship
Inn also serves food, plus plenty of
picnic spots along the route

Enjoying a stroll at Dunwich, where much has been lost to the sea

START & ROUTE DIRECTIONS

Start

The ancient Borough of Southwold lies on the coast south of Lowestoft, 4 miles (6.5km) east of the A12 along the A1095. Parking (pay-and-display, toilets) is on Pier Avenue beside the sea, or free on York Road (Southwold Common).

Directions

1 🚲 From Pier Avenue cross straight over Station Road into Blyth Road with a garage and cycle hire business on the left. Alternatively, from York Road turn left on to Station Road with The Kings Head on the right, then left into Blyth Road. Blyth Road becomes a stony track (Old Southwold Railway), with the common on the left. Enter Southwold Common through a gap between gates, fork left beside a sign warning of adders and in ½ mile (1km) cross the River Blyth by footbridge into Walberswick Nature Reserve. Continue straight ahead. When the tarmac path climbs uphill and bends left through gorse after ½ mile (1km), turn right on to a narrow grass bridleway, (signed 'B R'). Fork right and continue to a metal five-bar gate, with signs of an old railway track on the right. Once through the gate keep straight ahead, across a sandy track. Go through another gate and turn right on to the B1387. In ½ mile (1km) turn right on to a bridlepath, signed 'Blythburgh', through heath and woods with the Blyth estuary beyond. On reaching the B1125 turn left; Blythburgh is to the right.

2 🚲 The road climbs out of Blythburgh; keep straight on at a crossroads with a water tower on your right. Continue downhill to the next crossroads, turn right, signed 'Hinton' and go straight on at next junction along an unhedged lane. In ½ mile

Westleton Heath is a pleasant place for a family ride

The River Blyth at Walberswick is popular with fishermen

(1km) turn left beyond Poplar Farm along a very narrow lane. At a T-junction in ½ mile (1km) turn left, signed 'Westleton', then right and left at the next T-junction, signed 'Westleton'. In Westleton follow the road left in front of The White Horse Inn and immediately right with the village pond on your right.

3 🚴 Cross straight over the B1125 into a narrow lane (blue sign, 'Unsuitable for Coaches') with a flint cottage on the right. Climb from the village on to heathland and bear left at the next road junction. Go straight over at a crossroads, noting the 'Minsmere Reserve' sign and watch for speed-humps. Turn left through a narrow entrance on to a path into woods just before a five-bar gate ('Private Please Keep Access Clear'). When a footpath joins from the right, join a wide track on the left and keep straight ahead, but watch for deep sand. Continue, heading north-east and in 1½ miles (2.5km) turn left on to a road, then right at a T-junction for Dunwich. Keep right at the next road junction for the beach.

4 🚴 Leave Dunwich with The Ship Inn on your left and climb sharply into Dunwich Forest, straight over the crossroads. On reaching the B1125, turn right on to the heath through the car park. Follow the sandy track that skirts the trees, past a cottage on the left, and climb a hill past another cottage where the track becomes a tarmac lane at Westwood Lodge. Continue to Walberswick.

5 🚴 Turn left on to the B1387, signed 'Blythburgh 3' (or right for Walberswick, or for ferry). Take the first right into Palmers Lane which leads to the footbridge over the River Blyth and the track across the Common back to Southwold.

PLACES OF INTEREST

Southwold: This small, busy seaside town is blessed with nine village greens and a 15th-century church that looks more like a cathedral. Built of coloured flints and stone, in a time of great prosperity, it is representative of the common building materials of the area. Visit Southwold's museums for local history.

Westleton: In 1086 this attractive village had two churches, plus two beehives, 20 pigs, and 24 goats. Today it makes a pleasant place to stop for lunch, and the 17th-century Crown Inn has accommodation with four-posters. The 14th-century thatched church stands on rising ground in the west of the village, a strategically placed bench making this a good place to rest.

Walberswick and Minsmere Reserves: The route passes through Walberswick and close to the RSPB reserve of Minsmere, with public hides at Minsmere, where the avocet, bittern and marsh harrier may be seen. The two reserves offer a wide variety of habitat, from heath to mudflat, and even where hides are not available birds are accustomed to human presence and seem unconcerned. Watch the normally shy heron stalking its prey in the shallows of the Blyth estuary. Picturesque Walberswick village, almost surrounded by a nature reserve which stretches from the Blyth to the Westwood marshes, can be reached from Southwold by a tiny 'rowing-boat' ferry across the River Blyth.

Southwold's lighthouse overlooks the Sole Bay Inn

Dunwich: The Domesday Book states that the landholder has lost half his land to the sea, yet the following centuries saw Dunwich grow in size and wealth to become the capital of East Anglia. Today its six churches, two monasteries, chapels and houses have mostly disappeared into the sea. Only a few cottages and some mysterious, crumbling walls remain, an awe-inspiring reminder of the power of nature. Dunwich Museum has the full story.

WHAT TO LOOK OUT FOR

In an area so diverse the possibilitites are immense. Dragonflies, frogs and toads may be glimpsed while watching for birds along the marshes and mudflats. Watch also for basking adders and woodpeckers across the heaths. Note tall pines and stunted oaks, and look for the thatcher cutting reeds or thatching, and houses built of flint. At Blythburgh look for waders on the mudflats of the silted-up River Blyth, and note the impressive 15th-century church, visible for miles around.

Hunstanton and Sandringham

RIDE 22
NORFOLK
TF673408

Using minor roads and off-road tracks this ride takes in gently rolling quiet countryside. Starting in a seaside town the ride soon takes you away from the traffic and into a superb nature reserve. It continues through villages, all waiting to be explored, visits a working windmill and the royal estate of Sandringham. A 4-mile (6.5km) loop to pretty Wolferton is included, but may be omitted if more time is needed in nearby Sandringham.

INFORMATION

Total Distance
28 miles (45km), with 4½ miles (7km) off-road

Grade
1

OS Map
Landranger 1:50,000 sheet 132 (North West Norfolk)

Tourist Information
Hunstanton, tel: 01485 532610

Cycle Shops/Hire
Searles of Hunstanton, tel: 01485 534211; A E Wallis, Heacham, tel: 01485 571683; Howlett's Cycles, Dersingham, tel: 01483 543774; Great Bircham Mill, tel: 01485 578393

Nearest Railway Station
King's Lynn (16 miles/27km)

Refreshments
Many cafes and restaurants in Hunstanton and Heacham. En route are Great Bircham Mill tea room, Sandringham Country Park tea room/picnic areas and The Feathers, Dersingham. Wolferton Station Museum has toilets and a picnic area.

The famous striped cliffs at Hunstanton

START & ROUTE DIRECTIONS

Start

Hunstanton is a busy seaside resort on the A149 some 16 miles (26km) north of the ancient port and market town of King's Lynn. The town is well served with adequate on-street parking and designated car parks. If possible, park near The Green at the bottom of Greevegate. The route starts from the Town Hall which also houses the local Tourist Information Office.

Directions

1 🚴 Ride up Greevegate to the junction with the A149. Turn right, signposted 'Heacham', and after 500 yards (300m) pass the fire station and turn left into Downs Road, a gravelly track which improves. After ½ mile

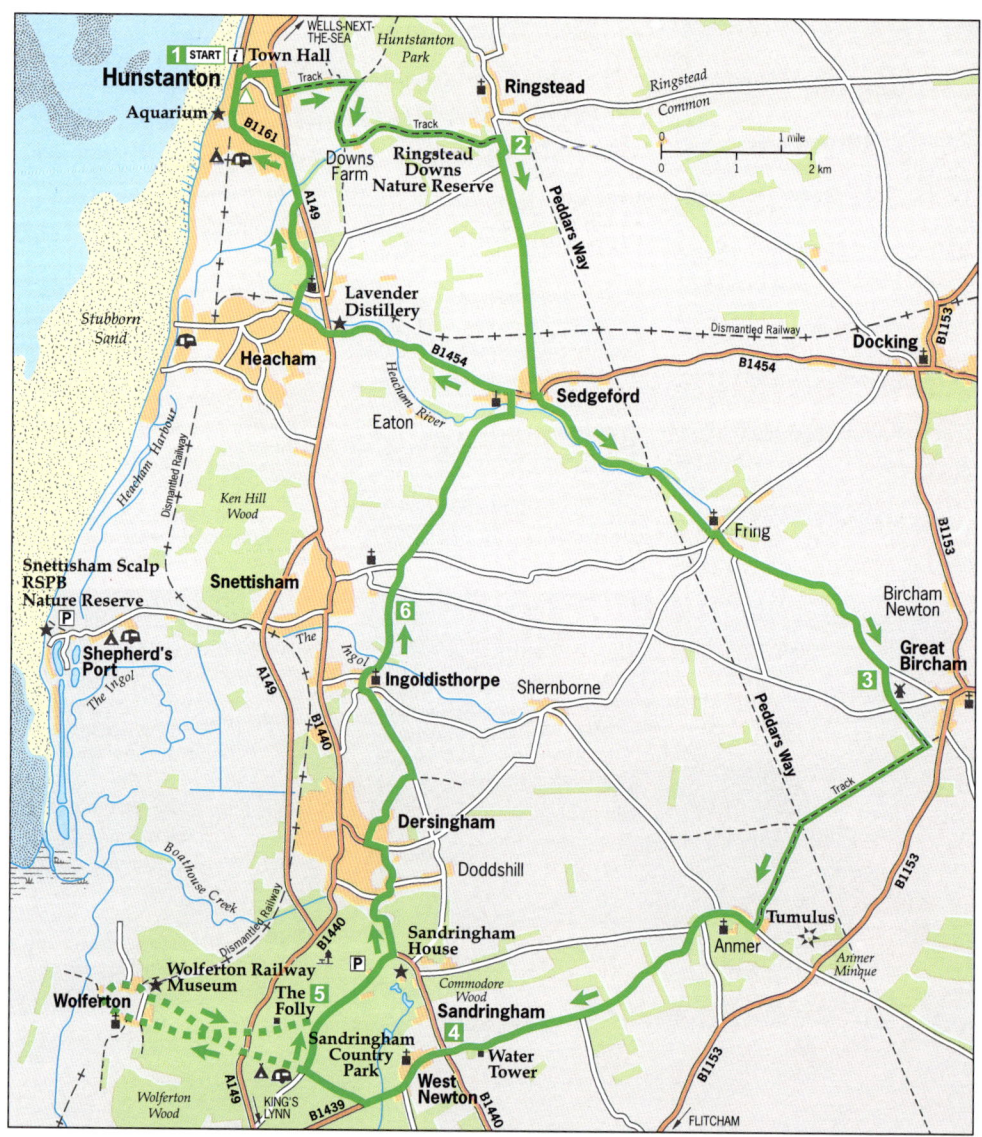

Flower borders and smooth green lawns at Hunstanton

(1km) bear right and after another ½ mile (1km) bear left, keeping Downs Farm on your right. The lane crosses Ringstead Downs on a grassy surface.

2 On reaching a metalled road, turn right and cycle gently uphill to Sedgeford. If time permits turn right to visit the picturesque Heacham River and the round-towered church, whose graveyard gate commemorates a typhus epidemic of 1852. Otherwise turn left at the first junction and immediately right, on to the Fring Road. After about 2 miles (3km) Fring's All Saints' Church will appear on the left, and then the village. At the junction, turn left and immediately right, past a dried-up village pond, towards Great Bircham. Before you reach the village, note the windmill on the right after about 2 miles (3km). Turn right into the lane leading to it.

3 The Mill stands beside a narrow lane. Continue along this lane and, at the next crossroads cross over on to a hard-surfaced lane and continue for 600 yards

(500m) before bearing right and keeping on a similar track for 1 mile (1.5km). Come to a crossroads with the Peddars Way, an ancient track, now part of a long-distance path traversing north-west Norfolk; cross the Peddars Way, taking the left-hand fork, (this lane soon becomes tree-lined), and soon reach Anmer at an unusual Boy Scouts monument. Turn right, keeping the church on your left and, after the church turn second left on to a very narrow metalled lane. The brick water tower above West Newton soon comes into view; follow the road to the crossroads at West Newton.

4 Go straight over the crossroads, past the church, and take the first right into Sandringham Country Park. After visiting the park, follow the road to the next crossroads. For an optional loop via Wolferton, continue over the crossroads. Otherwise, turn right (see section 5) and continue for ½ mile (1km) flanked by silver birches to meet the A149. Go straight over, then turn left and downhill, past the old railway level-crossing cottage

which retains its 'Beware Of Trains' notice; follow the road round and back up to Wolferton Railway Museum. Continue uphill and soon fork left to reach the A149. Go straight across into Sandringham Country Park, past the folly on the left to a junction to re-join the route which omitted Wolferton.

5 Soon come to refreshment facilities and picnic areas on the left near Sandringham House. Continue for ½ mile (1km) and leave the park, turning left on to the B1440 soon to reach the village of Dersingham, with the Feathers Inn on the left and St Nicholas's Church on the right. After the church bear left and then soon turn right up steep but short Fern Hill which becomes Mill Road. Soon turn left and continue to Ingoldisthorpe. Bear left at the junction, then right, keep the tree-surrounded church to your right. Cross Ingol stream and cycle uphill to the crossroads before Snettisham.

6 With Snettisham village and church to the left, go over the crossroads and bear right, then left to reach Sedgeford. At the junction turn left along the B1454 and continue to the A149, by the Lavender Distillery at Heacham. Go across on to Lynn Road and in 440 yards (500m) turn right on to Hunstanton Road, soon to reach the A149 which leads back to Hunstanton to complete the tour.

PLACES OF INTEREST

The royal estate of Sandringham is well worth a visit

Hunstanton: This popular seaside town was founded as a resort in 1846. Its sandy beaches, shallow sea waters and striped cliffs – a geologist's dream – make it popular with holiday-makers of all ages. Children particularly enjoy the Oasis Leisure and Sealife Centres.

Ringstead Downs: Much of this area of mature woods and grassland with out-cropping chalk is a Norfolk Naturalists' Trust nature reserve, and its beech and ash trees are alive with woodland birds.

Great Bircham Mill: As the only windmill in the area open to the public (from Easter to September), this is worth a visit. The mill comprises five floors, and visitors may also see the bakery, with its 200-year-old Peel oven, the tea rooms and gift shop, and the stables. The mil also offers cycle hire facilities, and has a play area for under 7s.

Sandringham: This famous estate was bought by Queen Victoria in 1862 for the future Edward VII. There is a huge parkland with woodland, picnic areas, restaurants, and gift shop. The museum and house grounds, and the house itself when the Royal family is not in residence, are open to the public.

Wolferton Station Museum: Once the Royal Station on the Sandringham Estate, the old station and platform are set in a secluded wooded valley beneath the impressive heights of Sandringham Warren. The museum includes the former Royal Retiring rooms, items of furniture from Royal trains and other memorabilia.

Norfolk Lavender: Situated beside the A149 at Heacham, this lavender farm with free admission is where visitors can discover how lavender is grown, harvested and used. You can also buy a variety of products. Refreshments are available at Millers Cottage Tea Room.

WHAT TO LOOK OUT FOR

Do not miss the striped cliffs of Hunstanton, the only hard rocky cliffs on the East Anglian coast, formed of white chalk over red chalk and carstone – a rust-brown sandstone. Look out for churches with round towers, nationally rare but common in East Anglia, as at Sedgeford. On Ringstead Downs in summer you should see stemless thistles, whilst great mullein and hoary mullein can be seen on roadside verges. The hawthorns, ash and beech trees on Ringstead Downs, and the extensive woodlands of Sandringham, are alive with birds, and a quiet wait with binoculars is sure to be rewarded.

RIDE 23
LEICESTERSHIRE
SP426937

Hinckley and Bosworth Field

The superb Ashby Canal forms a large part of this ride. Built along the 300-foot (90m) contour, this lock-less waterway meanders through the countryside, passing the site of the Battle of Bosworth Field, and accompanied for several miles by the Battlefield Line, a standard-gauge steam railway. The route also takes in quiet country lanes, rural villages and the pretty town of Market Bosworth.

Note: Riders on this towpath must have a permit, available free from British Waterways Board, tel: 01923 226422.

INFORMATION

Total Distance
26 miles (42km), with 13 miles (21km) off-road

Grade
1

The extensive Ashby Canal, near bridge 36

Tourist Information
Hinckley, tel: 01455 635106

Cycle Shops/Hire
Bikes & Sports, Hinckley, tel: 01455 617202; Townsend Cycles of Hinckley, tel: 01455 635776

Nearest Railway Station
Hinckley

Refreshments
There are cafés and restaurants in Hinckley. En route facilities are available at the Bosworth Battlefield Visitor Centre, there are tea rooms in Market Bosworth and near bridge 52 of the Ashby Canal in Shackerstone. The Rising Sun pub is also near by as well as The Horse and Jockey at Congerstone

START & ROUTE DIRECTIONS

Start

Hinckley is a growing town on the A47, 14 miles (23km) south-west of Leicester. Park in one of the car parks near the bus station between Brunel Road and Lancaster Road. The ride starts from the library/Tourist Information Centre in Lancaster Road.

Directions

1 🚲 At the library turn left on to Rugby road, and immediately right at the traffic lights, up Trinity Lane. The road soon turns left and becomes Hollycroft. After ½ mile (1km) keep right on the Stoke Golding road to reach a new roundabout on Hinckley's north perimeter road (A47). Keep straight on to Stoke Golding. Turn left into the village, right into Main Street and then left into Station Road, with the church and the George and Dragon pub on the right. In ¼ mile (0.5km) reach Ashby Canal bridge 25 and go down to the towpath.

2 🚲 The path varies; here it is single-file and solid, further on it is wider, surfaced with grass or bark chipping, but always good cycling. The path is often close to the water, so take care and give way to walkers. Continue for 4 miles (6km) to bridge 35 and leave the canal, turning right over the bridge to visit Shenton Station and the Battle Trail. The latter is short and waymarked, and includes the spot where Richard III was killed, and where his

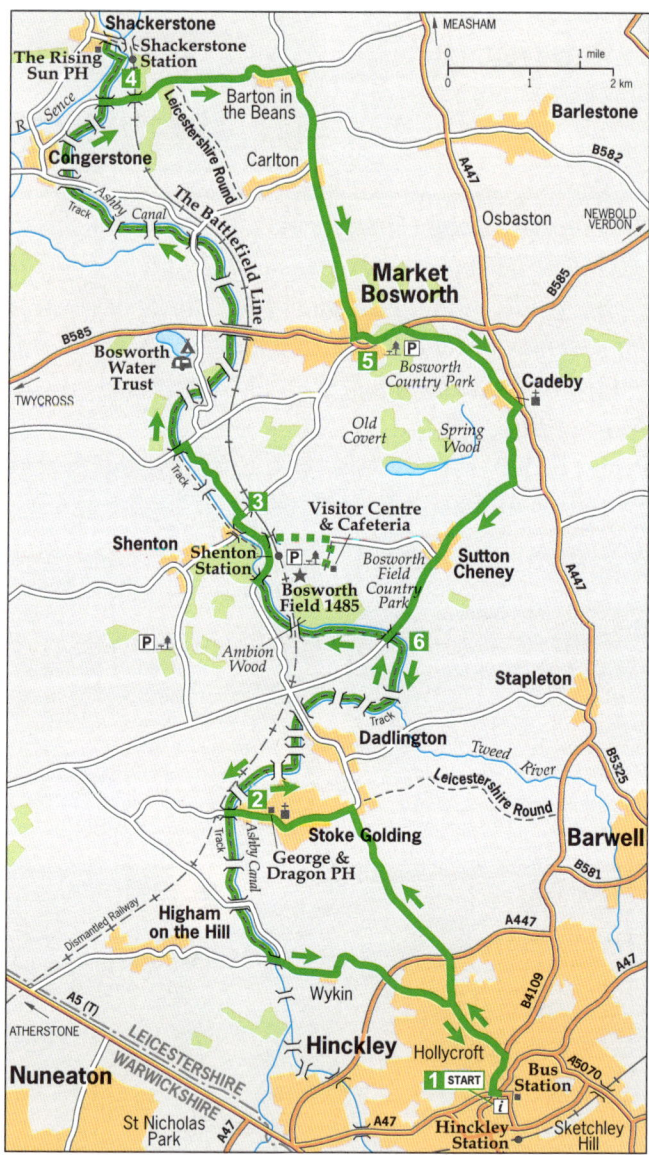

Royal Banner is often flown. You may also divert right, to visit Bosworth Field Country Park.

3 🚲 Continue on the road for ¼ mile (0.5km) and turn left, signed 'Far Coton'. After

½ mile (1km) turn left to rejoin the canal at bridge 37; follow the path for 5 miles (8km) to bridge 52 at Shackerston. At the bridge turn left for the Battlefield Line and tea, and/or right into the village and the Rising Sun.

Narrowboats are a common sight along the Ashby Canal

4 🚲 Return along the canal path to bridge 51 and go over it on to the metalled road, soon crossing over the railway bridge to reach Barton in the Beans after 1 mile (1.5km). Turn right at the crossroads, keep straight on at the next crossroads and continue to Market Bosworth.

5 🚲 Turn left into Newbold Verdon Road and after ¼ mile (0.5km), with Bosworth Country Park on your right, turn right towards Cadeby, soon passing the Gatehouse Tea Room on your left. Cadeby is a further 1 mile (1.5km); note a cruck house (Church Cottage) on entering the village. Passing the village hall, turn right opposite the church and, with the tiny church school on the right corner, right again to Sutton Cheney. Keep straight on at

the junction and after 1 mile (1.5km) reach the Ashby Canal at bridge 34 and rejoin the towpath.

6 🚲 Ride south for 3½ miles (6km) to bridge 21. Leave the canal, turning left over the bridge into Hinckley Lane to

soon reach tiny Wykin. After the village you will come to another roundabout on the A447 perimeter road. Go straight over and back into Hinckley.

The colourful sight of Hinckley in full bloom

WHAT TO LOOK OUT FOR

The Ashby Canal abounds with birds, plants and insects, including coot, water hen and mallard, stately bulrushes and tiny-flowered water figwort, and several species of dragonfly. The lane-side hedges have an unusual abundance of holly. Do not miss the market place in Market Bosworth, with its timber-framed and thatched cottages. The Church of St Margaret in Stoke Golding is one of the most beautiful in Leicestershire.

PLACES OF INTEREST

Hinckley: This large bustling town, served by good roads and a railway, is an excellent centre from which to experience a wide range of leisure facilities. It has an extensive and fascinating history, although its Norman motte and bailey castle is now a mere mound topped by the war memorial. Among its old buildings is the Unitarian chapel of 1722, linked with the hymn writer Philip Doddridge.

Market Bosworth: This historic small town has a Wednesday market in the Square, and a good variety of shops. To the north-west of the Square is the Grammar School, built in Tudor style in 1828; other picturesque buildings, some thatched, front the Square.

The Ashby Canal: Begun in the late 1790s, this canal meanders for some 25 miles (40km), linking the Coventry Canal with Moira, near Ashby. The stretch along this ride, between Hinckley and Shackerstone, has some 35 bridges, all numbered and named, including Wooden Top, Geary's and Fox. The canal passes through open countryside and the Battle of Bosworth Country Park. Boat trips are available from Stoke Golding and Sutton (Cheney) wharves, bridges 25 and 34.

Bosworth Battlefield Country Park and Visitor Centre: These are based on the Battle of Bosworth Field (1485) in which Richard III was killed, bringing medieval England to an end. There is a battle trail close to the cycle route and a comprehensive visitors' centre, including: exhibitions and models, films, gift shop and café. The Country Park is near by, not to be confused with Market Bosworth Country Park.

The Battlefield Line: This railway line, running close to the Ashby Canal, is a 5-mile (8km) standard-gauge steam passenger service, linking the villages of Shackerstone and Shenton. Shackerstone has a railway museum, tea and gift shop and extensive parking.

Cadeby Light Railway and Brass-rubbing Centre: At Cadeby rectory is a narrow-gauge and 5-inch gauge railway, and a model layout of the Great Western Line in 1935 – the work of a former rector of Cadeby, Reverend Teddy Boston. The Brass-rubbing Centre in the church contains some 70 replica brasses from churches all over the country.

Historic Market Bosworth

RIDE 24
STAFFORDSHIRE
SJ918229

Staffordshire Villages

The gently undulating landscape of western Staffordshire is ideal for cycling. The charm of the area lies in its villages, which are often nestled around the parish church and inn. There are no hills of any consequence and little traffic. Between Stafford and Haughton is a 'greenway' which is open to cyclists, a traffic-free escape out of the county town of Stafford.

INFORMATION

Total Distance
24 miles (39km), with 6 miles (10km) on traffic-free Stafford Greenway

Grade
1

OS Map
Landranger 1:50,000 sheet 127 (Stafford & Telford)

Tourist Information
Stafford, tel: 01785 40204/214668

Cycle Shops/Hire
None on the route

Refreshments
There are cafes in Stafford and a pub in every village, all of which welcome children. The Fox in Marston is popular with cyclists and has a large rear garden. The Vaughan Arms at Lapley is gloriously decorated with flowers in summer and welcomes children. There is a picnic site (Haughton Station) on the Greenway

The High House in Stafford was built in 1595

START & ROUTE DIRECTIONS

Start

Stafford lies on the A34 between Birmingham and Stoke-on-Trent, 2 miles (3km) from junction 14 on the M6. Go to Stafford railway station, just off the A518, where there is a car park.

Directions

1 🚲 From Stafford station turn immediately left into Railway Street. At the end go right up Peel Street and left into South Street, noting the old windmill at Broadeye on your right. Go left into Castle Street, rising up over the railway and descending by a factory to reach a kissing gate at Martin Drive. Go right and ride straight on at the roundabout. Turn next right, then left on to a metalled lane which is also a bridleway leading up to Burleyfields Farm. About 220 yards (200m) before the buildings is a gap on the right leading on to the Stafford Greenway. Go on to the old railway trackbed and turn left out of town. The track continues beneath the M6 motorway and by the village of Derrington. It then crosses a road at Stalbrook and runs above pastureland to the former Haughton railway station (picnic site).

2 🚲 Go left through the car park up to a road. Turn left over the bridge; the road descends to a junction. Go right here along Brazenhill Lane to rise over the old railway again before passing a cottage and farm to

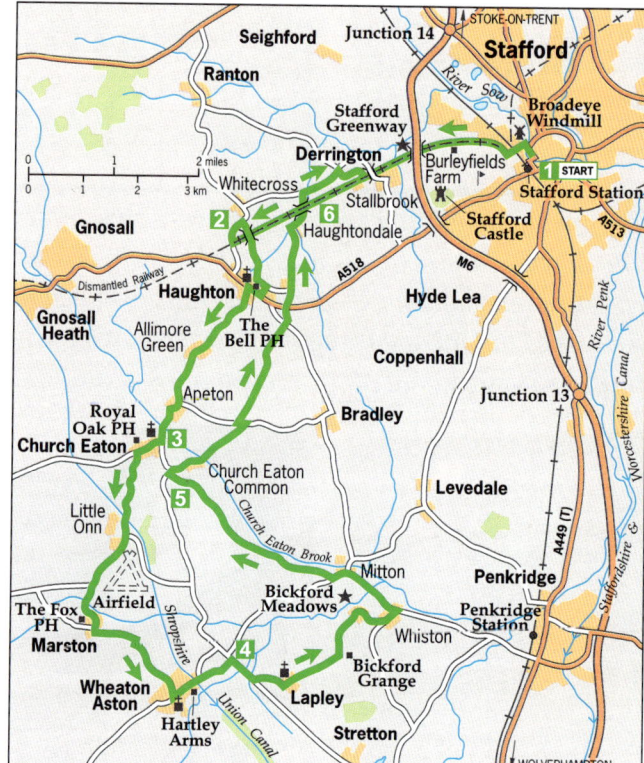

Haughton. As you enter the village go left at the junction with Rectory Lane and then right into Prince Avenue. At the top of this road reach the main A518 and turn right with care (or dismount and walk across). Pass The Bell pub and the church on your right and go next left into Jolt Lane, signposted 'Church Easton'. Follow this winding road, passing through the hamlet of Allimore Green and also Apeton (ignore a turn to the left), to enter Church Eaton by the church.

3 🚲 Go right at the junction here and ride through the village. Pass the Royal Oak pub on the right and then

take the next left towards Little Onn and Marston. The road winds between fields for about 1¼ miles (2km) then crosses the Shropshire Union Canal. Shortly beyond, pass a road leading off to the left and an old airfield landing strip. At the next junction keep left for Marston, a settlement of farms gathered around the pretty Fox Inn. Go left at the junction for Wheaton Aston village and turn left in the main street. Cross the Shropshire Union Canal again and at the fork, keeping straight ahead.

4 🚲 At the next junction go right and dip down to cross a brook. Reach another

junction and go left, the road rising up to Lapley Church. Follow the bend of the road left, past the Vaughan Arms and through the village and to the entrance to Bickford Grange, where the road bears left. The road then runs straight, then bears right. Look for a bridleway on the left allowing access to Bickford Meadows. It is best to wheel your bike along this route, as there is no cycling at the meadows.

Otherwise follow the lane as it bears right and continue to a junction where you keep left. At the next junction turn left and ride for 1mile (1.5km) to a triangular junction at Mitton. Keep ahead for ¼ mile (0.5km) to a junction where you turn right. This is a very quiet lane with access to local farms so ignore all those on the left. Continue along the lane for 2½ miles (4km) towards Church Eaton.

5 🚲 On reaching a junction turn right and right again along a quiet lane through Church Eaton Common. Cross the Church Eaton brook and climb gently for ½ mile (1km) to a junction. Go left and then next right along Alstone Lane which weaves its way for just under 2 miles (3km) to a junction with Watery Lane which you ignore, but within a few yards/metres you reach a much wider road. Go left here and up to the crossroads with the main A518. Cross straight over into Dale Lane; pass Back Lane and a large farm on the left. Continue ahead to the hamlet of

Norman Stafford Castle bears evidence of the original town

Haughtondale, then ride to a bridge beneath the old railway trackbed. Go under the bridge and on the left you can climb up to the cycle route above and turn left.

6 🚲 If you prefer, continue to a junction with Long Lane where you turn right. Ride ahead for ½ mile (1km) to a crossroads. Go right, into the appropriately named Crossings Lane, and at the crossing go left on to the cycle route. Either way, retrace your route back into Stafford along the Greenway cycle route, passing Derrington and with fine views over to Stafford Castle, and return to the start point.

Stafford: Stafford is a good base to explore the central and western parts of the county. The old quarter around the parish church is particularly attractive, as is the restored half-timbered Ancient High House which houses the tourist information office and a museum. Stafford allows easy access to nearby Shugborough Hall, set in landscaped parkland, as well as Cannock Chase, which has become increasingly popular with mountain bikers. Another important attraction is Stafford Castle which sits on a hillside above the town.

Bickford Meadows: This nature reserve is a haven for wildlife in a heavily cultivated area. The tall herb grasses attract a variety of birds and the luxuriant growth near Whiston Brook includes a wide range of plant life. In the summer the site attracts butterflies such as the small skipper, red admiral and peacock, as well as damselflies and dragonflies. The Staffordshire Way, a long-distance path, allows access on foot to the site.

Staffordshire Villages: The most charming aspect of this ride is the Staffordshire villages en route, many of which retain a degree of tranquillity, and there are a number of delightful parish churches too. Each village has its special features: Haughton boasts a fine half-timbered 16th-century manor house, and a number of Georgian houses; Wheaton Aston depended much on the Shropshire Union Canal,

probably the last mainline rural canal to be built, and also the most beautiful. It is a pleasure to sit by the Hartley Arms and watch the narrow boats pass

Bickford Meadows Reserve, off the Staffordshire Way footpath

by; Church Eaton and Lapley are equally charming.

WHAT TO LOOK OUT FOR

Ancient parish churchyards are one of the endearing features of rural life in England, not only offering a haven for plantlife and animals, but a rich insight into local history. Look out for features which were once commonplace such as the water pump at Church Eaton church. Fascinating Lapley church, built on the site of a former Benedictine priory, with its large central tower, dominates the surrounding landscape – sheep often graze between the gravestones.

RIDE 25
NOTTINGHAMSHIRE
SK651676

Ollerton and Sherwood

This ride takes in three distinctly different forest parks within Sherwood Forest. The woodland roads and tracks vary but all are sound and suitable for cycling, the routes being well way-marked. A countryside loop at the beginning and end of the journey takes in interesting villages and good views to complement the forest riding.

INFORMATION

Total Distance
30 miles (47km), with 10½ miles (17km) off-road

Grade
2

OS Map
Landranger 1:50,000 sheet 120 (Mansfield & Worksop)

Tourist Information
Newark, Notts, tel: 01623 824545

Cycle Hire
National Trust at Clumber Park

Nearest Railway Stations
Worksop (10 miles/16km); Newark (12 miles/19km)

Refreshments
Ollerton Watermill Teas Shop, Wellow - Durham Ox and Olde Red Lion, Sherwood Pines Forest Park, Sherwood Forest Visitor Centre. Carburton (B6034) The Olde School tearoom. Clumber Park

Cyclists enjoying the peace and quiet of Clumber Park

Start

Ollerton lies on the main
A614/A616 junction about
15 miles (22.5km) north-east
of Nottingham. Start from
the roundabout at this
junction, where there is car
parking at the Tourist Information Centre at Sherwood
Heath Nature Reserve.

Directions

1 🚲 From the roundabout
go along the narrow bus
route into Ollerton (old
village). At the first junction
turn right, with the church
on your left, and then right
again at the Back
Lane/Wellow junction on to
the A616 towards Wellow.
Reaching Wellow, turn right
at the Durham Ox pub,
passing the village green and
maypole, to Eakring, with an
old windmill on the left as you
enter the village. Turn right
at the junction (with the
Saville Arms on your right)
and follow the Bilsthorpe road
for 2½ miles (3.5km) to the
A614. Go straight across,
signed 'No through road',
into old Clipstone Forest.

2 🚲 After 1 mile (1.5km)
reach a small car park at the
entrance to Sherwood Pines
Forest Park. Go straight on,
following the red posts
indicating a circular cycle
way, past the official start of
this route, to the main (north)
car park and refreshments.
(Other tracks in the forest can
be cycled, but do not cycle on
any white or blue signed
footpaths.) Turn right into the
car park and follow the exit

signs for ½ mile (1km) to a
metalled road; turn right and
cycle uphill and down,
bearing left and keeping on
this road for ½ mile (1km) to
the B6030.

3 🚲 Turn left downhill and
immediately right uphill, to
soon reach Edwinstowe
village. Turn left at the first
junction (Mill Lane), follow
the one-way system to the

Ollerton road, and turn right.
After this turn left, with the
church on the left, and after a
further 200 yards (180m)
turn left into Sherwood
Country Park.

4 🚲 Go through the car
park and follow the signs
'Bridleway to Gleadthorpe'
and 'Major Oak' on a single
track. Soon fork left following
clearly marked horseshoe and

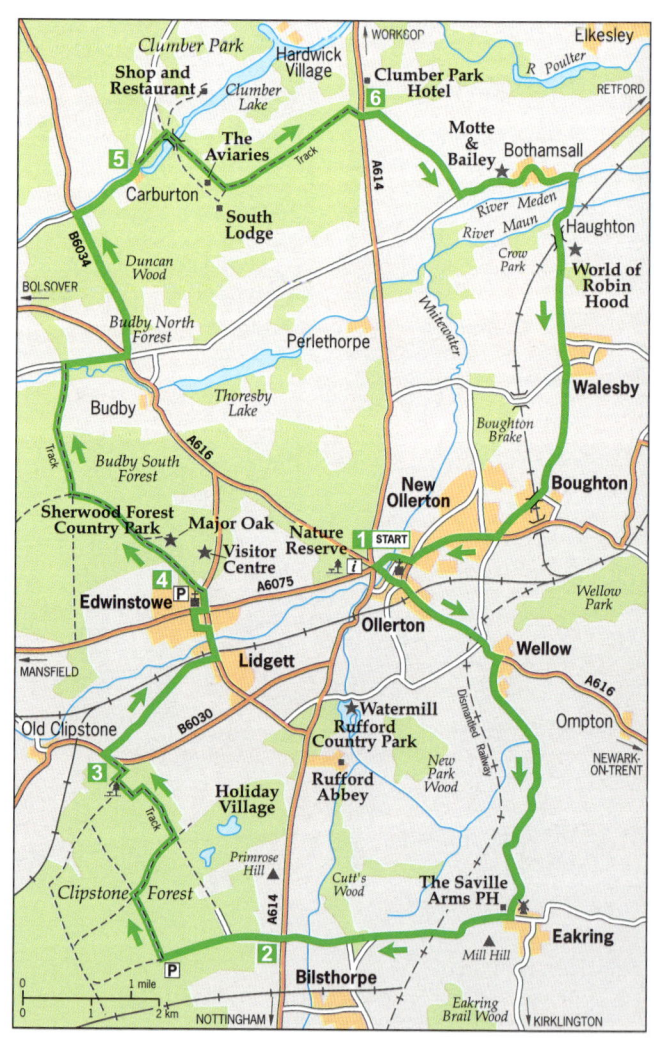

A dense carpet of warm-coloured foliage covers Sherwood Forest

blue 'public bridleway' signs. Shortly turn right on to a broader, solid bridleway at the Dukeries Training Area (Budby) sign which includes 'Blank firing & troop movements; warning'. There is open heath to your right, conifer plantation to your left, and then soon open arable field to the right and conifers to the left (also yellow-marked posts). After ½ mile (1km) pass a barrier and soon reach a metalled road at the forest exit. Turn right to the A616 junction, cross over, then turn left on to the B6034.

Continue to Carburton crossroads, turning right through Carburton and into Clumber Park.

5 🚲 After ½ mile (1km) cross the stream and fork right, signposted 'Shop/Restaurant/Chapel'. At the next crossroads go right and cross the lake bridge (divert left for refreshments). Bear right (South Lodge – No Through Road) and immediately leave the road left, past a wooden barrier, on to a solid grass track to reach thick woodland with rhododendrons and soon come to a low wooden barrier; turn left, by another barrier, and go straight on for 1½ miles (2.5km) taking care over exposed tree roots, to the A614.

6 🚲 Cross over and after 1½ miles (2.5km) branch left to Bothamsall. Soon after the village turn right, passing through Haughton and by 'The World of Robin Hood' to Walesby. Keep straight on through the village and along the B6387 to Boughton. Turn right on to the A6075, go across the roundabout and back to the start.

PLACES OF INTEREST

Sherwood Heath Nature Reserve: The charming starting point of the route includes an area of grassland with ling and bell heather, and mixed broadleaf woodland. Common lizards may be seen and the shy nightjar is a regular visitor.

Ollerton: Together, Ollerton old village and New Ollerton form a complementary self-contained township – an ideal centre from which to explore Sherwood Forest. Among a number of fine buildings is the Hop Pole Hotel, its name derived from the hop fields which once lined the River Maun. The Watermill, an 18th-century flour mill, has been restored and is the last working mill in Nottinghamshire. About 2 miles (3km) south is Rufford Country Park where the remains of a 12th-century Cistercian abbey stand in many acres of park and woodland. The lake hosts many species of wildlife, the formal gardens contain a variety of herbs and roses, and the Orangery dates

This gargoyle can be seen inside Rufford Abbey

from 1730. There is an extensive craft shop and gallery, and refreshments are available from the Buttery and Coach House restaurants.

Sherwood Forest Country Park: Just outside Edwinstowe, the park covers 50 acres (20ha), mainly of mature oak, including the magnificent 800-year-old Major Oak, and silver birch. It has many way-marked footpaths, and cycling is on

well-surfaced public bridleways. There is a year-round programme of activities and events based on the Robin Hood legend, plus a visitors' centre, shop and exhibition.

Clumber Park: Once one of the vast ducal estates from which this area of Nottinghamshire (The Dukeries) derives its name, this National Trust property centres on a fine lake with magnificent bridge, and a long double avenue of lime trees. With full refreshment facilities and many rideable tracks and roads, the park and extensive woodland are ideal for cycling.

The World of Robin Hood: This centre at Haughton recreates the 'magic and medieval' atmosphere of the times of Robin Hood, including the Crusades, and features a medieval market place – with chickens and pheasants. There is deer park near by and the lovely twin rivers of Meden and Maun are a short walk away.

WHAT TO LOOK OUT FOR

The byways, woods and waterways of this ride are most picturesque, so do take a camera. Look out for Ollerton's watermill before leaving town en route for Wellow, with its exceedingly tall maypole. Once in the woodlands look for the many birds, from the shy tree-creeper to the voluble and visually gaudy jay. In the silver birches of Sherwood you will see many 'witches' brooms' – like tufty nests – made by plant galls. Stand on the bridge at Clumber and look along the lake for the spire of the chapel – a cathedral in miniature. Do not miss the twin rivers of Meden and Maun between Bothamsall and Haughton, nor the remains of the Norman motte and bailey at Bothamsall.

RIDE 26
LINCOLNSHIRE
SK891755

The Celtic Kingdom of Lindsey

With glorious views of Lincoln Cathedral, quiet country lanes lead the explorer on a historical tour through relatively flat countryside. Along the way are a Roman canal, the sites of deserted medieval villages, the ruins of an Elizabethan castle and a rest home for horses.

INFORMATION

Total distance
18½ miles (30km)

Grade
1

OS Map
Landranger 1:50,000 sheet 121
(Lincoln)

Tourist Information
Lincoln, tel: 01522 529828;
Gainsborough, tel: 01427 615411

Cycle Shop/Hire
Barron Cycles, Stow,
tel: 01427 788417;
Arrow Cycles, North Hykeham,
tel: 01522 694564 ;
Lincolnshire Lanes, East Firsby;
tel: 01673 878258

Nearest Railway Station
Saxilby (the station is closed but trains
do stop), Lincoln (6 miles/10km)

Refreshments
There are take-aways and pubs in
Saxilby (The Sun serves meals), and
picnic benches beside the canal. Also
available: a picnic site at Bransby, two
pubs serving food in Sturton by Stow
and The Cross Keys (pub/restaurant)
in Stow. In Torksey The Hume Arms
(hotel/pub, children's play area)
serves food and welcomes families

The Gothic splendour of Lincoln Cathedral

START & ROUTE DIRECTIONS

Start

Saxilby stands where the A57 crosses the Fossdyke Roman canal 5 miles (8km) west of Lincoln city. There is free parking in the village hall car park on Sykes Lane, west of the High Street.

Directions

1 🚲 Turn right out of the car park and right again on to Saxilby High Street. Follow the road as it bends left with the canal on your right. Turn left at a T-junction on to Mill Lane (B1241 signed 'Lea'). From the farm entrance of Ingleby Grange, after 1¼ miles (2km), the site of South Ingleby's moated manor house can be seen and the fields are a maze of humps – the sites of the deserted medieval villages of South and North Ingleby. Continue uphill to a crossroads and turn right on to a minor road for Bransby, with Lincoln Cathedral on the skyline.

2 🚲 From Bransby continue for ½ mile (1km) and

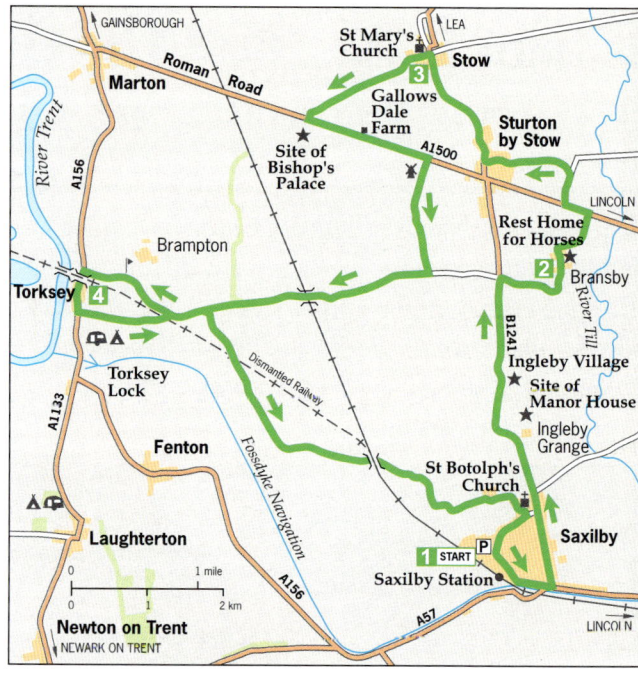

turn left at a T-junction on to Till Bridge Lane (A1500, Roman Road), signed 'Sturton'. Shortly turn right into a narrow lane, signed 'Thorpe'. Take the first left and left again at the next junction. At the T-junction turn right on to the B1241 (or left to visit Sturton by

Stow). Note a sign for Lincolnshire Cycle Trail on the right. In 1¼ miles (2km) reach Stow village sign on the left and Barron Cycles workshop on the right. Continue into the village and turn left at a crossroads, signed 'Stow Park'. St Mary's Church and The Cross Keys pub are on your right.

3 🚲 Leaving Stow, pass a cemetery and in 1 mile (1.5km) turn left at a T-junction. Opposite is the moated site of Stow's Bishop's Palace from the Middle Ages. Pass Gallows Dale Farm (note the lines of ancient rig and furrow on left), and take the first turning right (Mill Lane), with a sail-less windmill on

Small boats on the Fossdyke Roman canal

Colourful narrow boats at Torksey Lock on the Fossdyke Navigation

the right, and soon turn right at a T-junction for Torksey. Continue for 3¼ miles (5.25km) with Cottam Power Station ahead, over the railway bridge and through the golf course. Turn left at a T-junction on to the A156 into Torksey village.

4 🚲 Take the A156 through Torksey, turning left into Sand Lane, passing a cemetery for 1 mile (1.5km). Turn right at the T-junction, then fork right on to an unfenced lane, signed 'Saxilby'. Continue for 3¼ miles (5.25km), crossing a disused railway track, past Harkwick turning and under a railway bridge. Turn left

beside a sign 'Sykes Lane' into Church Lane, Saxilby, and the steepest section of the route. With St Botolph's

Church on your left, turn right, then right again into Sykes Lane for the car park.

The imposing statue of George III in Lincoln

PLACES OF INTEREST

Saxilby: A large village of warm red-brick and pantile houses and a 15th-century church. At Saxilby's centre is a riding club, supermarkets, and other shops, including a fabric shop that is an Aladdin's cave.

The Fossdyke: This Roman canal, linking the Witham and Trent rivers, was originally used to transport grain to the legions. It has enjoyed a chequered history, silting up several times. This century a magnificent Roman silver statuette of Mars was dredged from its bed at Saxilby. Today the canal carries narrow boats between Boston and the Trent, and supports many water birds.

North and South Ingleby: These two deserted medieval villages on private land were not necessarily depopulated by the Black Death, though it may have contributed. The site shows clearly where cottages stood and the lines of ancient roads. The villages were probably last inhabited in the 16th century.

Bransby Home of Rest for Horses: A treat for the children, Bransby was founded in 1968 and now cares for 250 animals, including horses, ponies, donkeys and goats. There is also an excellent gift shop, plus toilets, and a picnic site.

Stow: A village where history and legend entwine creating a romantic past. Reputedly, when St Etheldreda stopped to rest here, her staff instantly took root and gave her shelter. Her husband, King Egfrid of

The village of Stow has an impressive old church

Northumbria, built a church here in AD 678 which became the Saxon cathedral of Lindsey.

Stow Park: The route passes close to this moated site of the Bishop's Palace, which was once surrounded by a large deer park and known as a place of retreat and entertainment throughout the Middle Ages. On private land, the site is bounded by a massive ditch visible from the road.

Torksey: A major port in Roman times and winter base for Danish invaders (AD 873) who sailed up the Humber and Trent to attack settlements inland. The Romans established potteries in the area and examples of more recent items, known as Torksey Ware, can be seen at The Usher Gallery, Lincoln. Elizabethan Torksey Castle suffered during the Civil War, particularly on 1 August 1645 as Royalists and Parliamentarians fought for control of the county.

Lincoln: Only 6 miles (10km) from Saxilby, Lincoln offers not only steeply cobbled streets, a castle, a museum and a magnificent cathedral, but also all the attractions of a modern city, including shopping malls and markets.

WHAT TO LOOK OUT FOR

Since the 13th century bricks have been Lincolnshire's main building material. Handmade, they were cast from wooden moulds, stacked, covered with brushwood, and fired. The resulting variety of size, shape and colour can help to date old properties. Look at the first houses on the right and left in Bransby; compare old and new. Look also for views of Lincoln Cathedral. Listen to the silence, and while trying to spot skylarks watch for kestrels. See ducks and mute swans on the wing and watch for great-crested and little grebes. Stoats could be busy amongst the rabbit warrens under thick hedges full of nesting birds.

Ashford in the Water

RIDE 27
DERBYSHIRE
SK195698

This scenic ride through the heart of the Derbyshire Peak District tackles the hills on their easiest gradients and has only two sharp descents. There are magnificent views across high sheep pastures and into craggy, wooded dales. The local white limestone creates distinctive dry-stone walls and farmsteads in the hills and charming cottages in the villages.

INFORMATION

Total Distance
20 miles (32km), with 220 yards (200m) off-road, 17½ miles (28km) using the two off-road short cuts or 13 miles (21km) using off-road short cuts and omitting Over Haddon

Grade
3

OS Map
Landranger 1:50 000 sheet 119 (Buxton, Matlock & Dove Dale)

Tourist Information
Bakewell, tel 01629 813227; local information displays at Tideswell Dale picnic area, Millers Dale Station, and Over Haddon Craft Centre.

Nearest Railway Station
Grindleford (Manchester/ Sheffield line)

Refreshments
The Bulls Head, Ashford in the Water, a favourite cyclists' pub, has a room for children and sunny seats outside. At Great Longstone the Crispin Inn welcomes children and has a beer garden. The Monsal Head Hotel Stable Bar and Tea Room is open all day every day except Christmas or you may prefer the Monsal View Cafe next door. Opposite the Millers Dale Station car park, the Wriggly Tin Cafe is open Friday 11-5, Sat/Sun 10.30-5, whilst at Over Haddon, Yew Tree Tea Room offers home baking every day of the week. There are picnic spots at Monsal Head and in Tideswell Dale

Cressbrook Mill was originally a cotton mill

START & ROUTE DIRECTIONS

Start

Ashford in the Water is bypassed by the A6, 1½ miles (2.5km) north-west of Bakewell. Take the A6020 over the River Wye and go immediately left into the village. The small free car park is on the right in about ½ mile (1km). Miller's Dale Station pay-and-display car park, on the Monsal Trail, provides an alternative start from the west.

Directions

1 ڶڶ Turn right out of the car park and immediately right again to climb gently to the B6465. Cross on to a narrow lane which rises through the tangled woods of Thornbridge Hall towards Longstone Edge and the village of Great Longstone.

2 ڶڶ Go left at the T-junction, past Longstone Hall, and climb again to recross the B6465 at spectacular Monsal Head. Descend with care to Upperdale for an idyllic ride on a single-track lane beside the River Wye.

3 ڶڶ At Cressbrook Mill there is a choice. For a short, flat route join a concessionary path, part of the Monsal Trail, by turning left through the second gateway (there are two stone balls on the wall) and walking your cycle through lovely Water-cum-Jolly Dale for about 1 mile (1.5km), to join a narrow lane at Litton Mill leading to Miller's Dale. Alternatively,

continue on the road for 2 miles (3km) as it leaves the dale and winds up through woodland to emerge amongst hill pastures. Turn left and then left again at the junction on the outskirts of Litton down tiny Litton Dale, go left on the B6049 and climb slightly past the Tideswell Dale picnic area before swooping down to Miller's Dale under a fine viaduct.

4 ڶڶ Over the river the road starts to rise, and around the corner is a further choice of routes. With low gears you can take part of the walker's Limestone Way, a steep tarmac byway on the left. This levels off to become a good stone and grass lane which joins the road towards Priestcliffe. For a gentler

climb remain on the B6049 for a further 1 mile (1.5km) and go left towards Priestcliffe, ascending steadily to the A6. Cross the A6, turning left and immediately right (with care) through the outskirts of Taddington. Leaving the village, turn right at the crossroads and climb to the edge of Taddington Moor where The Jarnet offers a smooth descent. Turn left at the crossroads for a short climb on to High Low and views of the old Magpie Mine.

5 ڶڶ Past the mine entrance, at the Ashford turn, is a short cut left, straight down Kirk Dale. Otherwise continue, and in ¼ mile (0.5km) take a broad stone track right to descend Bole Hill. At the crossroads take

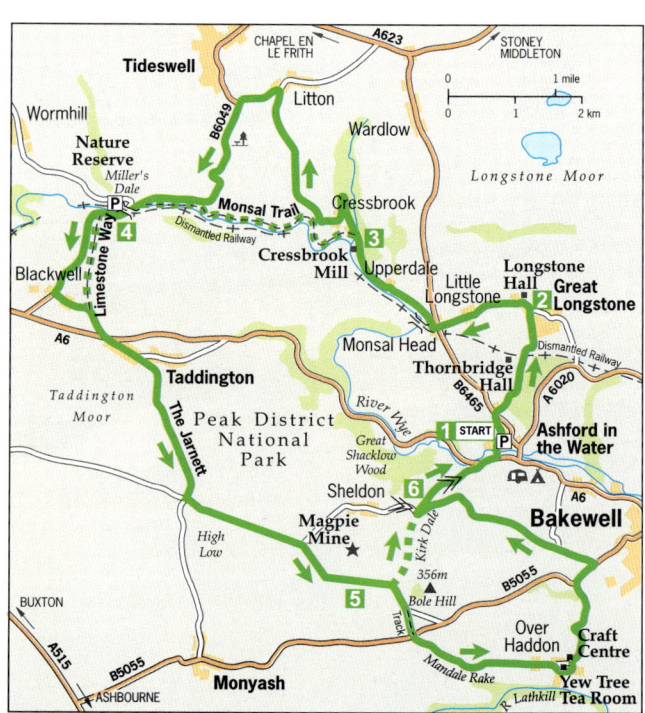

On the banks of the River Wye at Ashford in the Water

the tiny lane opposite along Mandale Rake and down to Over Haddon, perched on the hillside above Lathkill Dale. Immediately after the 30 mph sign turn right into the hamlet. Follow the road round to the left in front of Yew Tree Tea Room and keep left, with views over the dale to the right, passing the Craft Centre and Information Office. As you leave the hamlet, the road dips and Bakewell and the eastern gritstone edges appear ahead. At the B5055 go right and soon left. Stay on this quiet lane above the Wye Valley, as far as the T-junction.

6 ⏷ Turn right for a thrilling descent of Kirk Dale and at the A6 go right and

look for the old Sheepwash Bridge almost immediately on the left. Dismount and cross the bridge into Ashford. Rejoin the road by the well

and turn left; you will shortly see the car park on the right.

The Monsal Trail near Miller's Dale by the River Wye

PLACES OF INTEREST

Ashford in the Water: This is a typical Derbyshire village which keeps many of its old customs. Five wells are dressed for Trinity Sunday and paper garlands of maidens who died before their wedding day hang in the church. There is an attractive information plaque on the wall by the 17th-century Sheepwash Bridge.

Cressbrook Mill: An impressive, partly ruined Georgian building, this was originally a cotton mill, taking water from the Wye to power two large waterwheels before steam turbines were introduced in 1890. Conditions at this mill were reasonable, but at Litton Mill pauper apprentices were cruelly treated and many children died.

The Monsal Trail: This long-distance trail uses part of the disused Bakewell/Buxton railway line which was bought by the Peak National Park

Authority in 1980. Only short stretches are currently suitable for cycling as several tunnels are closed. The information board at Miller's Dale Station details four mountain bike circuits using the trail and byways.

The Limestone Way: Following 26 miles (42km) of footpaths and lanes from Matlock to Castleton, this walkers' trail is waymarked with the Derby Ram logo.

The Magpie Mine: With its ruined engine house, the Magpie Mine is a prominent relic of Derbyshire's lead mining past, accessible by footpath. Near by, Mandale Rake is a long scar from which a seam of lead has been extracted, and Bole Hill is the site of early lead smelting. Rakes and boles are frequently wooded to prevent livestock grazing the poisoned ground.

Lathkill Dale: This nature reserve is one of Britain's best wildlife sites and well worth exploration. There is a concessionary footpath through the dale alongside the river and its mill pools, old lead mines, natural caves and cliffs. The old Ricklow Quarry spoil heaps, towards the dale head, are covered in wild flowers, including the rare Jacob's Ladder. Visit the Information Room in Over Haddon Craft Centre for full details of the current flowers in bloom and of bird sightings.

A beautiful early spring orchid at Cressbrook Dale

RIDE 28
PEMBROKESHIRE
SM932394

Cycling around Strumble

Using quiet country lanes through the delightful Pembrokeshire countryside, this route takes you past many sites of historical and prehistoric interest. There are extensive views from several points, while at others the tall hedges are filled with colour from the wild flowers, for which the area is noted. The first half of a mile (1km) can be muddy and the climb up to Garn Fawr is quite tough, with two sections of 1 in 4.

INFORMATION

Total Distance
13½ miles (21km)

Grade
2

OS Maps
Landranger 157 (St David's & Haverfordwest); Outdoor Leisure 35 (North Pembrokeshire)

Tourist Information
Fishguard, tel: 01348 873484

Cycle Shops/Hire
Preseli Venture Outdoor Centre, Mathry, tel: 01348 837709 (ring in advance)

Nearest Railway Station
Fishguard

Refreshments
Tea rooms at Melin Tregwynt Woollen Mill and the Llangloffan Farmhouse Cheese Centre.

Strumble Head viewed from Garn Fawr

START & ROUTE DIRECTIONS

Start

This route starts from the quiet hamlet of Llanwnda, at the end of a minor road some 1½ miles (2.5km) north-west of the A40 at Goodwick, following signs for 'Town Centre', then 'Church Tour' and finally 'Llanwnda'. Roadside parking is available on the green in the centre of the hamlet.

Directions

1 ᢒᶞ From the green, take the old road Feidr Pont Eglwys (Church Bridge Road), signed 'unsuitable for motors', past Llanwnda House, taking the right (major) fork at the initial junction. This takes you down to a minor road where you turn right. Follow the road for 1¼ miles to a junction past Trehowel Farm. Turn left, signed 'Tremarchog St Nicholas Abermawr' and 'unsuitable for coaches', and climb up to the car park at the

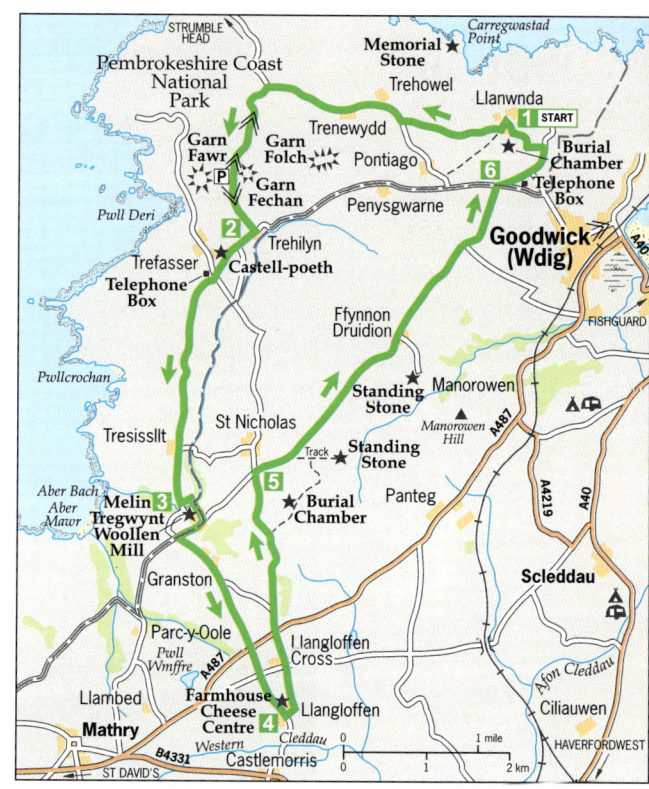

foot of Garn Fawr, before continuing down to the T-junction at Harmony.

2 ᢒᶞ Turn right, signed 'Pwllderi Tremarchog St Nicholas', and follow the road – ignoring a T-junction – for ½ mile (1km) to the staggered crossroads at Trefasser Cross. On your right as you come to the cross are the overgrown and inaccessible remains of Castell Poeth Iron-Age fort. Go straight over (the second right immediately past the telephone box) at the crossroads signed 'Abermawr and Tregwynt Woollen Mill', and enjoy the mainly downhill ride for 2 miles (3km) to a T-junction opposite glasshouses at the

The distinctive rocky outcrop at Garn Fawr

It is well worth pausing to take in the view at Strumble Head

bottom of a steep descent signposted 'Tregwynt Woollen Mill'.

3 🚲 Turn left to soon reach Melin Tregwynt Woollen Mill. After visiting the mill, continue up to the T-junction, turn right and follow the road to a crossroads. Turn left and follow the road signposted 'Fishguard' for 1½ miles (2.5km) to Llangloffan, bearing right at the first junction and going straight over two crossroads, following the signs 'Castle Morris and Llangloffan Cheese Centre', to enter the village via the Llangloffan Farmhouse Cheese Centre.

4 🚲 Leaving the Cheese Centre, drop the few metres to the T-junction in the centre of the village and turn left, signed 'Tremarchog and St Nicholas'. Follow this road, enjoying extensive views, across two crossroads as you generally descend for 2 miles (3km) to a third crossroads at St Nicholas' Cross.

5 🚲 Turn right, signed 'Wdig Goodwick 3'. Up to your right is Ffyst Samson burial chamber which, along with a standing stone and tumuli, can be visited by walking down the track on your right (footpath only) found 450 yards (400m) from

the crossroads. Continue for 3 miles (5km) from St Nicholas' Cross past Ffynnon Druidon Farm (where a short diversion to the right takes you down to another standing stone), gently climbing to Henner Cross, a staggered crossroads, ignoring all the side turnings on the way.

6 🚲 Go straight over into the road signed 'single track road' by the telephone box. After 550 yards (500m) turn left at the T-junction and turn left again, signed 'Llanwnda', after another 400 yards (350m). This road takes you past a cemetery and back down to the starting point of the ride.

Look out for the 'Holy Well' in the hamlet of Llanwnda

American, General Tate, had surrendered by the evening of the 24 February, thus ending the last invasion of Britain. The surrender was signed at the charming farmhouse of Trehowel which is passed on the route.

Garn Fawr: This rocky hill offers superb views from its craggy summit and held an Iron-Age fort and settlement, while the remains of a wartime look-out can be found near the top. On the western side near the road is a small corbelled hut, variously described as a Celtic monk's cell, a prehistoric hut or an ancient pigsty!

Melin Tregwynt Woolen Mill: In its quiet wooded valley, this fascinating working woollen mill, can be visited free of charge. You can see the traditional skills of the woollen textile industry, or enjoy a rest in the restaurant/tea rooms, the picnic area and shop.

Llangloffan Farmhouse Cheese Centre: Another place to enjoy displays of traditional skills in a charming location. As well as watching the cheese-making process, you can sample the products in the farm shop, take coffee in the museum tea room, stroll around the farm and meet the friendly Jersey cows, or expend more of the children's energy in the play area. The farm shop is open every day except Sunday. Tours of the Cheese Centre take place on selected mornings according to season (tel: 01348 891241).

PLACES OF INTEREST

Llanwnda: This tiny hamlet is full of historical interest. The rocks on the green in the centre formed part of a prehistoric stone circle, while on the crag above the farm is a well-preserved burial chamber. Just over the fence, by the stile marked 'Carregwastad Path', is a 'Holy Well', and the outer walls of the Celtic bellcote-style church have ancient inscribed stones, showing crosses and a spectacular Celtic head.

The French, who landed at nearby Carregwastad Point, tried to burn down the church in 1797, but the short-lived invasion was routed by the local militia, aided, it is said, by the appearance of local ladies who came to watch the fun and were mistaken for Redcoat reinforcements by the French who mistook their tall Welsh hats and red shawls for shakos and uniform coats. Landing on 22 February, the drunken convicts and mercenaries of the invasion force, led by the

WHAT TO LOOK OUT FOR

Pembrokeshire is noted for the variety of its wild flowers and animals. Prominent on this ride are gorse, with its 'coconut ice' perfume, foxgloves, heathers on the uplands, and a myriad of other plants. The area is also famous for its birdlife, from cliff-nesting seabirds to wrens, while buzzards are very likely to be seen soaring overhead.
Several burial chambers, forts, standing stones and tumuli are to be found by taking short walks from the route, the best being burial chambers a Ffyst Samson and Garnwnda, and standing stones near Manorowen.

The Malvern Hills, Eastnor and Castlemorton Common

A steep climb providing views right across Worcestershire takes you straight up to the centre of the Malvern Hills before an easier ride to British Camp offers equally splendid views in the opposite direction. After Eastnor Castle a narrow lane – sometimes muddy, but tarmac throughout – leads through a ford. The route passes through woodland before dropping down across Castlemorton Common and past a children's zoo.

RIDE 29
WORCESTERSHIRE
SO779458

Castlemorton Common (which provides afternoon teas) offer refreshments en route. Hot and cold snacks are also available at the Children's Zoo at Welland, as are light lunches and cream teas within the grounds of Eastnor Castle. There are plenty of informal picnic sites on the hills and on the common

Eastnor Castle reflected in the waters of its lake

INFORMATION

Total Distance
22 miles (35km)

Grade
3

OS Map
Landranger 1:50 000 sheet 150
(Worcester & The Malverns)

Tourist Information
Great Malvern, tel: 01684 892289

Cycle Shops/Hire
Mycycles Sport and Leisure, Malvern, tel: 01684 574836; Spokes & Saddles, Malvern, tel: 01684 576141

Nearest Railway Station
Great Malvern (½ mile/1km)

Refreshments
There is a wide choice of cafés, tea rooms, restaurants and pubs in Great Malvern. The Kettle Sings Café, Jubilee Drive and the Plume of Feathers pub,

START & ROUTE DIRECTIONS

Start

Great Malvern is on the A449 between Worcester and Ledbury. The town's main pay-and-display car park is behind the swimming pool in Priory Road, ¼ mile (0.5km) east of the junction of the B4211 with the A449.

Directions

1 🚲 Turn left out of the car park (away from the swimming pool) and cycle along Priory Road, following the curve up to the right for ½ mile (0.5km) until it joins Abbey Road. Turn sharp left here and follow Abbey Road for ½ mile (0.5km) to the junction with the A449. Cross straight over this main road (with care) and take the small road leading up to the right, through the trees. Very shortly turn sharp left on to Wyche Road and continue ahead for 1 mile (1.5km) up to Wyche Cutting.

2 🚲 Immediately after the summit turn left into Jubilee Drive, signposted 'Ledbury'. If you wish to walk the mile (1.5km) to the top of the Worcestershire Beacon, turn right into West Malvern Road and immediately right again up Beacon Road; afterwards retrace your steps to Wyche Cutting. Continue for 2 miles (3km) along Jubilee Drive and turn right on to the A449 towards Ledbury. It is a ½-mile (1km) walk from the car park at this junction to reach the summit of the Herefordshire Beacon and British Camp.

3 🚲 Enter Herefordshire and enjoy a long freewheel, straight on past the turning to Colwall and the Wellington Inn, and just after 2 miles (3km) cross a railway bridge. After a further ½ mile (0.5km) turn left down a narrow lane opposite a farm. Turn left at the main road, pass the village sign for Eastnor and in a short distance fork right (with care), signposted 'Bromsberrow'. Pass to the right of the village green in

Eastnor and enter Clencher's Mill Lane.

4 🚲 Pass the entrance to Eastnor Castle car park and continue along this narrow lane, crossing a ford, for 2½ miles (4km). Bear left, signposted 'Malvern and Worcester', at the grass island with the war memorial and then immediately fork right to stay on the larger lane. Continue along Allbright Lane for 1½ miles (2.5km) and

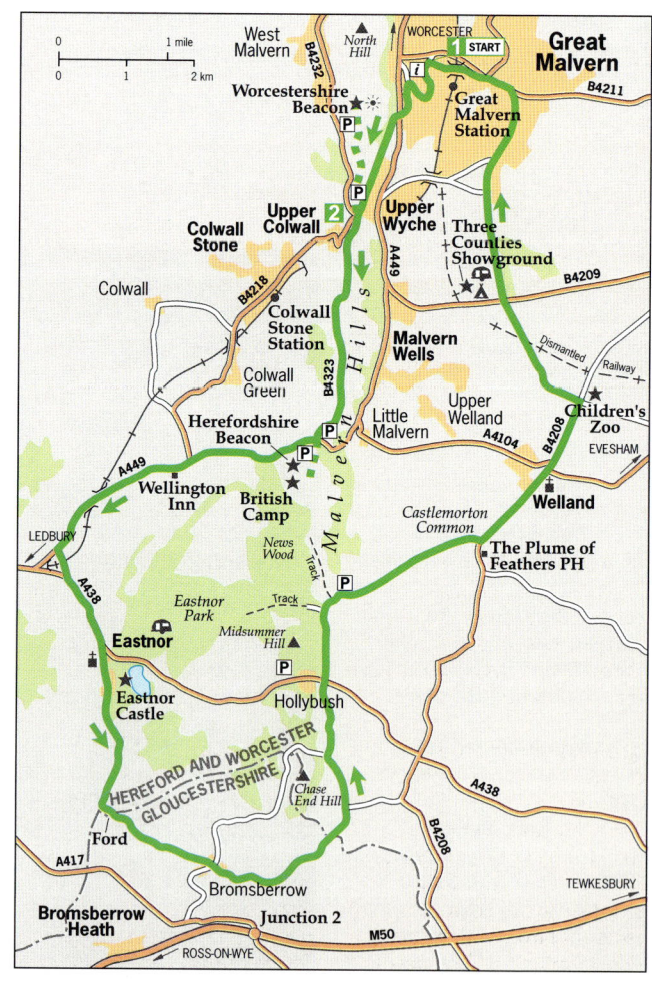

then go straight on, signed 'Hollybush' (do not follow the road to the right, signposted 'Camers Green'). In ½ mile (1km) fork right and continue up to the main A438.

5 🚴 Carefully cross straight over this road into another narrow lane between woodland and a converted wooden barn. Bear right at the fork and drop down a short steep hill before emerging from the trees to ride 1½ miles (2.5km) across

Castlemorton Common. At the main road, opposite a bus shelter, turn left. If you need refreshment The Plume of Feathers is just to the right. Follow the B4208 through Welland to the next crossroads. Turn left here, signposted 'Malvern', to stay on the B4208; the Children's Zoo is on the corner.

6 🚴 Continue for 3 miles (5km) towards Malvern, passing the Three Counties Showground on your left.

Sunrise over the Malvern Hills from Worcestershire Beacon

Bear left at the junction with the B4211 and soon right around the complex roundabout, turning left into Barnards Green Road. Immediately turn left into Avenue Road, signposted 'Railway Station and Tourist Information'. Continue for ¾ mile (1km), passing the railway station, before turning left into Priory Road to return to the starting point.

PLACES OF INTEREST

Malvern: As well as the hills themselves, the towns which make up Malvern – a Victorian spa – are full of hidden delights, including gas street lights and a large number of public wells. Leaflets giving details of trails to find these are available from the tourist information office near the start.

The Malvern Hills: Nearly 1,400 feet (422m) high and 9½ miles (15km) long, the hills divide Worcestershire to the east from Herefordshire to the west. Eastwards the view extends across the flat plain of the Vale of Severn (a desert millions of years ago) to the Cotswolds. To the west lies undulating farmland (which in equally ancient times lay under varying depths of tropical ocean, leaving a variety of fossils). The hills themselves are solid granite and are far older still, pre-dating any living creatures. The Worcestershire Beacon is the highest point, offering magnificent views in all directions. At the opposite (southern) end is the Herefordshire Beacon where the British Camp – a large Iron-Age fort – stands dramatically on the skyline.

Eastnor Castle: This imposing 19th-century building is set in the foothills of the Malverns, surrounded by a deer park, an

The Abbey Gatehouse at Malvern, a fashionable spa town

arboretum and a lake. Attractions include a garden centre and a recently constructed children's maze.

Castlemorton Common: This, together with several other local commons, is protected by the same authority – the Malvern Hills Conservators – which guards the hills themselves. The vegetation ranges from well-grazed pasture through woodland to blackberry, bracken, broom and gorse to dry grassland with patches of heather and bilberry. The composer Edward Elgar lived locally and enjoyed cycling around the hills – perhaps thus gaining much inspiration for his enduringly popular works. Note: off-road cycling is permitted on bridleways, but riders are asked not to ride on the ridge of the hills or on other open land or commons. Give way to horse riders and walkers and avoid damaging the ground by cycling in wet or muddy conditions or by harsh braking. Inconsiderate riding could lead to a total ban on all cyclists on the Conservators' land.

Children's Zoo, Welland: A few miles south of Great Malvern on the B4208, the zoo contains around 100 different species of animals and birds, as well as a narrow-gauge railway, an adventure playground and a picnic area.

WHAT TO LOOK OUT FOR

A good source of free Malvern Water is a spring just below Jubilee Drive at the junction with a lane leading down to Evendine, ¾ mile (1km) past the 'Kettle Sings' sign.

RIDE 30
POWYS
SO284726

The Teme Valley

The Teme rises on the high ground of the Radnor Forest. One of the purest rivers, it is rich in wildlife, including otters which have returned to its banks. The ride follows lanes which shadow the river upstream from Knighton, returning through Knucklas. There are climbs and descents on the outward section but the lanes have little traffic.

INFORMATION

Total Distance
14 miles (22.5 km)

Grade
3

OS Maps
Landranger 1:50,000 sheet 148
(Presteigne & Hay-on-Wye)

Tourist Information
Knighton, tel: 01547 528753

Cycle Shops/Hire
Offa's Bikes, Knighton,
tel: 01544 230534;
Wheely Wonderful, Elton near Ludlow,
tel: 01568 770755;
Greenstiles, Llandrindod Wells (hire),
tel: 01597 824594

Refreshments
The pubs in Knighton all serve food,
and there is a café and a fish and chip
shop. The Red Lion at Llanfair
Waterdine has a pleasant beer garden
overlooking the River Teme (children
are not allowed in the lounge). The
Lloyney Arms at Lloyney and The
Castle at Knucklas both welcome
children but there are only a few
seats outside

The junction at Skyborry Green along the route

START & ROUTE DIRECTIONS

Start

Knighton, lying on the border of England and Wales, is on the A488 road from Shrewsbury and Llandrindod Wells. It is also served by the Heart of Wales railway line. There is parking at the Offa's Dyke Centre in West Street.

Directions

1 🚲 Turn left from the Offa's Dyke Centre into West Street, then take the second left (Church Street) to the parish church. Follow this road to the main A488, Station Road, and turn left. The road bears left over the Heart of Wales railway line and then swings to the right.

Go left here, signposted 'Skyborry'. The road runs beneath Kinsley Wood to Panpunton Farm where it crosses Offa's Dyke Path before rising steadily to a group of houses at Skyborry. The route then descends steeply before levelling out for ½ mile (0.5km) to reach a T-junction at Skyborry Green.

Look for the church when in Llanfair Waterdine

At the T-junction keep left for Llanfair Waterdine. The road now runs above the watermeadows and passes a farmstead, Monaughty Poeth, where the road to the left is for Knucklas. Your route is straight ahead, climbing to

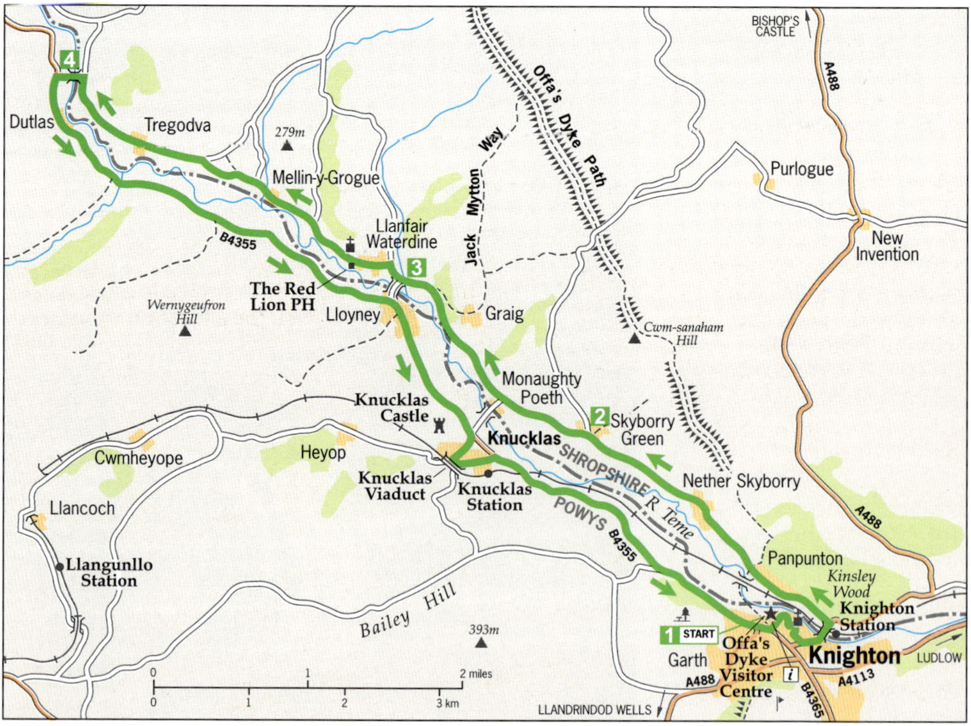

Knucklas Viaduct is a most impressive sight

Graig, with Jack Mytton Way coming in from the right.

3 🚲 At the next junction, cross the bridge over the River Teme on the left and go right for a sharp climb up into Llanfair Waterdine. Keep ahead at the junction. Go past The Red Lion and the church, leave the village and shortly reach a junction. Keep ahead again to Mellin-y-Grogue where you descend to a brook. This climbs steeply to a point where you meet an old track. Stay on the road and climb again to a junction; continue ahead, passing Tregodfa and Runnis Chapel, dating from 1837. The road now descends to the river's edge. Go left, cross the bridge to Dutlas and ride back into Wales again.

4 🚲 Climb up to the B4355, turn left and cycle down the valley for 3 miles (5km) to Lloyney, where the pub is on the right. Continue along the B4355, mainly downhill, to Knucklas. At the crossroads turn right to the centre. Above on the right you can see Knucklas Castle. Pass the Bridge Stores and keep left for the Castle Inn and the main road. On leaving Knucklas go right on to the B4355 to climb over the railway. The road reaches a summit and descends into Knighton, and the Offa's Dyke Visitor Centre, the start point of the ride, is on the left as you enter town.

Sheep graze on Offa's Dyke at Springhill, near Knighton

PLACES OF INTEREST

Knighton: The Victorian Clock Tower stands proudly in the town centre, and from it radiate streets with much older buildings, notably the 'Narrows'. Knighton grew up as a crossing point of the River Teme and Offa's Dyke and has always been a market town. Although very hilly, it is a superb area for walking and cycling. Knighton is also served by one of Britain's most rural railways. It is worth planning a trip, for the scenery is magnificent and there are several feats of railway engineering to marvel at, including the ornate 13-arched Knucklas Viaduct which stands high above the village. If you plan to take your bike you need to book in advance.

Knucklas: Above the sleepy village of Knucklas stand the scant remains of Knucklas Castle, reputed in local legend to have been the home of Arthur and Guinevere. The castle was sacked by Welsh champion Owain Glyndwr and it is said that much of the stonework was dismantled to build the Knucklas Viaduct.

Jack Mytton Way: This popular 70-mile (112km) route for walkers, cyclists and horse riders, through Shropshire to Llanfair Waterdine, is named after an 18th-century rake who enjoyed life to the full in the borderlands.

This Victorian clock tower dominates the centre of Knighton

Offa's Dyke: Those wishing to combine a trip to Knighton with a walk along Offa's Dyke will not be disappointed for there are well-preserved sections of the Dyke, created by King Offa of Mercia in the 8th century as a boundary between his kingdom and the Welsh tribes to the west. The Offa's Dyke Centre provides an exhibition and much information about the Dyke and the area.

WHAT TO LOOK OUT FOR

This is high country where sheep farming dominates. Famous breeds such as the Clun Forest and Kerry Hill are still popular. Look out for birds of prey such as kestrel and buzzard hovering above the valley, as well as for ravens and crows high in the trees. By the riverside you will catch glimpses of the grey heron searching for fish.

RIDE 31
SHROPSHIRE
SJ514288

North Shropshire

INFORMATION

Total Distance
20 miles (32km) omitting
Hawkstone Hill

OS Map
Landranger 1:50 000 sheet 126
(Shrewsbury)

Tourist Information
Shrewsbury, tel: 01743 350761

Nearest Railway Station
Wem

Cycle Shops/Hire
Top Gear Cycles, Wem,
tel: 01939 235485;
Wem Cycle and Toy Centre,
tel: 01939 233686

Refreshments
There is a good selection of pubs and
the Maypole Tea Rooms in Wem.
Welcoming hostelries on the route are
the Horse and Jockey in Northwood
and the Waggoner's Inn, Platt Lane,
Whixall, popular with passing barges;
both are open all day, and have
children's menus and a beer garden.
Hawkstone Park has a tea room and in
nearby Weston the village post office
is also Gino's Wine Bar, a tempting
little sun-trap

The heath and farmland of the Welsh Marches provide a network of quiet flat lanes with unspoilt villages ideal for family cycling. The meres, parkland and Llangollen Canal are rich in wildlife and worth further exploration. If you tire the route can be shortened, avoiding the climbs to Hawkstone Hill which could be visited as a separate short ride.

*Dusk settling in over Colemere
Country Park*

START & ROUTE DIRECTIONS

Start

Wem is a small friendly town about 10 miles (16km) north of Shrewsbury. It lies west of the A49 on the B5063/B5065/B5476 crossroads. The town's large free car park is signed opposite the Maypole Tea Rooms on the junction of the B5065 and B5476. Alternative starts are from Colemere free car park or Hawkstone Park free car park.

2 🚲 On reaching Noneley junction, turn right to Loppington. Pass the church, then turn left at the Dickin Arms and then turn immediately right, by the post office. Follow this lane for 1 mile (1.5km) through Brownheath to turn right at English Frankton and climb gently on a narrow lane overlooking the attractive parkland of Frankton Grange. Ride straight through enchanting Colemere hamlet for a fine view over Cole Mere itself.

4 🚲 Follow this road past a variety of smallholdings and tracks, for about 2 miles (3km) and then turn left. The lane is not signposted but a white painted bridge is visible from the road. Cross the Prees Canal on the unusual lift bridge, built slightly askew, and carry on to a T-junction to go right and soon left to rejoin the main Whixall road. Continue through this scattered community, now with views over Whixall Moss on the left, to the friendly Waggoner's Inn at Platt Lane.

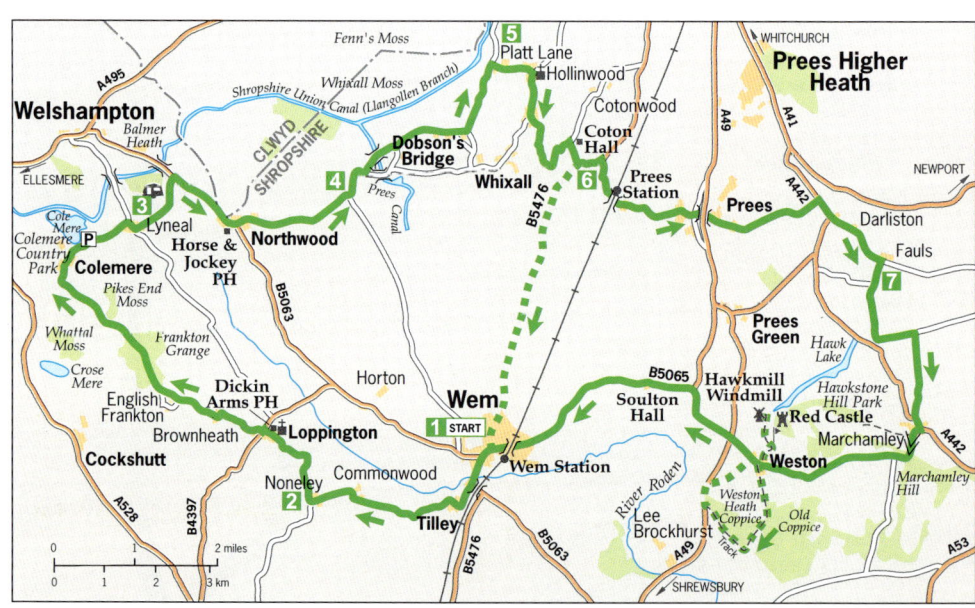

Directions

1 🚲 Turn left out of Wem car park on to the B5063 and left again on the B5476. In ¼ mile (0.5km), before the railway bridge, go right on to a quiet lane to Tilley. In ½ mile (1km) turn right opposite Rhuewood Grange to follow a single-track road through CommonWood.

3 🚲 Continue to Lyneal. Turn right at the first T-junction, and left at the second, towards Balmer Heath. At the B5063 turn right to skim the Welsh border at Northwood. Here, just past the Horse and Jockey pub, take the lane left to explore the charming village of Whixall.

5 🚲 Here turn right and, at Hollinwood, turn right again in front of the chapel. In 1 mile (1.5km) turn left, as the road bends right, towards Cotonwood and soon bear right and right again in front of Coton Hall, keeping the grounds of Coton Hall on your left. Continue to the B5476.

6 🚲 You can now take a short cut back to Wem by turning right along the B5476. To continue, go left and soon right, passing Prees Station. Over the old A49 in Prees, the road rises steadily under the bypass to the A442. Turn right and soon left through Darliston, climbing imperceptibly for 1 mile (1.5km) to Fauls hamlet.

7 🚲 Turn right and descend, on a single-track road (rough and grassy in places). At the T-junction go left and in ½ mile (1km) right. Turn right again at the next T-junction for the steepest climb of the route to the A442 at Marchamley. Here go left

Highly interesting, Loppington church dates from Norman times

and almost immediately right (with care) on to a narrow sunken lane which cuts through woodland over Marchamley Hill then dips sharply past the white lime-stone cliffs.

8 🚲 Turn right at the bottom of the hill through parkland, passing the Hawkstone Hill follies on the right and rising imperceptibly to Weston under Red Castle for fine views of the Welsh hills ahead. Continue over the A49 and turn left at the B5065 to return to Wem, passing Soulton Hall on your left.

Strolling beneath a green canopy in Colemere Country Park

PLACES OF INTEREST

Loppington: Of particular interest here is the church. Originally Norman but with many additions, its medieval angel beneath the clock is visible from the road. Worth closer inspection are vertical cuts in the wall under the south window, made by archers sharpening their arrowheads, and modern tapestries inside, particularly the 'four seasons' altar-rail cushions. The post office has a key.

Cole Mere: This is one of seven large meres formed by icebergs from the last Ice Age. It is a valuable water and woodland habitat which shelters the rare least waterlily. Visit in winter to see great-crested grebes; or on a summer evening when bats skim the water. There are attractive walks from the car park and day fishing by permit from the site warden.

Prees Canal: This unfinished branch of the Llangollen Canal is popular for holiday cruising.

WHAT TO LOOK OUT FOR

To the west, with distant views of the Welsh Hills, look for migrating birds in autumn, and in summer listen for breeding reed and sedge warblers. To the east catch intriguing glimpses of Sir Rowland Hill's monument and some of his follies and crags as you circle Hawkstone Hill. You will lose count of charming old timber-framed homesteads; notable are Oak Cottage, Tilley, Manor House Cottage, Prees, and Moat Farm House, an 11th-century fortified tenement in Fauls. Churches feature massive red sandstone blocks, also seen occasionally in walls, barns and cottages, particularly at Brownheath. Do not miss the majestic little stone owls and frogs on the banisters in front of Soulton Hall, a Tudor brick manor house, now a hotel.

This stretch, including two fine little lift bridges, has been restored to access a new marina at Dobson's Bridge.

Whixall and Fenn's Moss:
These two areas are an important habitat for peatland flora, particularly the insectivorous sundew, and insects including the large heath butterfly and white-faced darter dragonfly. Traditionally, Whixall inhabitants extracted peat but this is no longer undertaken commercially. The

edge of the moss can be visited by a short detour across the Llangollen Canal from the Waggoner's Arms.

Hawkstone Hill Park:
Described by Dr Johnson as a place of 'terrific grandeur', this was created in the grounds of the ruined medieval Red Castle by Sir Rowland Hill in the 18th century. There is a strenuous walk (3–4 hours), through woodland with concealed grottoes, secret tunnels, a precipice and a remarkable collection of follies (tickets required).

Weston under Red Castle:
The village has two delightful off-road detours: the bridleway to Hawk Windmill (disused) has views over the beautifully landscaped golf course where Sandy Lyle first learned his game. The byway around Weston Coppice is cycleable clockwise with care, giving fine views of mature mixed woodland.

Time for a quick visit to the post office in Wem

RIDE 32
CHESHIRE
SJ487473

Malpas and the Peckforton Hills

A circuit of the pretty Peckforton Hills, this ride offers views of a dozen castles and halls dating from prehistory to the 19th century. The lanes roll gently through wide fertile pastures with no major climbs, the highest point being Hampton Post (435 feet/133m). There are delightful villages and a watermill to explore, and a diversion into the hills for the energetic.

INFORMATION

Distance
29 miles (47km), excluding diversions

Grade
2

OS Map
Landranger 1:50 000 sheet 117
(Chester)

Tourist Information
Nantwich, tel: 01270 610983

Nearest Railway Station
Whitchurch

Refreshments
The Red Lion, a popular cyclists' pub in Malpas, is open all day. Good pubs en route are the Cholmondeley Arms, the Nags Head, Bunbury, and the Fox & Hounds, Tilston, all with gardens and play areas. Cholmondeley Castle gardens have a tea room and picnic area and you pass the Clifden House Restaurant in Tattenhall. Beeston Castle car park has a picnic area and a snack wagon on Sundays (daily Whitsun to September) and Stretton Mill is an attractive picnic area by the mill pond, whilst the Cheshire Ice Cream Farm may tempt you away from the route

Cows grazing untroubled in the foothills of Beeston Castle

START & ROUTE DIRECTIONS

Start

Malpas lies west of the A41 at the junction of the B5069 and B539, about 5 miles (8km) north-west of Whitchurch, itself south-east of Chester. Begin the ride from the free car park on the B5069, opposite the Fire Station. Beeley Castle free car parks provide an alternative start from the north.

Directions

[1] ⛵ Turn right out of the car park, right again on the B5069 and descend 3 miles (2km) to the outskirts of Hampton Heath. Immediately after the disused railway bridge go right, signposted 'Cholmondeley', and cross the A41. The lane climbs steadily to Hampton Post and winds gently to a junction at Cholmondeley Castle gatehouse.

[2] ⛵ Go right, through mature woodland, past the garden entrance, and cross the A49 by the Cholmondeley Arms. In ½ mile (1km) turn left and follow the Nantwich Road for 2½ miles (4km) through Chorley to the outskirts of Larden Green.

Take the second left, Hearns Lane. Alternatively, to visit Woodhey Chapel, at Larden Green turn left immediately after The Gables on Woodhey Lane, then fork left in front of Cooks Pit Farm and left by the old stone cross. The tiny chapel, dating from 1699, is on the right. (Woodhey Hall Farm has a key, and a donation is appreciated.) Retrace your tracks to the cross and continue to the A534 to turn right and first left at Brindley.

[3] ⛵ On the main route, follow this narrow road past well-kept cottages to a

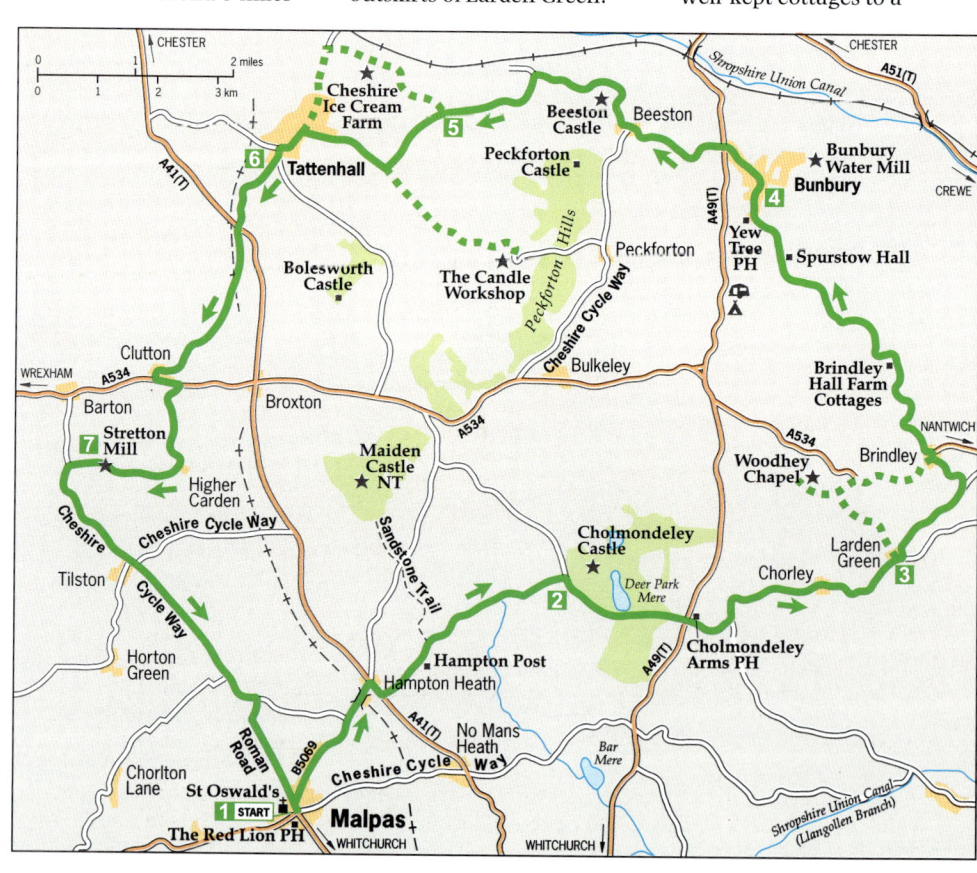

T-junction and go right, then immediately left, on to Ikey Lane, and soon left again on Kidderton Lane to cross the A534 at Brindley. After the newly landscaped Brindley Lea Hall the lane winds past Brindley Hall Farm Cottages to a striking residence, once Spurstow Primary School. Turn left here, pass Spurstow Hall, and then in ½ mile (1km) go right at the Yew Tree pub into Bunbury.

4 🚲 In the village centre bear left by Bunbury Cottage and cross the A49 with care, approaching Peckforton and Beeston Castles, perched ahead on opposing hills. Go left at the junction in Beeston hamlet, then immediately right and right again, to join briefly the Cheshire Cycleway and Sandstone Trail circumnavigating Beeston Castle on its spectacular wooded crag.

5 🚲 At the next T-junction turn right and follow this lane for 1¾ miles (2.5km). To the right is a road signed to the Ice Cream Farm; decide here on a detour or continue past Owler Hall Cottages to a junction. (The left turn is a strenuous detour to the Candle Workshops.) Turn right to ride through Tattenhall, a quiet market town.

6 🚲 At the outskirts go left, opposite the Beehive Stores, to climb gently between sandstone banks. Over the A41 take Chowley Oak Lane and continue parallel to the Peckforton Hills for 2 miles (3km) to turn left and rise to

Neat cottages in front of the church in Malpas

cross the A534. The lane opposite, signposted 'Carden only', ascends gradually through Carden golf course to Higher Carden before sweeping down to a fine gatehouse. Turn right here on to the single-track road ahead and descend to charming Stretton Mill.

7 🚲 Continue ahead to a T-junction and go left, past the recently restored Stretton Hall. The route is now a very direct lane which follows the Roman road through the village of Tilston, climbing steadily, to return to Malpas on the B5069 and the start point of the ride.

PLACES OF INTEREST

Cholmondeley Castle: The gardens and farm of this 19th-century romantic Gothic castle are open to the public, and attractions include a rose and lavender garden, water garden, lakeside picnic area, tea room and rare breeds of farm animals.

Bunbury Water Mill: On a 700-year-old corn milling site, the building is worth a short detour, just past the church. The present mill machinery, dating from 1850, worked commercially until 1960 and has been fully restored.

Beeston Castle: This noted landmark was begun in 1220 by Ranolf de Blundeville. After its capture for the King in the English Civil War by Captain 'Big Letter' Sandford, the castle was retaken by Parliamentary forces and reduced to an impressive crag-top ruin. The site includes a museum.

Cheshire Ice Cream Farm: This welcome detour just off the route provides a first-hand look at life on a working dairy farm. Using milk from its herd of over 300 cows, the farm produces 30 flavours of ice cream, offering free samples and, of course, the opportunity to buy.

Stretton Mill: This small rural watermill, believed to have the oldest working wooden machinery in the country, has parts dating from the 17th century. The friendly miller's tour is illuminating, but there is also much to be explored when the mill is closed.

WHAT TO LOOK OUT FOR

St Oswald's Church in Malpas has fine gargoyles outside and intricate 16th-century tomb effigies inside. Look for castles in the hills throughout the ride: the site of Maiden Castle prehistoric fort viewed from Hampton Post; Peckforton and Beeston Castles from Beeston and Bolesworth Castle, south of Tattenhall. Numerous impressive halls and traditional black-and-white cottages line the route, especially at Bunbury and Beeston. In late spring you ride through stupendous flowering rhododendrons in Cholmondeley woods. Passing Brindley Hall Farm Cottages, note the attractive hexagonal window panes.

Cholmondeley Castle stands proud in its grounds in Malpas

Dinas Dinlle and Foryd Bay

This route enjoys exceptional views across to the mountain range of Snowdon to the east and to the island of Ynys Mon in the west. Ride the traffic-free Lôn Eifion out of Caernarfon then on back lanes to Llandwrog and the nearby golden sands of Dinas Dinlle. The highlight of the ride has to be Foryd Bay where wader birds can be seen at close quarters. There are very few hard climbs on the route and most of the roads are lightly trafficked.

RIDE 33
GWYNEDD
SH477627

INFORMATION

Total Distance
22miles (35km), with 4miles (6km) off-road

Grade
2

OS Map
Landranger 1:50,000 sheet 115 (Snowdon)

Tourist Information
Caernarfon, tel: 01286 672232

Cycle Shops/Hire:
Don's Bikes, Caernarfon, tel: 01286 672606; Beics Beddgelert, Beddgelert, tel: 01766 890434

Refreshments
There are several pubs and cafés at Caernarfon and also at Dinas Dinlle. There is also the Harp pub at Llandwrog (children welcome.), and a pleasant picnic site by Foryd Bay

Caernarfon Castle stands imperiously above the harbour

START & ROUTE DIRECTIONS

Start

Caernarfon lies south-west of Bangor on the A487. Follow the signs to Caernarfon Castle and the car park beneath (pay on entry) on Slate Quay. There are other car parks in the town.

Directions

1 🚲 From Slate Quay car park, pass by the magnificent 19th-century Harbour Offices to join a road which passes between the old railway line and a row of warehouses. Join the old trackbed on the left as signposted, and bear right. The cycle route begins to climb above the harbour and leaves town. Climb up to an old crossing by a house, signposted 'Hendy'. Continue ahead, crossing another road, and on to Bontnewydd where you bridge the flowing waters of the Afon Gwyrfai. The route sweeps through a cutting, ahead to Llanwnda where you reach a road known as Glan Rhyd. The village church is to your left.

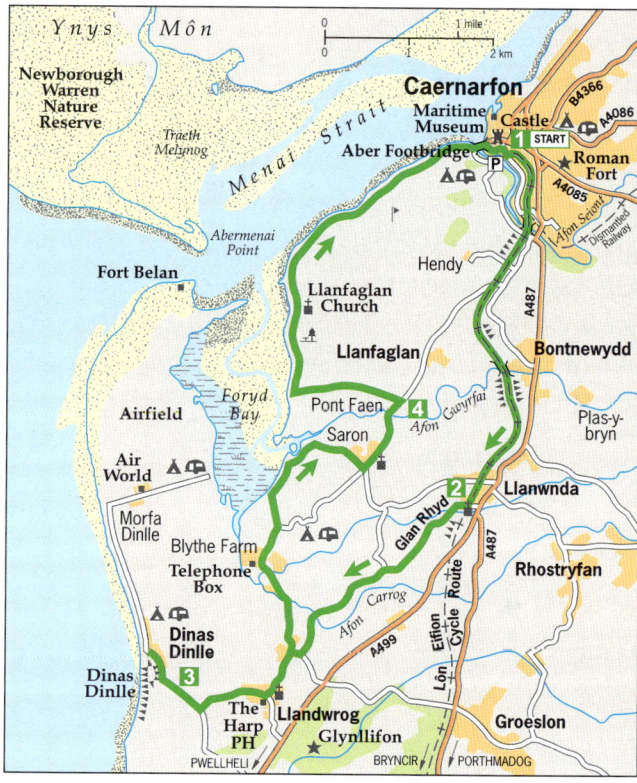

2 🚲 Go right along this road, rising through farmland for 2 miles (3km), ignoring a turning on the right and eventually dropping down to

the waters of the Afon Carrog. Climb to a junction beyond a white house, go right and then left at the next junction to Llandwrog. Turn right by The Harp pub; the road descends to a junction in less than ½ mile (0.5km). Go right for Dinas Dinlle. There is more traffic but you soon arrive at the seafront at Dinas Dinlle, named after the mound to your left.

3 🚲 Retrace the route to Llandwrog. Turn left before The Harp and begin the journey back to Caernarfon, but not without a deviation or

Caernarfon's museum of the Roman fort of Segontium

![Dinas Dinlle, with fine views overlooking the bay]

Dinas Dinlle, with fine views overlooking the bay

two. Ride for ¾ mile (1km) to cross the Afon Carrog and pass a small cluster of buildings. Once through this hamlet, pass Blythe Farm (telephone box) and keep ahead until the road bears right. You, however, turn left along a quiet road leading to Foryd Bay where the Afon Gwyrfai enters. The lane bears right and reaches a crossroads. Go left here, through the hamlet of Saron.

4 ⬮ The road then drops to a bridge at Pont Faen, crossing the Afon Gwyrfai, and rises to a junction. Turn left and continue on this busier road for less than ½ mile (0.5km) to the water's edge at Foryd Bay, with excellent views across to Ynys Môn. Pass a picnic spot on the right, and later look out for the small windswept Llanfaglan church on the right. If you wish to visit, dismount and walk across the field. The road bears right and runs along the front to the harbour at Caernarfon. Wheel your cycle across the Aber footbridge and return to the castle and the start point of the ride.

The mound of Dinas Dinlle dates from the Ice Age

PLACES OF INTEREST

Caernarfon: The centrepiece of this medieval walled town is its magnificent 13th-century castle built by King Edward I, splendidly sited by the lapping waters of the Menai Straits. The Slate Quay and Harbour Offices near by are reminders of later centuries when the port bustled with commercial vessels loading Welsh slate for distant parts. There are several other attractions, such as Seiont II Maritime Museum at Victoria Dock, the Regimental Museum of the Royal Welsh Fusiliers and the roman fort of Segontium.

Dinas Dinlle: The large mound known as Dinas Dinlle is a natural deposit dating from the Ice Age which has evidently been used several times as a fortification by different peoples. Roman coins, dating from the time of Emperor Alectus (AD293), have been found here. It is also a site rich in legend, a place woven into the tales of the Mabinogi. The great leader Arianrhod, who once lived here, laid a curse on her son by refusing to give him either a name or weapons. Gwydion, a magician of high regard, chanced this way and by a measure of charm and sorcery managed to cajole Arianrhod into restoring the powers of her offspring.

Lôn Eifion: Families may wish to ride Lôn Eifion, a cycle route from Caernarfon to Bryncir, 14 miles (22.5km) each way. It is also possible to detour into Parc Glynllifon Hall and gardens, where there are walking trails.

Poetic Landscape: On the walls of The Harp at Llandwrog you will see a tablet featuring a poem by the well-known Welsh poet Evan Fardd:

'On level ground the finest inn
With plenty of food and beer within
And every hour of the day
The song and birds to make one gay
On holidays and Sundays too
Beware of drunkenness, be true
Enjoy you life but don't betray
The good old beer come what may.'

WHAT TO LOOK OUT FOR

Foryd Bay is a large shallow estuary rich in wildfowl which love the habitat of mud and reeds and saltmarsh. It is now a local nature reserve where you will see shelduck, oystercatchers dunlin, and many other birds, including the curlew with its distinctive beak and haunting call. Besides the ancient sights along the route, look out for the pretty chapel, dating from 1901, in the hamlet of Saron.

The town of Caernarfon, viewed from the castle

RIDE 34
LANCASHIRE
SD444124

Martin Mere

West Lancashire is an important farming area with crops still grown for local markets on rich peaty soils. The ride follows quiet back lanes through fields between the settlements of Burscough Bridge and Rufford. It is flat and therefore easy cycling. There are a number of short sections where traffic is heavier, especially crossing the A59 road.

INFORMATION

Total Distance
14 miles (22.5km)

Grade
1

OS Map
Landranger 1:50,000 sheet 108
(Liverpool)

Tourist Information:
Southport, tel: 01704 533333;
Wigan, tel: 01942 825677

Cycle Shops/Hire
None on route, but many shops in
Wigan

Preparing for a spot of fishing on the Leeds/Liverpool Canal

Refreshments
Facilities at the Martin Mere Wildlife Centre but only for visitors to the site. There is also the Brandreth Barn Tea Rooms and The Hesketh Arms at Rufford. Pubs in Burscough Bridge tend not to cater for families, unlike most of the canalside pubs located between Burscough Bridge and Wigan. There are also shops in Burscough Bridge

START & ROUTE DIRECTIONS

Start

Burscough Bridge is on the A59 between Liverpool and Preston, 2 miles (3km) north of Ormskirk. There is car parking near the railway station and elsewhere in town. The ride starts at the station, but visitors to the Martin Mere Centre could also start from there.

Directions

1 🚲 From Burscough Bridge station join the main A59 road which rises up to cross the railway tracks. It is busy so wheel your bike across the road and walk left down the pavement for 110 yards (100m) to Warpers Moss Lane on the right. Ride along the lane and soon reach the countryside; the lane winds its way beneath two railway bridges to a junction.

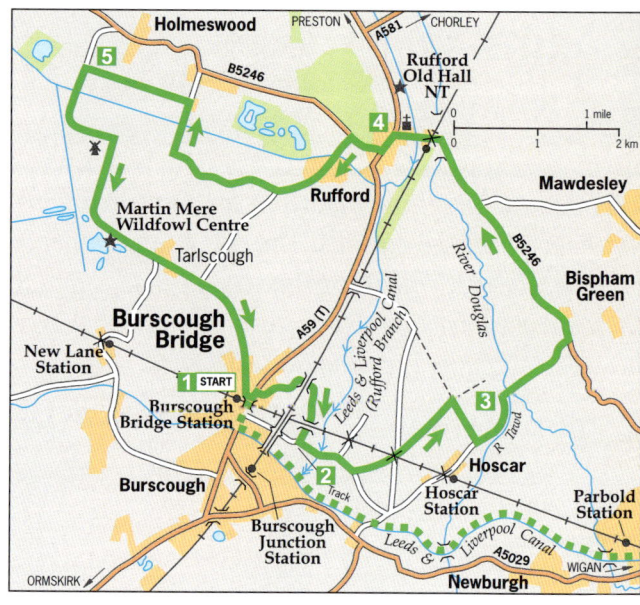

2 🚲 Go left and cycle along School Lane to cross the Leeds and Liverpool Canal. Ignore Sutch Lane but take the second left, Daisy Lane, which meets other roads at a level crossing. Proceed along Bleak Lane to a crossroads of tracks. Go right here along a road known as Wood Lane. At the

Boats at Burscough Bridge

The neatly kept approach to Rufford Old Hall

next junction turn left into Wanes Blanes Road.

3 The road bridges the River Douglas and in ½ mile (0.5km) meets the B5246 at Bispham Green. Turn left and continue for 2 miles (3km) to Rufford. The road bends left into the village, over the railway line and the Leeds and Liverpool Canal. Pass Rufford church and ride up to a busy junction to meet the A59. Rufford Old Hall is to the right, along the main road.

4 Cut left to ride along the old Liverpool Road, opposite the Hesketh Arms pub, where there is a right-hand feeder lane to the B5246. (It is better to dismount and walk across.) Ignoring the first bend, take the next left along Cousins Lane which joins Holmes Wood Road at a junction to become Tootle Lane. Keep right, and at the next junction

go right again into Mere Lane which runs through fields for ½ mile (0.5km) to a sharp right turn before reaching a T-junction by a few dwellings. Go left here and along a tree-lined road to a wider busier road.

5 Turn left and follow the road, passing a windmill and Windmill Animal Farm. The road bends right and then, after another straight section, left to Martin Mere Wildfowl Trust. Continue along Tarlscough Road to Burscough Bridge for just under 2 miles (3km), passing farmsteads and Brandreth Barn Tea Rooms. Enter the outskirts of Burscough Bridge and soon turn left back to the railway station.

Ducks at Martin Mere

PLACES OF INTEREST

Martin Mere: The Wildfowl and Wetlands Trust Centre is situated at Martin Mere, once an extensive lake covering the best part of 3,000 acres (1,200ha). Much of the area has been reclaimed but the Martin Mere Centre allows exploration of wildfowl of the world in a really entertaining way. There are ducks, geese, swans and flamingos of all shapes, sizes and colour, and many unusual birds seek refuge here during their winter migration.

Burscough Bridge: The town developed in the late 18th and early 19th centuries with the coming of the Leeds and Liverpool Canal and the

railways. It was known for corn milling and for basket making from reeds cut at Martin Mere, but textile mills grew up along the canalside, some of which have survived. From the towpath you can see classic examples of the development of mill and cottage at the junction with the Rufford Branch of the canal.

Rufford Old Hall: This 16th-century half-timbered hall was

home to the Hesketh family for centuries, but is now managed by the National Trust. One exceptional feature is the Great Hall, with its hammerbeam roof and an intricately carved movable wooden screen is on show. The hall also contains a range of fine furniture, arms, armour and tapestries from different centuries.

Towering chimneys of the brick wing of Rufford Old Hall

WHAT TO LOOK OUT FOR

The wetlands and surrounding peat mosses attract flocks of geese, so look out for them on the fields as you ride by. The landowners of the 18th century were keen to drain and improve the wetlands and each moss is threaded with drainage channels which attract ducks and heron.

Lanes and Villages of the East Yorkshire Wolds

This is likely to be a whole day ride, on lanes lightly-trafficked even on summer Sundays, providing a tranquil countryside experience. Views from the high points take in the broad Vale of York as far as the Humber and Trent. Most of the climbs are easily graded, the few steeper ones being quite short, though care is needed on some of the sinuous narrow descents. Opportunities arise along the way to shorten the excursion if necessary.

RIDE 35
HUMBERSIDE
SE804487

INFORMATION

Total Distance
23½ miles (38km)

Grade
3

OS Map
Landranger 1.50,000 sheet 106
(Market Weighton)

Tourist Information
No TIC at or near start. Local information: Town Clerk, tel: 01759 304851; Beverley/York

Cycle Shops/Hire
Wheelies, Pocklington,
tel: 01759 303353

Nearest Railway Station
York (13 miles/21km)

Refreshments
Pocklington has cafés, tea rooms, pubs and a noted Austrian restaurant. Food is also available at the shop/tea garden at Londesborough and Ramblers' Rest, Millington. There are pubs in only two villages: Bishop Wilton and Millington; both serve food. Just off the route is Millington Wood picnic area and nature reserve

Bankside plants abound at Warter, near Pocklington

Start

Pocklington is a market town just north of the A1079 York – Hull road, 13 miles (21km) east of York. Parking is free behind the old railway station (Sports Hall) on Station Road off the round-about near Presto's. Start the ride from a layby leading off the roundabout to Burnby Hall Park and Gardens.

Directions

[1] 🚲 From the layby in Pocklington, go west on the Balk for 110 yards (100m), turn right into New Street taking the first right into Burnby Lane, signposted 'Burnby 3'. Continue on this narrow lane for about 3 miles (5km) to Burnby. In the village turn sharp right by the church, signed 'Londesborough', and continue over a beck and out of the village, climbing gently for about 1 mile (1.5km) to a T-junction where you turn right. After a further mile (1.5km) go straight over a crossroads into the village of Londesborough, descend and bear left to the church; continue to the end of the street, take a sharp turn left, climb for 110 yards (100m) then take the first left to the shop/tea room. Turn right here to the crossroads to go north now following the signs for 'Warter'.

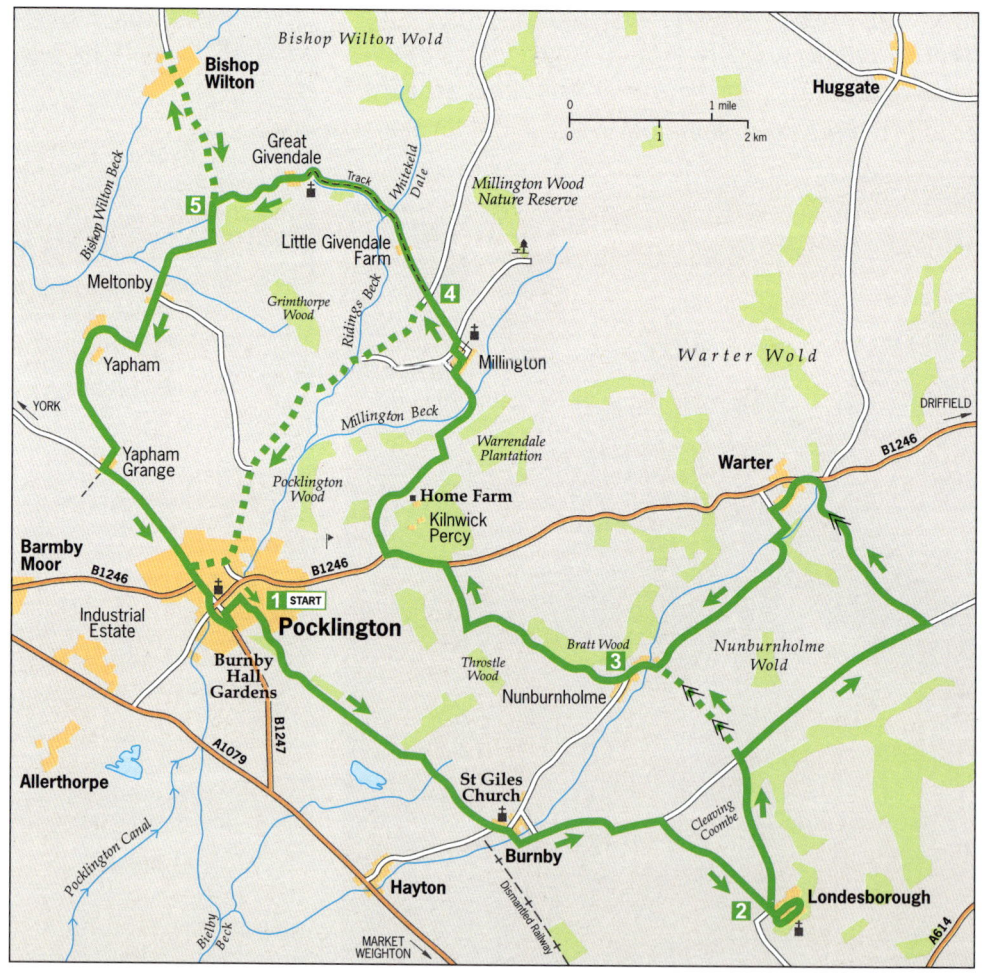

2 🚲 After leaving Londesborough, climb gently to a crossorads and turn right, signposted 'Middleton'. To shorten the route, keep ahead at the crossroads to Nunburnholme, then bear left into the village. Otherwise, continue for 2 miles (3km), turn left at the T-junction, signposted 'Warter' and descend with care to Warter. Once there, turn left at the junction with the B1246 into the village and fork left before the memorial. Shortly bear left on Mill Lane, signed 'Nunburnholme', descend to cross a beck and go up a short ascent. Continue on a narrow lane for 1¼ miles (2km) before turning right at a T-junction (give way). Descend to Nunburnholme, bearing left into the village, with the church at the far south-west end.

3 🚲 Fork right at a bus shelter, signed 'Pocklington', and continue to a junction with the B1246. Turn left towards Pocklington then right (take great care here), rising to Kilnwick Percy. In 1 mile (1.5km), at spot height 108m, bear left following a narrow lane down to Beck Cottage. Climb to Millington, going right at a T-junction. Take the first left opposite with care, pass the church and turn right to a crossroads. Turn left (not signposted), then take the first left opposite a café, passing a church, where you go right to a crossroads. Turn left here (no signpost), at The Balk, climbing to soon reach a T-junction. Note: If conditions are very wet or time is short, turn left to Pocklington.

4 🚲 Continue ahead along a farm track/bridleway, passing Little Givendale Farm. Follow bridleway signs (blue arrow on yellow) through two gates, then proceed north-west through pasture to a steep descent (or walk) into Whitekeld Dale. Cross a gated bridge and continue on the bridleway for ½ mile (1km) to the church at Great Givendale. On reaching a road beyond, cross over into Givendale village, continuing past a manor house. With care, descend this narrow winding lane for ½ mile (1km) to a T-junction.

5 🚲 To visit Bishop Wilton 2 miles (3km) on, turn right at this junction and retrace. Otherwise, turn left, signed 'Pocklington', continue for 1 mile (1.5km) to Meltonby, and go straight ahead, signposted 'Yapham'. After a further 1 mile (1.5km), at the next junction, go through Yapham, and forward to the next crossroads at Yapham Grange. Turn left and on to Pocklington, entering by Sherbuttgate. Near the church, fork right to a mini-roundabout and forward on Station Road to a large roundabout and the car park.

Yellow fields of rape near the town of Pocklington

PLACES OF INTEREST

Pocklington: This small market town with a leisurely air has broad squares and wide streets; market day is Tuesday and early closing Wednesday. Its 13th-century church with 15th-century perpendicular tower is visible from miles around. Slave reformer William Wilberforce was a pupil at the public school here. Burnby Hall Gardens is the town's most noted amenity. It features the Stewart Collection, a remarkable display of trophies and artefacts collected by Major Stewart during seven world tours from 1906–26. The lake has one of the finest collections of water lilies in Europe, and there is a seat dedicated to G H Stancer, OBE, born here in 1878 and for 25 years Secretary of the Cyclists' Touring Club.

Burnby: Well worth seeing is the small Church of St Giles, with its fine Norman-style doorway and west end and bellcote rebuilt in 1840. Beyond the village Burnby chalk pit can be discerned from far across the vale, though the distinctive Cleaving Combe is easily missed.

Londesborough: An estate village associated with the

Burlington's fine park, this was said to be location of the Northumbrian kings' summer palace, and where Edwin met Paulinus in AD627. After passing to the Cavendishes and later the 6th Duke of Devonshire, the Hall was pulled down in 1819. The park is laid out with superb lakes, waterfalls and terraces, along with extensive avenues. It was sold in 1845 to the notorious 'Railway King', George Hudson, who was then planning the railway from York to Market Weighton, and included his private station on the park's edge. The Hall's foundations and terraces can still be seen from the park gates, and there are public footpaths and bridleways

through the private estate. All Saints' Church is largely Early English, but has a Norman south doorway with an Anglo-Danish 11th-century crosshead. Its white limestone porch has a sundial of 1764.

Kilnwick Percy: Seen from the B1246, Kilnwick Percy Hall is impressive, with its estate lake and tiny St Helen's Church. The Hall, now a Buddhist Centre, was once part of the extensive estate held by the Percy family in Yorkshire. To the north, Home Farm is an intriguing collection of buildings.

Bishop Wilton: Sheltered by chalky hills with picturesque 18th- to 19th-century cottages set back on each side of the beck in its grassy hollow, this is a village not to be missed. St Edith's Church enjoys a lofty location and has a tall recessed stone spire set above the tower. With its hammerbeam roof, it is said to be one of Sir Tatton Sykes' best restorations.

An isolated cottage in picturesque Bishop Wilton

RIDE 36
NORTH YORKSHIRE
SE668756

Touring the Howardian Hills

RIDE 36
NORTH YORKSHIRE
SE668756

INFORMATION

Total Distance
22miles (35km)

Grade
2

OS Map
Landranger 1:50,000 sheet 100
(Malton, Pickering and
surrounding area)

Tourist Information
Malton, tel: 01653 600048;
Pickering, tel: 01751 473791

This gentle ride, with a choice of on- or off-road routes, takes you through the rich countryside around Castle Howard. The undulating roads pass castles and stately homes, visit pretty villages and woodland and offer panoramic views across the North York Moors and Ryedale.

Cycle Shops/Hire
Ryedabike, Malton, tel: 01653 692835;
Mad Mole, Malton, tel: 01653 690073

Nearest Railway Station
Malton (8miles/13km)

Refreshments
Bakery, tea room and pub in Hovingham, and tea room at Castle Howard; pub and shop in Terrington. The Fairfax Arms is a friendly pub in Gilling East, and Hovingham also has a pub

Castle Howard is a familiar sight to film and television viewers

Start

The attractive village of Hovingham is situated on the B1257 8 miles (13km) west of the market town of Malton. There is no roadside parking in the village.

and follow this track for ½ mile (1km) to the road. Go straight ahead, descending through woodland to the gatehouse at Coneysthorpe, looking across the Great Lake to Castle Howard.

2 🚲 The road option continues on the B1257 to

of elms. Descend to the Coneysthorpe junction and the Great Lake.

3 🚲 Cycle up to the obelisk (turn left to explore Castle Howard) and on through the stone gate house; look left for the Black Pyramid. Swoop down through a second mock

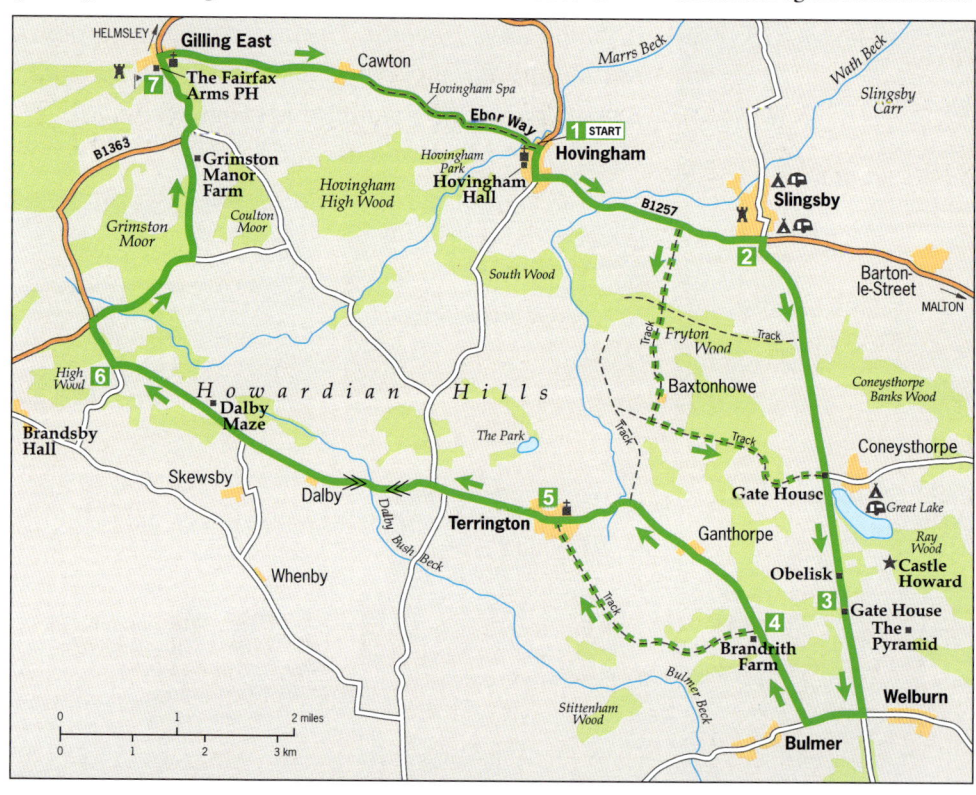

Directions

1 🚲 Cycle towards Malton on the B1257. Off-roaders: turn right after 1½ miles (2.5km), signposted 'Baxton Howe', and climb steadily to Fryton Wood. On the hill crest the lane becomes a farm track; descend to a stream, then ascend again to a T-junction on the woodland edge (2 miles/3km). Turn left

the village of Slingsby. Turn right here, signposted 'Castle Howard', and follow the quiet road as it climbs the Howardian Hills. Stop at the top to enjoy the view back over the North York Moors, and ahead to Castle Howard. The crest reveals a straight road with the obelisk (100 feet/30m tall, built in 1741) at the end of an avenue

fortified archway to a crossroads and turn right towards Terrington.

4 🚲 In just under ½ mile (1km) turn right towards Slingsby and climb gently to Brandrith Farm on the left. Off-roaders: turn left through a metal gate past the farmhouse (bridleway sign) and follow the track for ½ mile

(1km) across fields and down past fish ponds. Regain height, bear right into a farmyard, then left and continue to climb to reach the road. Descend for 1 mile (1.5km) into the hillside village of Terrington. Road riders continue past Brandrith Farm to tiny Ganthorpe and then to Terrington, with its pub and shop.

5 🚲 Bear right as you cycle up out of the village, then left along the ridge road, signed 'Hovingham', with views left to the ruined castle at Sheriff Hutton and right over the moors. Continue straight past a left turn to York, then bear left, signposted 'Dalby', as the road bends right. The road now swoops and climbs through Dalby, and on for the same distance to the Whensby/Skewsby junction. Stay on the ridge; just ahead on your right is the ancient Dalby Maze, protected by white rails.

6 🚲 Continue straight on to a T-junction and turn right towards Helmsley. At a major road junction turn right, signposted 'Hovingham', and follow the quiet lane to another T-junction. Turn right, then left in 330 yards (300m) along a lane to Gilling East. Soon descend past Grimston Manor to a T-junction; turn right on to the B1363 and enter Gilling East village.

Grazing peacefully in the grounds of Hovingham Hall

7 🚲 Turn right at the Fairfax Arms to the hamlet of Cawton. As the road turns sharp left at the village end, a chalk track continues straight on, with Spring Farm Cottages on the right. This is the Ebor Way, an easy off-road section to Hovingham, which can be ridden on slick tyres. Halfway along the 2-mile (3km) track pass Spa House; the track then bends right and left to run straight to Hovingham and the start point of the ride. Go through a gate by the children's playground, and follow the lane to emerge by the ford and bakery.

PLACES OF INTEREST

Hovingham Hall: Hovingham has been an estate village since Roman times, its shape determined by a junction of Roman roads. Hovingham Hall is owned by Sir Thomas Worsley, whose family's connection with the estate dates to 1661; the daughter of

stately home. The main building was commissioned by Charles Howard, 3rd Earl of Carlisle, from Vanbrugh between 1699 and 1726. The mansion is surrounded by ramparts whose tremendous length and 11 towers make it Britain's largest folly, as well as the first mock fortification for display rather than defence.

railing beside a quiet country road, is the only surviving example in North Yorkshire of an ancient game. The rules and origins of the game have long been lost but 'treading the maze' was once a common entertainment of village life.

Gilling East: This quiet village nestles in pleasant wooded

The neat and well-kept village of Hovingham

the house is now HRH the Duchess of Kent. The house is a family home and is not normally open to the public.

Slingsby: Riders taking the early road option will cycle by Slingsby, with its great ruined castle and the Wyville Hall. Slingsby dates from the 11th century, with the castle built in the early 18th century. It became a backwater when the Earl of Carlisle bought it in 1751, but the village continued to prosper.

Castle Howard: Over 1,200 acres (490ha) of parkland, with nature walks, a scenic lake and fountains, flank this magnificent

Home of the Howard family since the day it was built, the castle is open to the public from Easter to early November.

Dalby Maze: This little turf maze, protected by a low white

countryside beneath its castle (now part of a school). The village has old stone estate cottages, a welcoming inn (the Fairfax Arms) and a fine church with a strong, square turret of yellow limestone.

WHAT TO LOOK OUT FOR

This route ducks through several woodlands – keep your eyes open for wild deer and pheasants. Partridge abound in the open grassland areas and an array of hedgerow birds – yellowhammers, blue tits and dunnocks – can be seen. If you are lucky, you may catch a fleeting glimpse of these birds being pursued by a lightning-fast sparrowhawk.

Bransdale and the North York Moors

The valley of Bransdale is a delight. Drivers tend to pass it by, however, because it is effectively a cul-de-sac, with a road looping around both sides of the valley. This is good news for cyclists, with little traffic to mar their enjoyment of long moorland views and tiny villages. Start and finish at the bustling little market town of Helmsley, overlooked by its ruined but still imposing castle.

INFORMATION

Total Distance

26 miles (42km)

Grade
1

OS Map
Outdoor Leisure 1:25,000 sheet 26
(North York Moors, western area)

Tourist Information
Helmsley (summer daily; weekends only in winter), tel: 01439 770173

Cycle Shops/Hire
Footloose, Borogate, Helmsley, tel: 01439 770886

Refreshments
No pubs or cafes until you have covered about 18 miles (29km), so consider taking a picnic to enjoy at the head of Bransdale. Then pubs include the Royal Oak Inn, Gillamoor and the Plough Inn, Fadmoor. Helmsley boasts a number of welcoming pubs, cafés and tea rooms

Rolling countryside surrounds Bransdale, near Helmsley

START & ROUTE DIRECTIONS

Start

Helmsley lies on the southern boundary of the North York Moors National Park, at the junction of the A170 and the B1257. Here, in the Old Vicarage, is the headquarters of the National Park Authority. Park (pay-and-display) in the market place, except Friday (market day).

Directions

[1] From the market place in Helmsley take the A170 towards Scarborough. At the end of town, opposite a petrol station, take a road, left, signed 'Carlton'. Climb steadily uphill for half a mile (1km) into the little village of Carlton, after which the road levels out through woodland and is soon unenclosed.

[2] Pass the viewpoint of Cowhouse Bank to continue steeply downhill. Then climb steadily through conifer woodland, as fields gradually give way to a more rugged landscape of open heather moorland – particularly colourful in late summer.
The undulating moorland road is mostly unfenced, so beware of freely roaming sheep. Keep your eyes open, too, for the lapwings, curlews and red grouse that make the moors their home.
Soon you can enjoy views up and down Bransdale: a pattern of scattered farmsteads of honey-coloured stone, with the red-tiled roofs so typical of the North York Moors.

[3] Go through two gates across the road to arrive at the head of the valley (National Trust property). Ignore a road to the right, and continue to a T-junction. Left takes you to the little Church of St Nicholas, but your route is to the right, signed 'Kirkbymoorside'. Climb up and around the head of the valley to head back south. (A footpath sign on the right, immediately before the first farm you see – Cow Sike – offers a short walk down to Bransdale Mill.) The route is punctuated at regular intervals by handsome farms of well-dressed stone. Two miles (3km) past a pair of sharp bends, as the landscape reverts back to arable

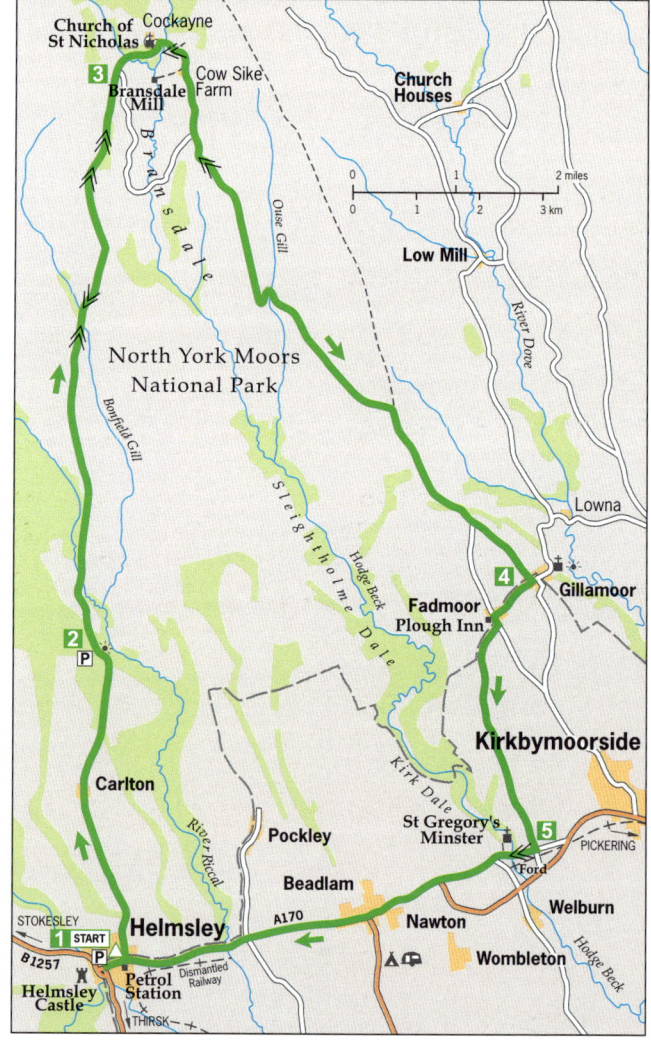

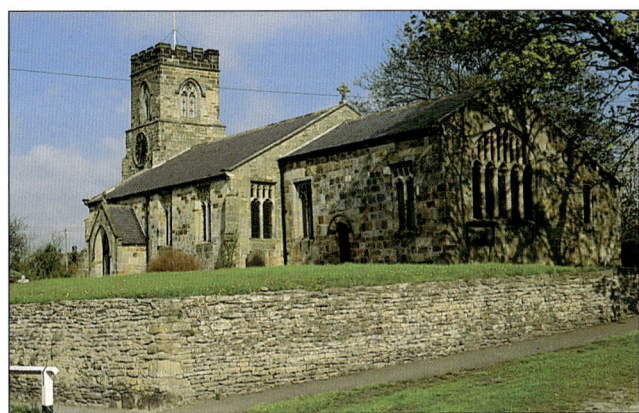

St Nicholas parish church in Stillington, near Helmsley

descent brings you to a crossroads.

5 🚲 Go right, signed 'Kirkdale & Helmsley'. After a ford look out on the right for a track that leads you straight to St Gregory's Minster, a solitary church of great age and interest. When you continue along the road, ignore the Welburn turn-off and keep straight on to meet the main A170 road once again. Now go right; the last stage – passing through two villages, Nawton and Beadlam, that have almost become one – is on the main road back into Helmsley to complete the tour.

farmland, the road forks. Keep left, signed 'Gillamoor', to arrive at a T-junction.

4 🚲 This is the village of Gillamoor, and your route is to the right. After just half a mile (1km) you arrive in Fadmoor, similar in that its houses cluster around a village green. Bear left at the Plough Inn, signed 'Kirkbymoorside', then almost immediately right, signed 'Sleightholmdale & Welburn'. Shortly after, keep straight on at a junction, towards Welburn. A long

Greenery and hanging baskets cover some of Helmsley's buildings

PLACES OF INTEREST

Helmsley: Little more than a village in size, Helmsley nevertheless feels like a county town, busiest on Fridays when the stalls are set up around the old market cross. The castle, standing 'head and shoulders' above the town, was built in the 12th century by Robert de Ros. The manor of Helmsley was his reward for fighting alongside William the Conqueror during the Norman invasion. Most of the fortifications were blown up after the Civil War, though enough of the Norman keep still stands to its full height to remind us what an impressive castle it once was.

Cockayne: This intriguing place-name appears on the map, at the head of Bransdale, although it comprises but a handful of buildings. The name probably derives, prosaically, from 'kirk', a church. The Church of St Nicholas, although dating back only to 1886, is a typical moorland church: small,

unfussy and with a splendid view. Inside, the barrelled roof is worth inspection.

Gillamoor and Fadmoor: Barely half a mile (1km) apart, these moorland villages are almost twins. Both are grouped around a village green, but Gillamoor has an extra surprise in store. Walk to the church at the end of the village to discover a panoramic view across the lovely valley of Farndale to the heather moors beyond. Look out, too, for an elaborate sundial in front of Dial House Farm, which was erected by public subscription in 1800.

St Gregory's Minster: This ancient and diminutive church – dedicated to St Gregory, the first monk to become Pope – is hidden away in secluded Kirkdale. A sundial mounted over the south door bears an intriguing inscription (the longest Anglo-Saxon example to have survived) that dates the church with some accuracy to between 1055 and 1066. The name 'minster' was originally used for a monastery church, and this was a site of worship many centuries before this date.

Helmsley Castle viewed from Duncombe Park

WHAT TO LOOK OUT FOR

An intriguing feature of the North York Moors is the great number of standing stones that have survived the centuries. Some are crosses built to give travellers guidance and reassurance in featureless terrain; the National Park's own emblem is derived from Ralph Cross, which is one of the best-known examples. Other stones are inscribed waymarkers, giving directions and mileage. Some examples can be spotted on the first part of the ride up Bransdale.

Wensleydale and the Yorkshire Dales

The main A684 is the principal east–west route through the Yorkshire Dales National Park, making Wensleydale probably the most accessible of the Dales. But this ride explores both sides of this attractive valley by using quiet side-roads. On the route you can see the highest market town in the country, two of Yorkshire's most famous waterfalls and some of the finest countryside in the Yorkshire Dales.

INFORMATION

Total Distance
25 miles (40km)

Grade
1

OS Map
Outdoor Leisure 1:25,000 sheet 30
(Yorkshire Dales,
Northern & Central areas)

Tourist Information
Hawes, tel: 01969 667450;
Aysgarth Falls, tel: 01969 663424

Cycle Shops/Hire
Ian Rawlins, Askrigg,
tel: 01969 650455

Refreshments
There are plenty of pubs and tea rooms along the route – in Hawes, Askrigg, Carperby, Aysgarth and Bainbridge – and a café in the National Park Centre at Aysgarth Falls. Semer Water makes a good picnic site

*The shimmering column of
Hardraw Force*

Start

The little market town of
Hawes lies on the A684, in
the heart of the Yorkshire
Dales, north-west of Ripon.
There is a free car park in the
town, plus pay-and-display
parking at the Dales
Countryside Museum.

landscape of this gently
sloping U-shaped valley.
Wensleydale's river – the Ure
– is visible at most points
during the ride. Half a mile
(1km) beyond a turn-off to
Bainbridge, you reach the
village of Askrigg.

3 🚲 The road winds up
through this compact village,
best-known today as a

steeply uphill to meet the
A684 at a T-junction. Go
right, towards Aysgarth,
Bainbridge and Hawes. After
half a mile (1km) you will
pass through the village
of Aysgarth.
Leave the village, turn left,
signed 'Thornton Rust'. The
roads climbs steadily to give
panoramic views across
Wensleydale.

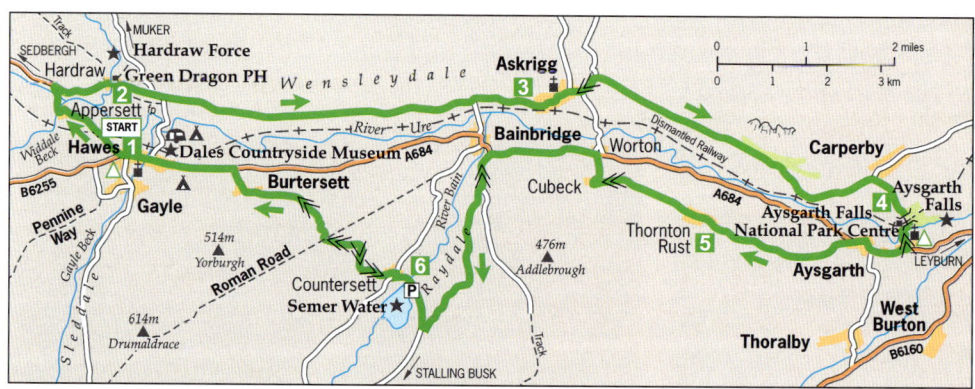

Directions

1 🚲 Leave Hawes
travelling westwards along
the A684, towards Sedbergh
and Kirkbymoorside. It is just
a mile (1.5km) to the little
hamlet of Appersett. Cross
two bridges – spanning first
Widdale Beck, followed by
the River Ure – before bearing
sharp right, signed 'Hardraw
and Askrigg'.

2 🚲 After a mile (1.5km)
you arrive in the village of
Hardraw. Make sure to visit
Hardraw Force, a spectacular
waterfall; entry is through
the Green Dragon pub.
Continue along the road
towards Askrigg (ignoring
turn-offs left and right, to
Muker and Hawes). The road
is level, through the enticing

Herriot 'film set', although
well worth exploring in its
own right. Leaving the
village, your route is signed
'Carperby and Leyburn'. A
steep climb is followed by
level riding, through a
typical Dales landscape of
dry-stone walls, field barns
and scattered farmsteads.
Just before the village of
Carperby, go right, signed
'Aysgarth Falls'.

4 🚲 To investigate the trio
of waterfalls (on foot) turn
right after half a mile (1km),
immediately beyond a
railway bridge, into the
Aysgarth Falls National Park
Centre. Afterwards, continue
steeply down the road, cross
the bridge over the River Ure,
and climb (or walk) very

5 🚲 After 2 miles (3km) of
level riding you reach the
characterful cottages of
Thornton Rust. A further 2
miles (3km) brings you to the
hamlet of Cubeck; freewheel
downhill to meet the A684
once again, at Worton. Go
left, signed 'Bainbridge and
Hawes'. Just before the road
descends into Bainbridge (a
lovely village whose green is
as big as a meadow), bear left
on a road signed to Semer
Water and Stalling Busk.
Climb uphill, keeping right
when the road forks, to arrive
at an almost Lakeland scene:
Semer Water in the valley
bottom hemmed in by hills.
Keep right at the next fork,
overlooking the lake (ignore a
sign to Stalling Busk), and
ride down to the lake.

The idyllic scenery of Aysgarth Middle Falls is typical of the region

6 🚲 Cross a handsome three-arched bridge over the River Bain, and negotiate a 1-in-4 hill up to a T-junction. Go right, and immediately left, signed 'Burtersett and Hawes'.

A steep climb is followed by a long descent (crossing the old Roman road from Bainbridge to Ilkley) to arrive in Burtersett village. Continue downhill to rejoin the A684 for the last time; bear left to cycle the last mile (1.5km) back into Hawes to complete the tour and for some well-earned refreshment.

The evocative ruins of the church at Semer Water

PLACES OF INTEREST

Hawes: The 'capital' of Upper Wensleydale, Hawes is a busy little town – especially on Tuesday, market day. The Dales Countryside Museum, occupying the old Hawes railway station, is home to a splendid collection of tools, bygones and curios that help to show what Dales life was like in earlier times.

Hardraw Force: Hardraw Force crashes over the lip of a limestone crag into a pool 90 feet (27m) below. It is England's highest waterfall and a spectacular sight – especially after heavy rain. Entry is via the Green Dragon pub (small fee payable) and the walk to the waterfall takes only a few minutes. An old tradition of holding brass-band contests here has been revived; they take place every September.

Askrigg: Until Hawes took on the mantle, Askrigg was the main market town of the upper valley; now only the stepped market cross remains. But Askrigg has known TV stardom: the village has featured in many episodes of James Herriot's *All Creatures Great and Small,* the long-running series written by

Market day adds to the usual bustle in Hawes

Yorkshire vet, James Alfred Wight. Viewers will recognise Cringley House as the vets' home, 'Skelgate House', and also the King's Arms pub opposite, which became the 'Drovers Arms'.

Aysgarth Falls: The waterfalls at Aysgarth have been much-loved landmarks as long as visitors have come to the Dales. The usually placid River Ure hammers over rocks in a series of three splendid falls, best viewed from a footpath at the visitor centre.

Semer Water: Nestling in the little side valley of Raydale, Semer Water is one of the few areas of open water in the national park. It drains into the River Ure at Bainbridge via the River Bain – reckoned, at 3 miles (5km), to be the shortest river in the country.
Legend has it that there is a lost village beneath Semer Water; at night a phantom church bell has been heard to toll.

WHAT TO LOOK OUT FOR

Most of the Dales (Swaledale, Wharfedale, Airedale etc) are named after the rivers that run through them. Wensleydale is an exception, taking its name from Wensley, a village further down the dale. The river is the Ure, and 'Yoredale' is an old name for the valley. There are many opportunities on this ride to stop by the riverside, for rest and refreshment. Look out for typical waterside birds, such as the dipper, yellow wagtail and the huge grey heron.

Cumbria and Northern Lakeland

This route explores the north-eastern fringes of the Lake District with its diverse scenery, offering good views of the area's mountains and lakes and an insight into rural Cumbrian life. The area is rich in history – raided and settled by the Romans, Saxons, Normans, Scandinavians and Scots – and castles and fortified farmhouses are evidence of the turbulent past. The middle section is hilly but the effort is rewarded by fine views.

INFORMATION

Total Distance
25miles (40km)

Grade
3

OS Maps
Landranger 1:50,000 sheet 90
(West Cumbria)

Tourist Information:
Penrith, tel: 01768 867466;
Pooley Bridge, tel: 017684 86530

Cycle shops/Hire
Arragon Cycle Centre, Penrith,
tel: 01768 890344; Harpers, Penrith,
tel: 01768 864475; Ullswater Caravan,
Camping and Marine Park,
Watermillock, tel: 017684 86666;
Tindals, Glenridding/Pooley Bridge,

The River Eamont flows past Brougham Castle

tel: 017684 82393/86282;
The Sun Hotel, Pooley Bridge,
tel: 017684 86205

Nearest Railway Station
Penrith

Refreshments
Numerous pubs and cafés along the route, plus tea rooms and plenty of picnic spots, particularly at Wetheriggs Pottery, Lowther Park and Pooley Bridge

START & ROUTE DIRECTIONS

Start

Penrith lies by the M6 at junction 40. Park in the Southend Road pay-and-display car park at the south end of the town.

Directions

1 🚲 Leave the car park going east, turn left into Southend Road then right into Crown Square. At the T-junction turn right into King Street then second left into Roper Street which becomes Carleton Road.

Continue to the junction, turn right on to the A686 then immediately left and right again passing the Cross Keys pub on your left (ignore the 'no through road' sign). Follow the road downhill. At the end pass through the gate and follow a track under the A6. Turn left immediately to reach the road, then right, crossing the River Eamont with Brougham Castle on your right.

2 🚲 Continue with views of Cross Fell and the Pennines to the left, shortly cross the B6262 and continue for

3 miles (2km) to reach a T-junction at Clifton Dykes. Turn left, signed 'Wetheriggs Pottery', and continue for ½ mile (1km) to Wetheriggs Country Pottery.

3 🚲 Continue for 650 yards (600m) then turn right, signed 'Melkinthorpe'. Follow this road, passing under the railway to reach the A6. Turn left then second right and follow signs for Lowther. Just past Lowther Village is the Lakeland Bird of Prey Centre.

4 🚲 Continue through Newtown; at the end of the

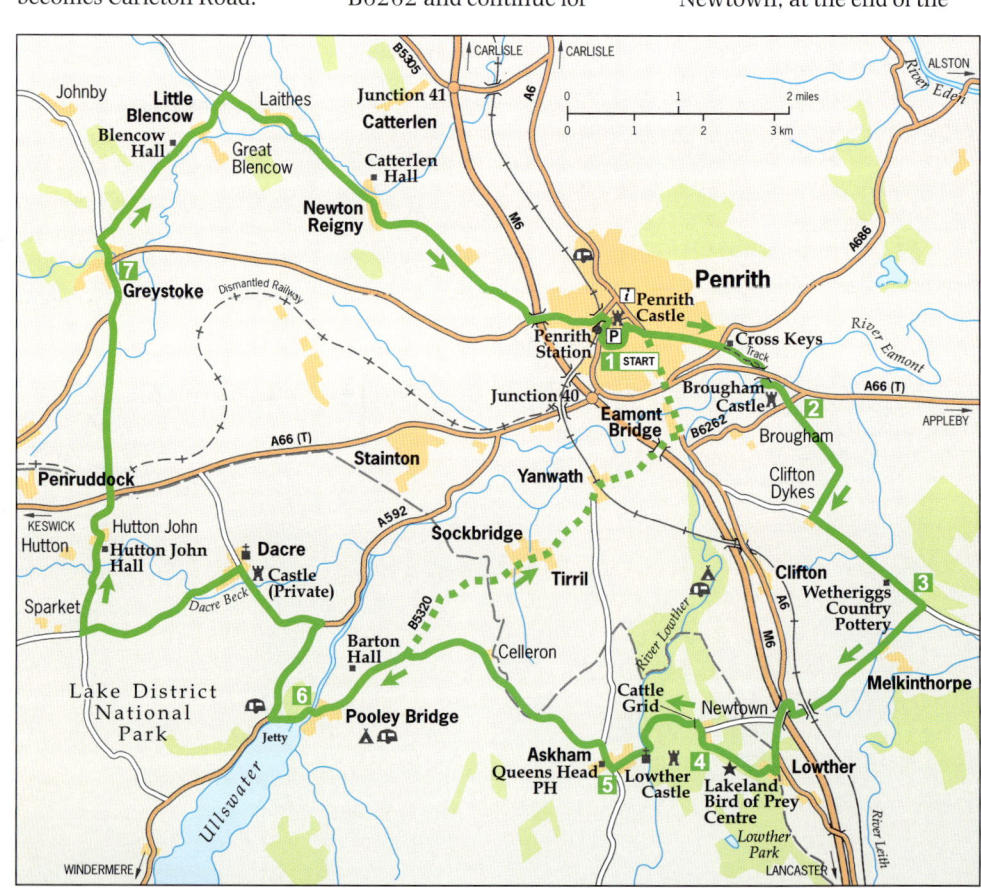

line of houses, where the road bears right, continue straight on following the sign for Askham and Ullswater. At the T-junction by the knobbly oak tree turn left, cross over the cattle grid, pass through the park with Lowther Castle on your left and carefully descend a steep hill to eventually cross the river and pass St Peter's Church and climb into Askham.

5 ۶ At the T-junction at the top of the green, turn right, signed 'Ullswater', passing the village shop and the Queens Head. Continue for 550 yards (500m) before turning left. signed 'Celleron', to climb with views of High Street on the left and the Pennines on the right. Continue ahead to the next T-junction (B5320) and turn left. Passing Barton Hall on the right, in 1½ miles (2km) enter Pooley Bridge. (From

here you may shorten the route by 5miles/10km if you return to Penrith by retracing the route along the B5320, continuing for 5 miles/8km through Sockbridge, Tirril, and Yanwath to the junction with the A6. Turn left and proceed with care over Eamont Bridge and back into Penrith.)

6 ۶ Go over the bridge and continue on the B5320, passing the ferry jetty on your left. Soon turn right on to the A592, signed 'Penrith', and after 1 mile (1.5km) left, signed 'Dacre'. Follow the lane, eventually descending to cross the beck, and shortly arrive in Dacre. Leave Dacre by the narrow lane on the left as you entered the village, signed 'Sparket and Thackthwaite'. After 1½ miles (2.5km), at a crossroads turn right, signed 'Penruddock'. Continue past Hutton John

Hall, enjoying views of the Lakeland Mountains as you climb, eventually crossing the A66 (with care), to join the flat lanes leading to Greystoke.

7 ۶ Leave the village following the road signed 'Johnby and Blencow', and shortly bear right, signed 'Blencow and Carlisle'. Pass Blencow Hall (a a fortified farmhouse) and continue through Little Blencow. After ½ mile (1km) turn right, signed Laithes. Follow this road, with fine views of Cross Fell, through Laithes (Cattellen Hall on the right) and Newton Reigny to return to Penrith. Follow signs for the town centre and return to the car park and the start point of the ride.

Barton Church at Pooley Bridge is an impressive sight

PLACES OF INTEREST

Historic Gloucester Arms in the busy market town of Penrith

Penrith: Gateway to the Northern Lakes, this former capital of Cumbria and now the hub of the Eden Valley is a busy market town with much to offer the visitor. An important site since the Bronze Age, Penrith has seen the Romans on their way to Scotland and experienced many invasions by Border raiders, evident in the intricate defensive street pattern. Richard III had connections with the Castle and the Gloucester Arms and Jacobite Rebels stayed in the George Hotel. William and Dorothy Wordsworth attended a Dame School in the churchyard. The old Elizabethan Grammar School is now incorporated in the new library and Devonshire Arcade and the historic Robinson's School, Middlegate, now houses the Tourist Information Centre.

Brougham Castle: On the banks of the River Eamont lie the ruins of one of the region's strongest castles, built in the 13th century and restored in the 17th by Lady Ann Clifford. An exhibition of Roman tombstones is near by.

Wetheriggs Country Pottery: At this working pottery you may throw your own pot, visit the museum housing a working steam engine or follow the nature trail.

Lowther: The Lakeland Birds of Prey Centre, situated in the walled garden of Lowther Castle, keeps a variety of birds of prey. There are daily flying demonstrations between March and October.

Pooley Bridge: From its location at the northern end of Ullswater, Pooley Bridge offers magnificent views of the Lakeland mountains. Steamer trips are available during the summer months.

WHAT TO LOOK OUT FOR

There are many opportunities to glimpse a wide variety of wild life, particularly red squirrel, roe deer, buzzard, kestrel and sparrow hawks. Look too for fortified farmhouses (halls) at Little Blencow, Laithes, Hutton John and Yanwath and castles at Penrith, Brougham, Lowther and Dacre.

The North-West Lake District

RIDE 40
CUMBRIA
NY125305

This route explores quiet lanes around the fringes of the Lake District before entering the National Park at Waterend. There are excellent views from the smooth round hills of the north, to the rugged, volcanic, central mountains of the Helvellyn and Scafell ranges. Approaching Loweswater there are spectacular views into the heart of the mountains from the solitary Melbreak to Grassmoor, the Buttermere Fells, High Stile range and beyond. There is one steep hill, otherwise the terrain offers surprisingly easy cycling.

INFORMATION

Total Distance
23 miles (37km)

Grade
2

OS Maps
Landranger 1:50,000 sheet 89
(West Cumbria)

Tourist Information
Cockermouth,
tel: 01900 822634

Cycle Shops/Hire
Derwent Cycles, Cockermouth,
tel: 01900 822113;
Track & Trail Mountain Bikes,
Cockermouth,
tel: 01900 827243

Nearest Railway Station
Workington (6 miles/9.5km)

Refreshments
There are several pubs and cafes in Cockermouth. On the route is Grange Country House Hotel at Waterend serving coffee, tea and meals. A good place for lunch is Kirkstile Inn, Loweswater; there are also pubs at Eaglesfield, Dean and Lorton and a village shop at Lorton. The route includes several suitable spots for picnics

The Earl of Mayo's statue, starting point of the ride

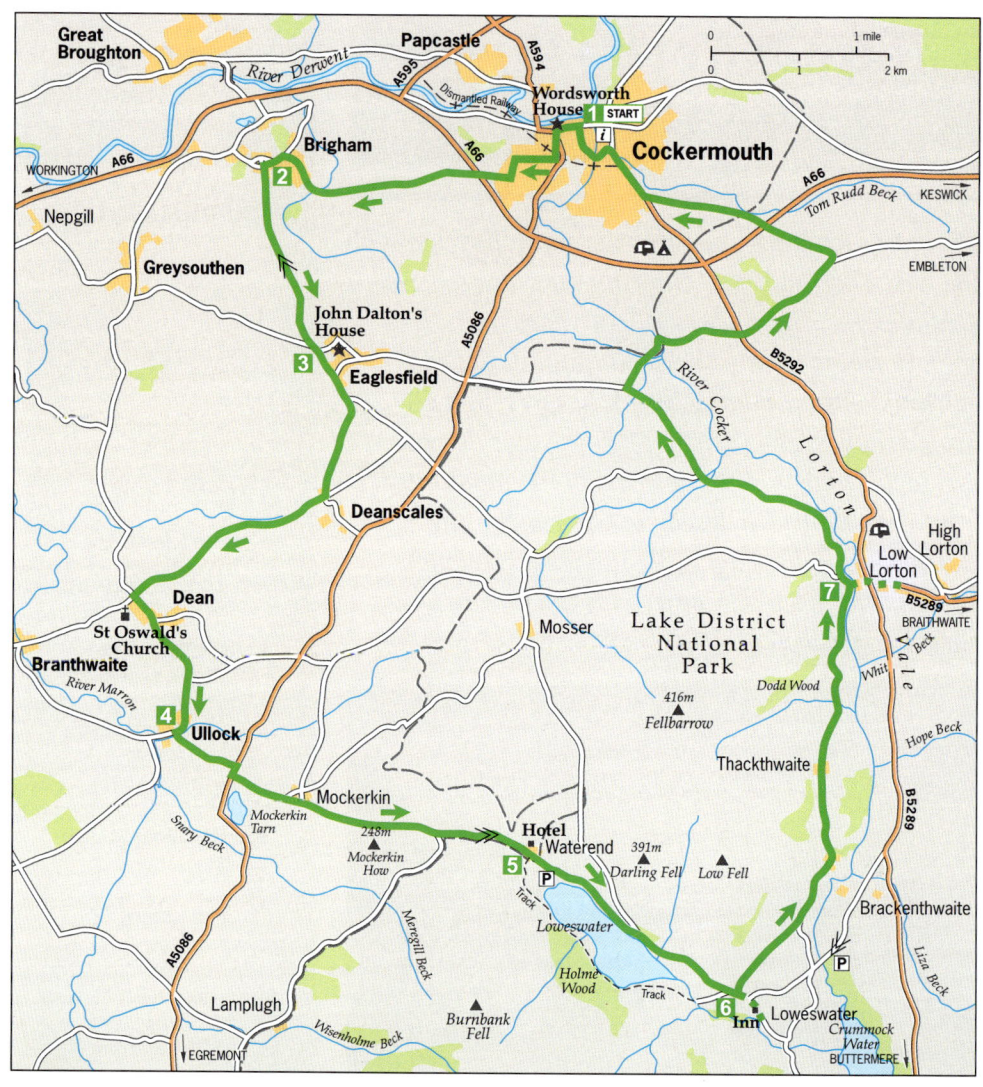

Start

Cockermouth lies just north of the A66, between the A595 and A5086. There are several car parks, including near the Tourist Information Centre, off Market Place. The ride begins in Main Street (parking, toilets) at the statue of the Earl of Mayo.

Directions

1 🚲 Go west along Main Street and turn left opposite Wordsworth House, signed 'A5086 Egremont'. After 110 yards (100m), ignoring the 'no through road' sign, turn right into the continuation of Sullart Street, go uphill to the end, take the footpath straight ahead (not the cycle path on the right) and walk for 55 yards (50m) to emerge at Fitz Road. Turn right here and go down the road for 450 yards (400m); turn left before the stone arch, into Mayo Street. At the T-junction turn right (no signpost). Follow this road

(ignoring 'no through road' sign) go through the gate, cross the A66 with care and follow the Brigham sign to Brigham.

2 🚲 In the centre of Brigham village, at the Apple Tree Inn, take the left fork, signed 'Eaglesfield', and soon turn left into Hotchberry Lane. Climb the hill, enjoying goods views of the Lakeland mountains, and descend into Eaglesfield. To explore the village turn left just past the village sign. John Dalton's House is at the end of this lane. Return to the Deanscales Road to continue on the main route.

3 🚲 Continue on this lane to Deanscales and, as the road bends left, turn right, signed 'Dean/Branthwaite', and proceed to the T-junction. To visit St Oswald's Church continue over the crossroads to see the church facing you. Otherwise, turn left, signed 'Mockerkin/Loweswater'. Shortly after entering Dean turn right, signed 'Ullock/Lamplugh', and soon enter Ullock.

4 🚲 At the end of the green turn left, signposted 'Lamplugh/Loweswater'. Cross the beck after ½ mile (1km), then cross the A5096 with care by turning right then left, signposted 'Mockerkin/Loweswater'. Climb steeply through Mockerkin, pausing at Mockerkin Howe at the top to rest and enjoy the expansive views from the west coast to the moutains in the east and south. Descend for ½ mile (1km), taking the next left turn, signed 'Loweswater Lake'. Continue the steep descent, stopping partway down for views of Loweswater and beyond.

5 🚲 At the bottom of hill pass Grange Country House Hotel. (From this point you may take a track on the right going along the south side of the lake for 2 miles (3km) to Loweswater.) Continue on the main route, passing Waterend Farm and as you ride towards Loweswater see the steep-sided Mellbreak immediately ahead. Shortly arrive at a left turn, signed 'Thackthwaite', and take this route along Lorton Vale. (To visit the hamlet of Loweswater, continue past this junction for 220 yards (200m) and turn right, signed 'Kirkstile Inn'.)

6 🚲 From the junction signed Thackthwaite follow the gently undulating lane for 3½ miles (5.5km), through Thackthwaite to a T-junction where you turn left, signed Rogerscale. (To explore Low Lorton/High Lorton turn right following the signs.)

7 🚲 Continue on this road for 2 miles (3.5km) and at a T-junction turn right, signed 'Embleton/Kerwick'. Continue downhill, crossing the bridge over the River Cocker to a T-junction with the B5292, and continue straight on, signed 'Embleton/Wythop'. In 1 mile (1.5km) turn left, signed 'Cockermouth', and continue, crossing the bridge over the A66. At the next T-junction turn right on to the B5292, descend into Cockermouth and follow the signs back to the town centre.

Lush hills around Loweswater

PLACES OF INTEREST

Cockermouth: This ancient market town standing at the confluence of the rivers Cocker and Derwent has plenty to interest the visitor. At one end of wide tree-lined Main Street is the castle in which Mary, Queen of Scots once took refuge. At the other end is Wordsworth House. This fine Georgian building, birthplace of William and Dorothy Wordsworth, is now owned by the National Trust and open to the public. Next door is the Printing House, a fascinating working museum describing

Eaglesfield: This village was the birthplace of John Dalton, discoverer of the atomic theory, in 1766.

Dean: St Oswald's Church, dating from the 12th century with later chancel and Sanctuary, lies picturesquely on

include the gargoyles, ancient gravestones and the Preaching cross (12th-century or earlier).

Loweswater: One of the Lake District's smaller lakes, Loweswater claims to be the only lake to flow inland, draining into Crummock Water.

Preparing lunch in Wordsworth House, Cockermouth

300 years of printing. Other attractions include Cumberland Toy and Model Museum, the Mineral and Mining Museum, Jennings Brewery (guided tours) and the Lakeland Sheep and Wool Centre, (working demonstrations).

the edge of the village. The interior includes renovated oak pews and pulpits bearing the carved mark of the famous 'mouse man', Robert Thompson. Other features

Sheep graze on the lush surrounding woodland and meadow and the woods, administered by the National Trust, are traversed by many leafy paths.

Blanchland and Slaley Forest

RIDE 41
COUNTY DURHAM/
NORTHUMBERLAND
NY966504

This tour through Hadrian's country takes in the lost-in-time village of Blanchland, pretty Derwent Reservoir and Slaley Forest. It rides the county line between Durham and Northumberland, with views north toward Hadrian's Wall and south to the mining country of Teesdale.

INFORMATION

Total Distance
20½ miles (33km), with
4½ miles (7km) off-road

Grade
2

OS Map
Landranger 1:50,000 sheet 87
(Hexham, Haltwhistle & the
surrounding area)

Tourist Information:
Hexham, tel: 01434 382069;
Stanhope, tel: 01388 527650.

Cycle Shops/Hire
Fewsters, Hexham, tel: 01434 607040;
Creswells, Hexham, tel: 01434
603823; Weardale Mountain Bikes,
Frosterly, near Stanhope,
tel: 01388 528129

Nearest Railway Station
Hexham (10 miles/16km)

Refreshments
Try the White Monk tea rooms in
Blanchland, plus pubs in Blanchland
(including the Lord Crewe Arms at the
start). The Rose and Crown Inn, Slaley
has a beer garden and public
telephone and there is another pub
near Shield Hall. There are picnic sites
at Derwent Reservoir and at various
points along the route

*Derwent Reservoir and Pow Hill
Country Park*

START & ROUTE DIRECTIONS

Start

Blanchland is on the B6306, 6 miles (9.5km) east, off the A68 near Consett, and 10 miles (16km) south of Hexham on the B6306. Park in the free estate car park at the top of the village.

Directions

1 🚲 From the car park, cycle past the Lord Crewe Arms and over the bridge. The B6306 climbs sharply through woodland and into County Durham before levelling out to follow the River Derwent. Just over 1½ miles (2km) after leaving Blanchland, turn left to pass Carricks picnic area and cross the river. Follow the north bank of Derwent Reservoir and pass the gates of the sailing club about 2½ miles (4km) after leaving the B6306. Now the road climbs gently, forking right to Millshield picnic area. Bear left and climb away from the reservoir to a T-junction. Straight ahead is the Passionist Monastery at Minsteracres.

2 🚲 Turn left and, in 660 yards (600m) fork right to Slaley. Descend through a larch and Douglas fir plantation (Kellas Plantation) to Slaley Hall. Continue for ½ mile (1km) to a crossroads and cycle straight ahead to Slaley village and the Rose and Crown Inn. From the inn, cycle through the village to a T-junction and turn right on to the B6306.

3 🚲 Shortly pass the Travellers Rest and 330 yards (300m) later turn left, (Whitley Chapel, Dukesfield). Follow the road to the right at the Dukesfield turn-off and descend past woodland to the Devil's Water.

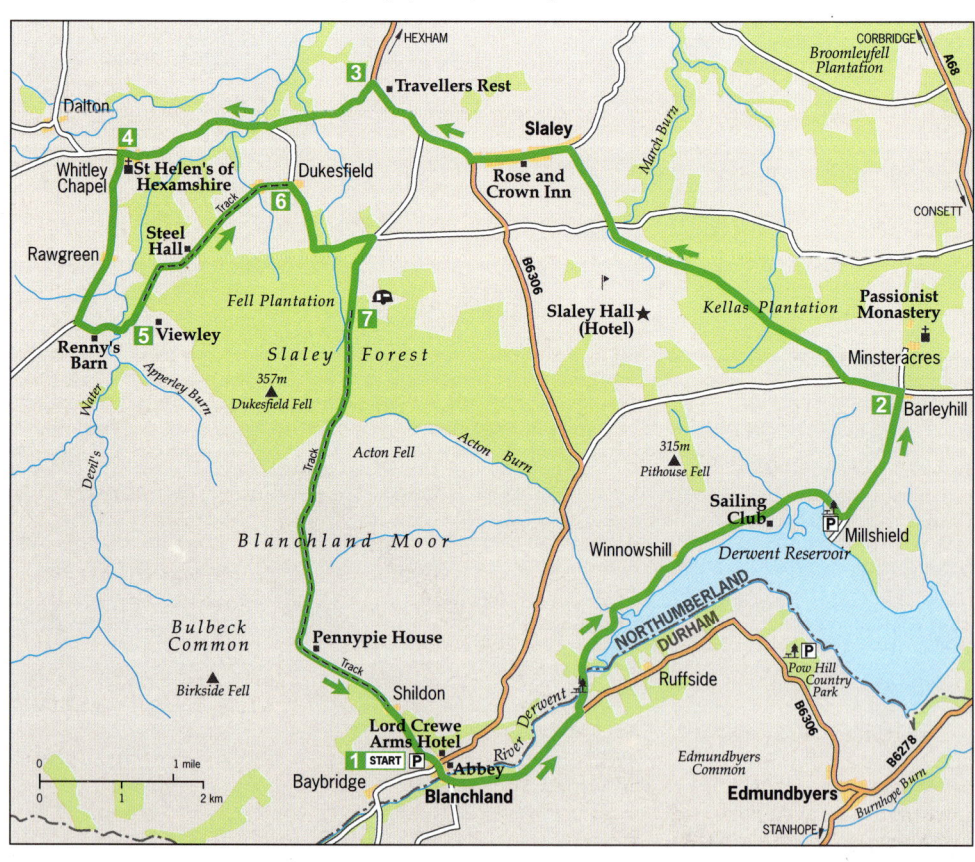

4 Cross the river, ascend and enter Whitley Chapel. Turn left past St Helen's of Hexamshire Church, follow the road for 1½ miles (2.5km) to a signpost for Renny's Barn, Embley and Viewley. Turn left, descend the steep lane to cross the stream. Follow the road as it twists and climbs steeply away from the river, taking the tight left bend towards Viewley, to a small crossroads at the forest edge ½ mile (1km) from Renny's Barn.

5 Go through the small gate ahead into the forest and ride along the wide track until it crests a small rise (110 yards/100m). The track dips and narrows; in about 55 yards (50m) turn off on a small track which veers right, rising slightly. Note: the main track continues straight on, downhill. If you have cycled downhill for more than 160 yards (150m), you have missed the turn-off and must go back. Follow the single track to the right, to meet a narrow gate leading into a field. Go straight through this and follow a rough farm track along a wall. The track swoops below Steel Hall; turn right away from the farmhouse at the track junction. Follow this well-made track for 1 mile (1.5km), veering right to go over a stream and past Dukesfield Farm, to emerge on a quiet road.

6 Turn left and climb gently for a mile (1.5km), to a crossroads. Turn right towards the caravan park and climb steeply for 550 yards

Shaded by trees is the River Derwent at Blanchland

(500m) before the ascent eventually eases to become a gentle climb through Slaley Forest. The tarmac ends 880 yards (800m) from the caravan park.

7 Continue straight on, along a wide, sandy track (bridleway to Shildon). A gate on the forest edge leads you on to moorlands; the wide track climbs gently to a gate in a new fence near the forest edge). Go through the gate and ride along fairly level ground for 1 mile (1.5km) to another gate in a stone wall. From here, descend to a gate by Pennypie House, leading on to a gravel farm track. Cycle down the track, parallel with the stream, past the settlement of Shildon and back to Blanchland car park.

PLACES OF INTEREST

Blanchland: This fascinating estate village grew around a monastery founded in 1175. Blanchland Abbey, a remnant of the monastery, can still be seen in the village. The monastery dormitory is now the Lord Crewe Arms Hotel; the quadrangle of cottages around the square was formerly the monastery forecourt. It is thought that Blanchland, which means White Land, was named after the white habits of the Premonstratensian Monks who settled here in the 12th century. Blanchland is often used as a setting for dramatised Catherine Cookson novels; it also features in *Jude The Obscure*, a film to be released in the UK in late 1996.

Derwent Reservoir: Completed in 1967, this is one of the largest reservoirs in England, and access to the shore is allowed only at the Millshield Picnic Area. The eastern tip, from Carrick's picnic site to Winnowshill, and the far western tip, are nature reserves. The reservoir, stocked with brown and rainbow trout, has 7 miles (10.5km) of bank available to anglers, with a fly-fishing season from May to October. Enquiries about wind-surfing and sailing can be made at the Derwent Reservoir Sailing Club (tel: 01434 675258).

Passionist Monastery: This large country house, built at Minsteracres in the 1800s, is a Catholic retreat. It is not open to the public.

Slaley Hall: The original estate owed its existence to Charles Samuel Hunting, who purchased the lands in the late 1800s. Today Slaley Hall is a modern hotel built around Hunting's country retreat, with 1,000 acres (405ha) of prime Northumbrian forest and moorland. Slaley Hall also has a Japanese garden which is open to the public (there is no charge) and a world-class championship golf course.

Blanchland is a popular setting for films and television drama

The Forth and the Pentland Hills

RIDE 42
LOTHIAN
NT334677

INFORMATION

Total Distance
24 miles (38km)

Grade
3

OS Maps
Landranger 1:50,000 sheet 66
(Edinburgh & Midlothian)

Tourist Information
Dalkeith, tel: 0131 663 2083/660 6818

Cycle Shops/Hire
Dalkeith Bike Shed, Dalkeith,
tel: 0131 654 1170; The New Bike
Shop Tollcross, Edinburgh (hire),
tel. 0131 228 6333

Refreshments
Emmaus Tea Room, Main Street,
Pathhead, open all day. Vogrie
Country Park, cafeteria. The Scottish
Mining Museum, open April to
September. Cavaliere Restaurant, High
Street, Dalkeith. County Restaurant,
High Street, Dalkeith. Continental
Café, Jarnac Court, Dalkeith. Excellent
picnic areas in Vogrie Country Park
and at Crichton Castle. There are
picnic tables at the Scottish Mining
Museum, Newtongrange

The early stages of this ride offer marvellous views of the Forth and Berwick Law. You then proceed across a ford to enjoy the Pentland Hills, and pause in the popular Vogrie Country Park; there is also the opportunity to visit The Scottish Mining Museum. The route includes three short steep sections which are easily walked if preferred.

A cyclist enjoys a shaded ride in Vogrie Country Park

START & ROUTE DIRECTIONS

Start

Dalkeith is just 10 miles (16km) south-east of Edinburgh on the A68, and the starting point of the ride is Dalkeith Country Park at the north-east end of the High Street (A6094) by St. Mary's Church.

Directions

1 🚲 Turn left from the car park following the sign to Whitecraig and Musselburgh (A6094) and at the roundabout, take the second exit towards Thorney Bank Industrial Estate (B6414). Turn left , still on the B6414,

towards Tranent. You will soon be on your first real hill of the ride but it quickly levels out as you reach the cottages and then a junction where you carry straight on. At the next crossroads carry straight on to Cousland (another short hill) and pass through the village of pretty cottages. After 2 miles (3km) turn right at the T-junction (not signed) and follow the road for a further 1 mile (1.5km) to reach the main A6093.

2 🚲 Turn left on to the A6093, then soon right, signposted 'Pathhead (B6367)'. Take the first left, continue for 650 yards (600m) then turn right on

to the B6371. Continue for 3¾ miles (6km) then turn right at a minor road, signed 'Windy Mains'. You really are off the beaten track now as you pass the Saw Mill and then cross the ford at the Salters Burn – there is a bridge if the water is high. (You could also walk the 55 yards/50m up the hill out of the ford.) Look for the pheasant farm on your left and a white dovecot in the distance on your right, with Whitburgh House beyond. At the next junction turn left then almost immediately right for 550 yards (500m) to emerge at a slightly off-set crossroads; go straight on until you reach the A68.

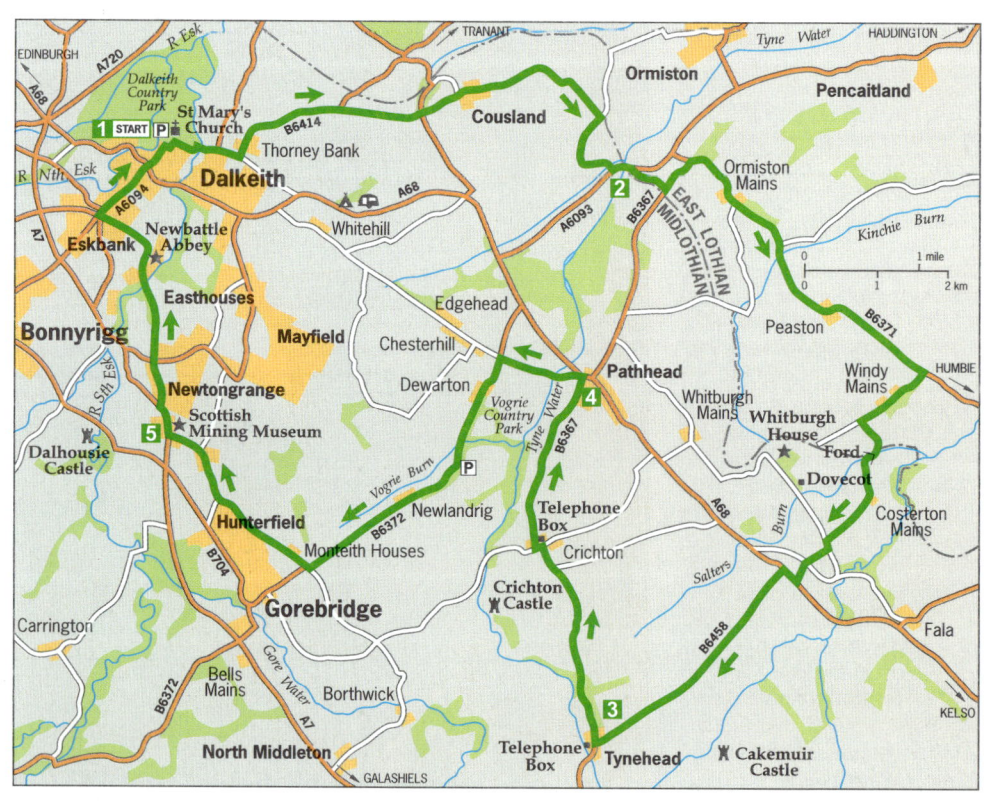

Outside the Scottish Mining Museum in Newtongrange

Turn right and stay on the A68 for 270 yards (250m), then turn left on to the B6458, signed 'Tynehead' (there is a pavement on this section where it is possible to walk your cycle).

3 Continue along the B6458 for 2½ miles (4km) to reach Tynehead where you turn right by the telephone box following the sign to Crichton Castle. At Crichton village turn left and then right at the telephone box, signed 'Pathhead'. (To visit the castle follow the signs from the village.) Continue along the B6367 to Pathhead, where there are shops, the Emmaus Tea Room and a village pub.

4 From Pathhead take the minor road, signed 'Ford and Edgehead' for almost 1 mile (1.5km) before turning

left on to the B6372, 'signed Dewartown, Newlandrig and Gorebridge'. Go through Dewartown to reach Vogrie Country Park, this would be an ideal picnic stop. Carry on for a further 2 miles (3km), turn right and carry straight on following the Newtongrange sign. Turn right at a T-junction after 1 mile (1.5km) and right again at the next T-junction to see The Scottish Mining Museum.

5 From the museum continue downhill and turn right after 330 yards (300m), signed 'Easthouses'. Continue through Newtongrange, going straight on at the crossroads and past Newbattle Abbey before coming to the roundabout at Eskbank Toll where you take the A6094 into Dalkeith. Keep going straight on at each junction to return to Dalkeith Country Park.

Experience a miner's life

Dalkeith Country Park:
Although part of the Duke of Buccleuch's estate, Dalkeith House (not open), dating back 700 years, is no longer a ducal seat. The park has nature trails and forests, walks along the River Esk, a woodland playground considered to be one of the best in Scotland, and Dalkeith Old Wood contains oak trees over 300 years old. Just inside the gateway to the park is St Mary's Church, which was built as the palace chapel. It is open on Saturdays and Sundays from May to September and teas are served in July and August.

Vogrie Country Park: This is a typical 19th-century estate with a formalised park, farmland and woods. A refreshment room and an adventure playground make this an ideal picnic spot all year round.

WHAT TO LOOK OUT FOR

In April and May there is a fine display of spring flowers on many parts of the route, but particularly in Crichton and in the window boxes of Dewartown village. The entrance to Newbattle Abbey has an impressive stone gateway well worth a photograph. The village of Tynehead is the source of the River Tyne that flows right across East Lothian through the county town of Haddington, eventually reaching the sea at Tynemouth by Dunbar. Roe deer, squirrels and many water birds can be seen in Dalkeith Country Park, and the Montagu Bridge, built by Adam in about 1792, is also a feature of the park.

Crichton Castle: Situated on the banks of the Tyne near Crichton village, the 14th- to 16th-century buildings of this Historic Scotland property include a fine Italianate arcade by the Earl of Bothwell. The castle is open from April to September.

The Scottish Mining Museum: This exhibition has been established at the Lady Victoria colliery in Newtongrange. Visitors can experience life in a coal-mining family in this realistic presentation, after being issued with a helmet and token to meet mining regulations! There is also a shop and refreshment room. The museum opens from April to October.

High chairs with a difference in Vogrie Country Park

Lanes and Disused Rail Routes of Renfrewshire

This pleasant route follows two former rail routes and some minor roads to give an extremely quiet, scenic ride through Renfrewshire. This belies the close proximity to the urban conurbations of Paisley and Glasgow, and gives the rider a taste of the Renfrewshire lanes.

RIDE 43
NORTH AYRSHIRE
NS355590

INFORMATION

Total Distance
23 miles (36km), with 14½ miles (23km) off-road

Grade
1–3

OS Maps
Landranger 1:50,000 sheets 63 (Firth of Clyde) and 64 (Glasgow)

Tourist Information
Paisley, tel: 0141 889 0711

Nearest Railway Station
Lochwinnoch (1 mile/1.5km)

Cycle Shops/Hire
Tortoise Cycle Centres, Johnstone, tel: 01505 335551,
Castle Semple Loch Visitor Centre, tel: 01505 842882 (hire)

Quarriers village was home to fortunate 19th-century orphans

Refreshments

There are plenty of facilities along the route. Brewers Fayre restaurant at the A737/A760 junction near Lochwinnoch welcomes families. Pubs in Kilbarchan, Quarriers and Bridge of Weir all welcome children; the Gryffe Inn and Gryffe Arms Hotel, Bridge of Weir, offer a children's menu and play area, respectively. Quarriers village has a coffee shop, and almost anywhere along the route you will find a suitable spot for a picnic

START & ROUTE DIRECTIONS

Start

Lochwinnoch lies at the south-west end of Castle Semple Loch ½ mile (1km) from the A760. Park free at the Castle Semple Visitor Centre car park (toilets available), adjacent to the old rail bridge.

Directions

1 🚲 At the left of the entrance to the car park is a ramp up to the disused rail track (see route information board). Proceed along the track towards the rear of the visitor centre and continue. After about ½ mile (1km), just after coming out of a short cutting, an access path crosses the route (Parkhill Wood). Continue along the track until you gain access to

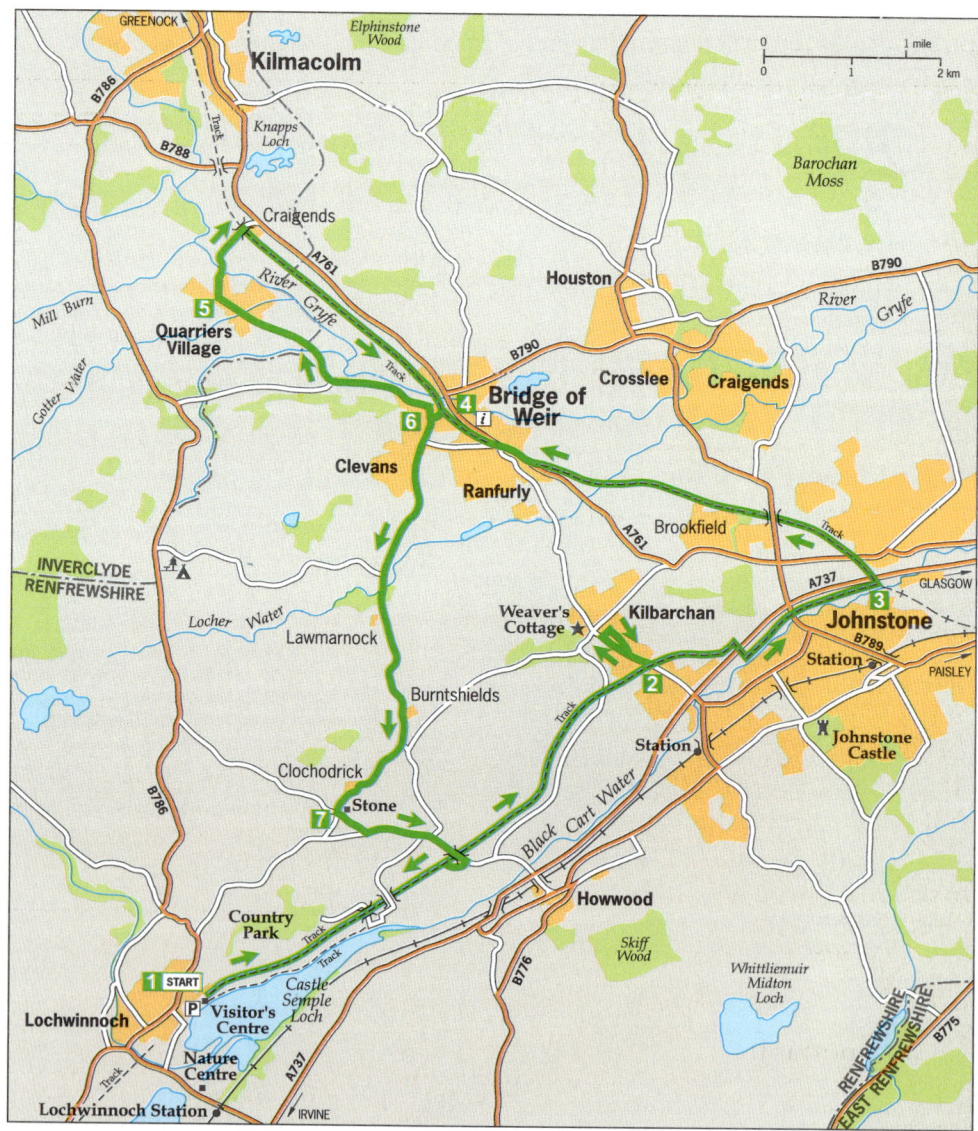

This unusual church can be found in Kilbarchan

Quarriers village. Bear right in 1 mile (1.5km), still following the signs, to shortly enter the village, with the coffee/craft shop on the right.

5 🚲 On leaving Quarriers take the right fork and follow this road to join a track in about ¾ mile (1km). Turn right along the track, passing the rear of Quarriers, and continue to return to Bridge of Weir.

6 🚲 Leave the track by same ramp as before, but this time on the right after crossing the bridge (again look for the builder's sign). Turn left at the road up a steep hill and continue straight across at a crossroads. Continue along this minor road, passing Lawmarnoch farm on your right after a steep hill, then descend to turn right in 1 mile (1.5km) after Lawmarnock road ends and just after a second set of overhead power lines. Continue for 1 mile (1.5km) to Clochodrick Stone.

7 🚲 Turn left here, left at the next junction and continue towards Howwood until you cross the rail track. Rejoin the track with access on your left immediately at the end of the bridge parapet. Turn left on to the track and retrace your route to Castle Semple Visitor Centre and car park. A variation at 2 miles (3km) is to take the track on your left opposite Parkhill Wood and return to the start along the shoreline.

Kilbarchan, on the left after 5 miles (8km).

2 🚲 Turn left at a bridge over the B787, go down a ramp (there is a barrier at the bottom) and turn left again and follow this road to the Square and the Weaver's Cottage. Return, passing the steeple, to the bridge where you left the track and then turn left uphill, signed 'no through road', to rejoin the track. Continue towards Johnstone, where the rail track crosses over the A737 Johnstone bypass.

3 🚲 Once across, turn left (still on the track) and in about ¾ mile (1km) cross over Barrochan Road (the traffic is controlled by pedestrian/cycle lights). Continue in the same direction (A737 on the left) to reach a tarmac surface and, a few yards further on, come to the junction of the rail track to Greenock. At this point arrows are marked on the surface of the track – Paisley is straight ahead. On the left is a concrete post with a route map.

4 🚲 Continue for 4 miles (7km) towards the Bridge of Weir until you come to a bridge over the River Gryfe (Bridge of Weir). Do not cross the bridge, but leave the track by a ramp on your left. Ahead is the gable of a building 'J Kerr – Builders'. Make for this and in a few yards/metres reach a road. Turn right, then left, following signs for

PLACES OF INTEREST

Lochwinnnoch: Originally a craft-based town, Lochwinnoch's Johnstone company supplied all the furniture for the great Cunard liners of the past, including the *Queen Mary, Lusitania, Titanic* and others. Today the town is recognised more for its watersports centre and the adjacent RSPB nature reserve on Castle Semple Loch. The watersports centre offers various activities, including sailing and canoeing, plus a small display area inside.

Kilbarchan: This town is renowned for its Weaver's Cottage, built in 1723. The last remaining link with the village's weaving heritage, it is looked after by the National Trust for Scotland. Across the square from the cottage is the steeple, and here, in a niche, is a statue of Habbie Simpson (1550–1620), piper of Kilbarchan.

Quarriers Village: This late-19th century settlement was built for orphans by William Quarrier who, instead of building institutional-type buildings, constructed stone two-storey houses to give the orphans as near as possible the chance to live in a house. Quarriers is now a conservation village, but some of the buildings are privately owned. The village also has a craft centre and tea room.

Clochodrick Stone: Lying in a grassy field north-west of Howwood, deposited there during the Ice Age about 18,000 years ago, this large volcanic rock was used by Druids as a place of judgement. It is claimed to be the burial site of Hael, Monarch of Strathclyde, who defeated the pagans at a battle fought near Carlisle which ended paganism in Scotland. An plaque by the stone gives full historical details.

Sunset over the evocative castle ruins beside Lochwinnoch

Kinross and Loch Leven

This route, using mainly B-roads, travels through gentle scenery in an area dominated by the Lomond Hills. Loch Leven itself is a vast nature reserve, while the whole area is deeply involved in conservation and preservation. The route highlights all these facets, including the area's links with Scottish history, and has plenty to offer so take your time and enjoy the ride.

RIDE 44
PERTHSHIRE & KINROSS
NO125018

INFORMATION

Total Distance
18 miles (29km)

Grade
1/2

OS Maps
Landranger 1:50,000 sheet 58
(Perth to Alloa)

Tourist Information
Service Area, junction 6, M90,
tel: 01577 863680

Cycle Shops/Hire
Loch Leven Cycle Tours, Kinross,
tel: 01577 850213

Refreshments
Kinross has a wide selection of hotels, pubs and cafés. There is pub food at Scotlandwell, Kinnesswood and at the Old Toll House at Wester Balgedie. All welcome children. Also Granada motorway services and Vane Farm (RSPB), with facilities for the disabled. There are picnic areas at Kirkgate Park, Gairney Bridge and Scotlandwell

Visitors cannot help but wonder at the view over Loch Leven

START & ROUTE DIRECTIONS

Start

Kinross lies on the west shore of Loch Leven, 12 miles (19km) south of Perth, just east of junction 6 of the M90. The main car park (free and with toilets adjacent) is in Kirkgate Park along the road leading to the ferry for Castle Island. An alternative parking area is near the pier, with a path link to the Kirkgate Park area.

Directions

1️⃣ 🚲 From Kirkgate Park proceed to the T-junction with the B996, turn left and continue, passing Loch Leven Mill and Shop on the left as you leave Kinross. Continue along the B996, with views over the loch to Bishops Hill and Benarty Hill ahead, to turn left in about 3 miles (5km) at Gairneybridge on to the B9097.

Exploring the grounds of Loch Leven Castle

2️⃣ 🚲 Proceed to Vane Farm Nature Centre 2 miles (3km) further on. Continue on the B9097, passing a picnic area and toilets on your left in

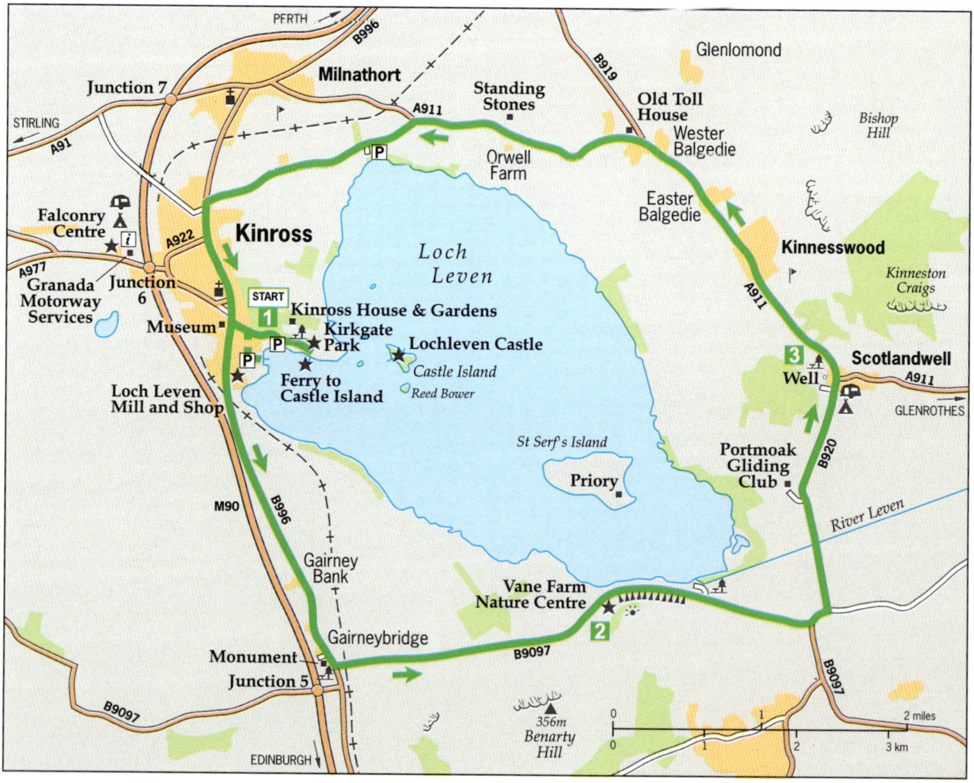

Lovingly manicured lawns at Kinross House

3 🚲 Fork left on to the A911, passing through Kinnesswood and Easter and Wester Balgedie, then fork left again at the Old Toll House, with the Inn on the right and Loch Leven Chalets on the left. Continue past Orwell Farm and turn left in 2 miles (3km) on to a minor road, signed 'Kinross'. Shortly after, in a small wood, is access to the loch on the left. Carry on to Kinross and turn left on to the B996. Continue through Kinross, passing the Green Hotel and Sands supermarket on the right to turn left for Loch Leven Castle and the car park at Kirkgate Park.

about 1 mile (1.5km), to turn left after 1 mile (1.5km) on to the B920, then turn left again to cross the River Leven, passing the Portmoak airfield on the left to eventually reach the village of Scotlandwell in 2 miles (3km).

Gardens in full bloom in front of Kinross House

PLACES OF INTEREST

Service Area Junction 6, M90: An unusual setting within a scenic tour, but no less interesting, the service area houses an information office, craft centre, and garden centre. The Queen of Scots Falconry and Conservation Centre, recently reopened under new ownership, will feature flying displays (weather permitting).

Kinross: The main attraction here is Kinross House, built between 1679 and 1693 by Sir William Bruce. The house is not open to the public, but the beautiful formal gardens can be visited from May to September. Bruce was the architect of the Palace of Holyrood House in Edinburgh. Although a quiet town, Kinross has plenty to offer the visitor, including a museum, bowling, tennis and a new leisure centre with swimming pool, 'moving floor' squash courts and a health suite. Fishing from boats in the loch is permitted, but limited for conservation. There is also a 17th-century tollbooth with decoration by Robert Adam. The Findlay-Clark complex includes a falconry centre and craft shop. Kinross also has possibly Scotland's biggest indoor market on Sundays.

Kirkgate Park: With picnic areas, putting, crazy golf and trampolines, this is the starting point for the Castle Island Ferry, which takes about 5 minutes to reach the island. Mary, Queen of Scots was imprisoned in the 15th-century castle here before her escape in 1568.

Vane Farm: This is the base for the Loch Leven Nature Reserve, one of the RSPB's major locations in Scotland. The loch attracts many species of bird, some stopping here to rest after long migratory flights. The picnic area on the left just past Vane Farm gives access to the shore and, at one end, the start of the River Leven Cut – a manmade channel dug in 1828 to lower the loch to reclaim land for farming. Shortly after joining the B920 cross this channel and you will see how straight it is. From the same vantage point look ahead to see gliders in the thermals around Kinneston Craigs/Bishop Hill. The airfield is on your left at Portmoak and you are welcome to go in and watch. Note: Stay

The well at Scotlandwell is thought to have healing powers

on the road to the clubhouse and restaurant (which you can use if quiet). Enquire at the clubhouse where you can watch; the gliders are silent and they land to the left of the clubhouse. These same hills are frequented by hang gliders, and the Scottish Aeromodellers Society use Bishop Hill.

Scotlandwell: The Red Friars founded a hospice here in 1250, and there is also evidence to suggest that Roman legions en route between Fife and Perthshire rested at the well. Robert the Bruce drank from the well, and its waters were also supposed to cure leprosy. There is a picnic and play area adjacent.

Kinnesswood: Birthplace of Michael Bruce, the gentle poet of Loch Leven, his parents' cottage is now a small museum. About 300 years ago the villagers manufactured vellum, probably for use by the monks of St Serf's island.

WHAT TO LOOK OUT FOR

At Gairneybridge is a large monument erected in 1883 to commemorate the first Succession Church and the right of its members to appoint their own minister. Birdlife abounds, especially at and around Vane Farm, with species including winter geese such as pink foot and grey leg. Also watch for most species of duck, grebes, muted whooper swans, greenshank and buzzards. Passing Orwell farm look to your right to see two standing stones (no access), one of which marked burial deposits from 2000BC.

Callander and Loch Lubnaig: In the Footsteps of Rob Roy

This route, following the disused rail track on the shore of Loch Lubnaig, travels through some fine scenery. A totally circular route is not recommended because of the area's popularity; the A84 can be busy at weekends in July and August. However, the repeated section of track (Strathyre to Barrier) has so much to offer scenically. The track is marked all along by white posts and arrowheads, with blue letters/numbers.

RIDE 45
STIRLING
NN624079

INFORMATION

Total Distance
28 miles (45km), with 16 miles (26km) off-road

Grade
1–3

OS Map
Landranger 1:50,000 sheet 57 (Stirling and the Trossachs)

Tourist Information
Callander, tel: 01877 330342

Cycle Shops/Hire
Wheels, Callander (hire), tel: 01877 331100

Spectacular scenery surrounds Loch Lubnaig

Refreshments
Callander has a full range of catering establishments. Pub meals are available at Lade Inn, Kilmahog, Strathyre and the Kingshouse Hotel (north of Strathyre); also a coffee shop at Kingshouse craft shop and teas at Stronvar House near Balquhidder. Food also available at Kilmahog and Trossachs woollen mills. There are ample picnic spots all along the route, especially on Loch Lubnaig

Start

Located some 15 miles (24km) north-west of Stirling at the junction of the A84 and A81, Callander lies on the banks of the River Teith. There are two large pay-and-display car parks with toilets; the one on the riverside at the western end of the town is adjacent to the rail track used on this ride. Drive through to the section near the children's play area.

trees in about 220 yards (200m), where it joins the rail track. Immediately ahead is a white post, signed 'Strathyre 9 miles', and an arrowhead pointing left. To the right of the post is an original semaphore rail signal marking the start if you come off the A84. Continue until you reach the A821, turn right towards Kilmahog, then left on the A84, signed 'Crianlarich'. Continue for about 1 mile (1.5km) until you reach a

after the falls or retrace your steps to the entry point. Continue towards Loch Lubnaig to turn left shortly at a Strathyre Forest Holiday Camps sign (Forestry Commission), crossing the River Leny.

2 🚲 Turn immediately right, go around a barrier and rejoin the track (do not continue along a surfaced road, signed 'no through road'). In about 1½ miles (2.5km) cross the Stank Burn and continue along the

This redundant church in Callander houses the Rob Roy and Trossachs Visitor Centre

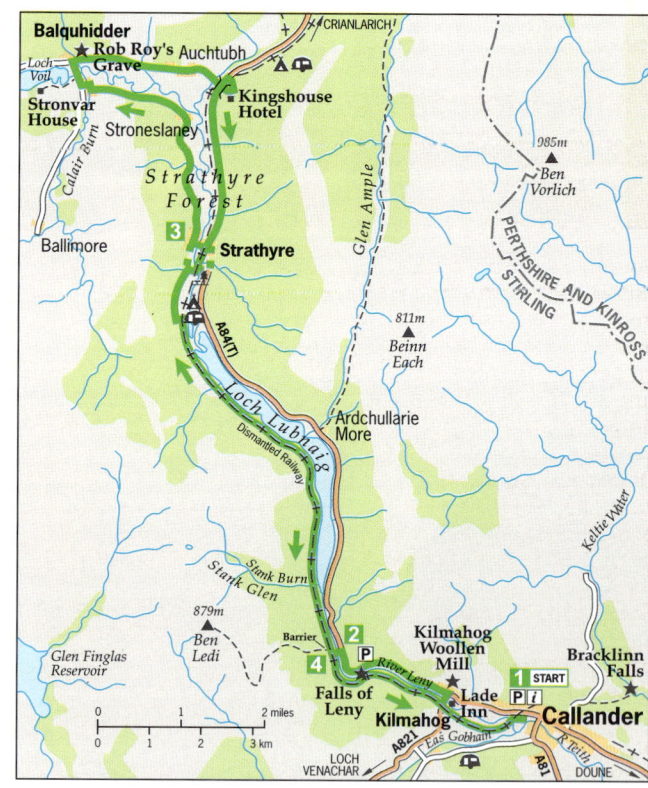

Directions

1 🚲 At the car park look towards the main road to see a log cabin and a path in front of it leading from the parking area. Follow this path, running roughly parallel to the road and into some

car park sign, dismount and go down a path to the Falls of Leny. Either continue along the path to rejoin the road

track close to the shore. At the bend in the loch look across towards the gap in the hills to see Glen Ample.

Continue ahead for 5 miles (8km), leave the track and go up a twisting waymarked path to the left for about 550 yards (500m) to join an unsurfaced forest road; continue to the right. The road eventually becomes surfaced. On reaching a few single-storey houses, follow the waymark signs to the right, passing between the gables of the last two houses to rejoin the track and arrive at Strathyre. You can leave the track following the signs to the picnic area/toilets and forest information. Continue along the main street, then turn left and right on a minor road, signed 'Stroneslaney'. If you do not wish to visit Strathyre, do not take the path between the houses. Instead, continue along the minor road and go straight on at a junction, signposted 'Stroneslaney'.

③ 🚴 In 3 miles (5km) turn right, over a hump-backed bridge, and follow the road around to the left to shortly turn right. Cross another arched bridge, passing an unsurfaced road to the left leading to Stronvar House, and enter Balquhidder. Turn right at the junction in the village and continue to the Kingshouse Hotel, going under the A84 and bearing left to join the carriageway above. Continue to Strathyre, where you have a choice: go to the south end of the village and turn right into a picnic site (toilets) to rejoin the track following waymarkers; or, turn right at

Rob Roy's grave at Balquhidder is popular with visitors

the crest of the hill entering the village, and turn left at a T-junction (signed 'Stoneslaney' to right). Continue left to reach some houses and the track on the left. Follow waymarked signs to Callander; after about 1 mile (1.5km) go down a way-marked path on the left to rejoin the track and continue alongside the loch.

④ 🚴 After a barrier over the track, continue across the road (bridge on left) to go along a track, with the River Leny on the left, crossing the A821 in about 2 miles (3km). Carry on for 1 mile (1.5km), then turn right into the path back to the car park.

PLACES OF INTEREST

Callander: Gateway to the Highlands, Callander is one of Scotland's most popular holiday resorts, and an excellent touring base for visiting the Trossachs. The town offers a wealth of activities, including bowling, fishing, cycling, tennis and golf, as well as walks and trails. The town's early history involves the Celtic St Kessog, and his former church building now houses the Rob Roy and Trossachs Visitor Centre, a fascinating presentation of the area and its notorious outlaw and folk hero 'Rob Roy' Macgregor. Other notable attractions in Callander include Bracklinn Falls, the dramatic Falls of Leny, the Queen Elizabeth Country Park and Ben Ledi, the mountain dominating the town.

Kilmahog: Famous for its woollen mills, this is where the River Leny reaches the Lowlands. A walkway and cycle path follows the river and the shore of Loch Lubnaig to the village of Strathyre.

Strathyre: This pleasant little village, overlooked by mountains on both sides, is popular with holidaymakers attracted by its location and its hills and forest walks.

Balquhidder: This tiny hamlet resting in a secluded glen alongside its neighbour Kingshouse, is famed as the resting place of Rob Roy, who is buried, along with his wife and two sons, in the kirkyard.

Ben Ledi looms large over Loch Lubnaig

WHAT TO LOOK OUT FOR

The route offers magnificent views throughout and the Trossachs area abounds with a great diversity of wildlife, much of it in the huge Queen Elizabeth Country Park, including deer, wildcats and foxes. If you are lucky you may glimpse a bird of prey, perhaps a peregrine falcon. The area also attracts many migrants from Africa.

Howe of the Mearns

This figure-of-eight route is a little longer than other routes, but it can be ridden as two separate rides of almost equal length. The area is at the foot of the Grampian Highlands and naturally involves some hills. However, almost half the route is on, or to the south of, the B966, which is a reasonably flat area, and there are no main roads on this route.

RIDE 46
ABERDEENSHIRE/ANGUS
NO650734

INFORMATION

Total distance
33 miles (54km), with 2 miles (3km)
off-road

Grade
2

OS Maps
Landranger 1:50,000 sheets 44
(Ballater) and 45 (Stonehaven)

Tourist Information
Arbroath, tel: 01241 872609;
Banchory, tel: 01330 822000

Cycle Shops/Hire
None on route

Nearest Railway Station
Montrose (12 miles/19km)

Refreshments
There are several cafés and hotels in
Edzell, and riverside picnic areas. At
Fettercairn are the Tea Rooms and the
Ramsay Arms Hotel with Victorian tea
room and garden (children welcome).
At the foot of the Cairn o' Mount is the
Clatterin' Brig Restaurant. There are
various other picnic sites, including
beside the cemetery in Auchenblae
(toilets), in Drumtochty Glen Forestry
Commission car park and at Fasque

*Edzell Castle features a beautiful
walled garden*

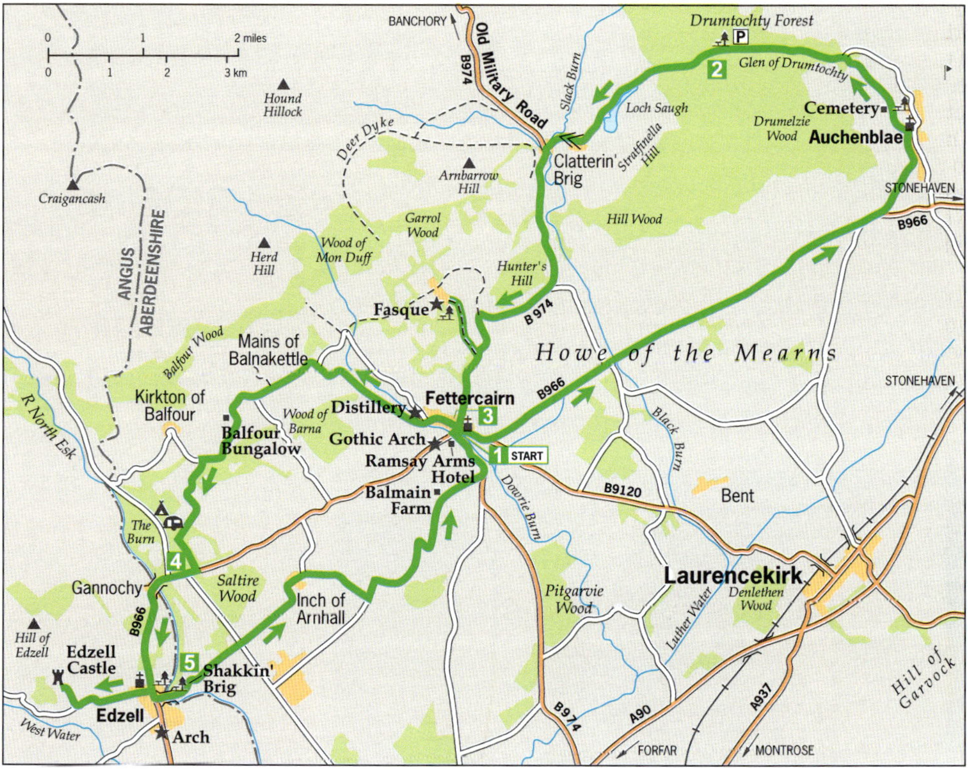

Map labels

BANCHORY
Old Military Road
B974
Slack Burn
Drumtochty Forest
Glen of Drumtochty
2
Loch Saugh
Strathfinella Hill
Clatterin' Brig
Drumelzie Wood
Cemetery
Auchenblae
STONEHAVEN
B966
Hound Hillock
Deer Dyke
Arnbarrow Hill
Garrol Wood
Hill Wood
Craigancash
ANGUS
ABERDEENSHIRE
Herd Hill
Wood of Mon Duff
Hunter's Hill
Fasque
B974
Howe of the Mearns
STONEHAVEN
Balfour Wood
Mains of Balnakettle
Kirkton of Balfour
Wood of Barna
Distillery
Fettercairn
3
B966
R North Esk
Balfour Bungalow
Gothic Arch
Ramsay Arms Hotel
1 START
Dovrie Burn
Black Burn
Balmain Farm
B9120
Bent
The Burn
4
Saltire Wood
Inch of Arnhall
Pitgarvie Wood
Lather Water
Denlethen Wood
Laurencekirk
Gannochy
Hill of Edzell
Edzell Castle
5
Shakkin' Brig
B966
Edzell
Arch
West Water
B974
A90
A937
Hill of Garvock
FORFAR
MONTROSE

Scale: 0 — 1 — 2 miles / 0 — 1 — 2 — 3 km

START & ROUTE DIRECTIONS

Start

The village of Fettercairn is 12 miles (19km) north of Montrose, at the junction of the B966 and the B974. Free parking is available in the central square around the Market Cross.

Directions

1 🚴 Leave Fettercairn on the B966, signed 'Auckenblae and Stonehaven' and after 5½ miles (9km) turn left, signposted 'Auchenblae'; pause to read the information board in the church yard above Auchenblae. Turn left on a lane, signposted

'Cemetery', then keep straight on at the next junction, signed 'Forest Walk', to Drumtochty Glen Forestry Commission car park.

2 🚴 Return to the road and continue through

Drumtochty Glen, pausing after 100 yards (100m) to admire the large Sitka spruce tree on the left, with an information board. Continue

Fasque House, home of the Gladstone family

by Loch Saugh to Clatterin' Brig to cross the ford on either of the two bridges. Turn left on to the B974 towards Fettercairn and continue for 3 miles (5km)then turn right on to the unsurfaced road into the Fasque estate. Return to the public road and turn right to Fettercairn.

3 🚲 Leave Fettercairn square, following the sign to the 'Distillery Visitor Centre'. Continue along the lane which turns left at Mains of Balnakettle farm. Again continue straight on, keep left at the entrance to Mains of Balfour farm, turn left at Balfour Bungalow, and left again at the next junction (where the right turn is to Kirkton of Balfour). Then keep straight on and turn right at the 'stop' sign on the B966 towards Edzell.

4 🚲 Stop just before Gannocky Bridge over the River North Esk. Go through the door in the wall on your right by the sign 'The London Goodenough Trust The Burn House' on to the permissive walk to see the river and gorge (lock your bike). Continue on the B966 to the edge of Edzell, turn right, signed 'Edzell Castle' and after 1 mile (1.5km) right again to the castle.

Return to the B966 and turn right along Edzell's main street. Turn sharp left between the post office and the petrol station, and go very slowly down the steep hill to the river and picnic area at Shakkin' Brig. Beware the steep hill, and people walking and children playing on this rough road.

5 🚲 From the picnic area walk on Skakkin' Brig over the River North Esk. At the end of the bridge turn right on the path to reach a surfaced road at the first house. After ½ mile (1km) continue straight ahead on the unsurfaced road for a further ½ mile (1km), perhaps dismounting and walking any sections with loose stone and soft sand. Continue straight across the road into the sur-faced lane to Inch of Armhall where you keep straight on at the crossroads; in 220 yards (200m) keep right at the Residential Centre. After 1 mile (1.5km) turn left, and soon left again. Continue on the surfaced lane, turning sharp right and sharp left. At Dalmain Farm follow the right of way through the farm buildings and turn left at the B974 back to Fettercairn.

Fettercairn features a splendid stone archway

PLACES OF INTEREST

Fettercairn: This town is noted for its distillery, where visitors can experience an audio-visual presentation of the history of life in the Mearns: farming, barley growing and making Scotch whisky. Be sure to accept a dram of Old Fettercairn Single Malt as a souvenir of your visit.
Also of note here is the Gothic Arch that commemorates the visit of Queen Victoria and Prince Albert in September 1861. Around the central square the houses are built of red sandstone. The Market Cross, in the middle of the square, has a sundial dated 1670, but out of the west side of the cross is a notch measuring 37½ inches (95.25cm) – an old Scottish 'ell' measure. See the information board on the building close to the cross. For the children there is a small park with swings on the B974 going south.

Drumtochty Glen: Also known as Strath Finella, this popular beauty spot has picnic tables and toilets, and a fairly steep climb from the car park leads to the Drumtochty Forest cycling route.

Fasque: Fasque House, former castle home to William Gladstone, four times Prime Minister, is one of the finest examples of a Victorian stately home. Built in 1809 and still used by his descendants, it retains its original appearance, with many rooms open to the public (May to September). In front of the House red deer roam in the park, whilst behind

WHAT TO LOOK OUT FOR

The geographical Highland Line traverses Scotland from Helensburgh in the west to Stonehaven in the east. At this geological fault the Central Lowlands meet the Highlands at a conspicuous line of hills in view for most of the ride. The broad valley of Strathmore continues north-east into the Howe of the Mearns, an area of fertile farmland separated from the sea by the Garnock Hills on one side, with the Highlands on the other. Crops include barley and daffodils. Although the route goes to Clatterin' Brig, it does not follow the Old Military Road northwards over the Cairn o' Mount – the only classified road in the country to climb 1,000 feet (300m) in 2 miles (3km).

the hills rise dramatically; there is also a picnic site.

Gannocky Bridge: The River North Esk, flowing through a picturesque rocky and wooded gorge, forms the boundary between Aberdeenshire and Angus. Salmon can sometimes be seen leaping on their way to their spawning grounds. Care should be taken on the riverside walk.

Edzell: Like Fettercairn, Edzell also has a stone arch over the

road. Situated at the southern end of the wide main street, it was erected in 1887 in memory of the 13th Earl of Dalhousie. Just west of this little inland resort stands Edzell Castle and Garden. In the care of Historic Scotland, it is open all year, with restricted opening in winter. A 16th-century tower still stands, but the most notable feature is the walled garden, laid out in 1604.

Edzell's stone arch is a little less prominent than Fettercairn's

INDEX

(numbers refer to cycle routes)

ACKNOWLEDGEMENTS

The Automobile Assoication would like to thank the following photographers and libraries for their assistance in the preparation of this book.

S L DAY 43, 44
J FENNA 121, 122, 123, 124
D HANNINGTON 16
D HEARN 85, 87b
H LINCOLN 94, 114
NATURE PHOTOGRAPHERS LTD 71b (P R Sterry)
I ROBINSON 19, 20, 23a, 24
WEALD & DOWNLAND MUSEUM 63

The remaining pictures are held in the Association's own library (AA PHOTO LIBRARY) with contributions from:
M ADLEMAN 73, 84; M ALEXANDER 179a; M ALLWOOD-COPPIN 141; A BAKER 47b, 48, 100; P BAKER 15, 25, 27b, 37, 40, 64, 115a; J BEAZLEY 175, 176, 187a, 187b; M BIRKITT 9, 11, 81, 101, 103a, 104, 109, 116; J BLANDFORD 211b; I BURGUM 52, 142, 143a, 143b; J CARNIE 189, D CORRANCE 179b; P DAVIES 96; S L DAY 5, 36, 77, 147b, 190, 191; M DIGGIN 8b; R EAMES 163b; D FORSS 41, 55, 57, 68, 95; S GREGORY 159a, 160; T GRIFFITHS 145, 146, 147a, 148; R HAYMAN 29, 31, 32; A J HOPKINS 6, 59, 71a, 72, 119a; D JACKSON 39; C JONES 7, 125, 127, 128, 129, 130, 131a, 131b, 132; S KING 167; A LAWSON 23b; C LEES 169; S & O MATHEWS 58, 61, 69, 78, 92, 93, 97, 99, 161, 163a, 173; C MELLOR 112; J MILLER 91; C MOLYNEUX 113; J MORRISON 140, 149, 151, 152, 155, 156, 157, 164; R MOSS 10, 13, 17; R NEWTON 138, 144, 153, 159b; K PATERSON 177, 180, 184, 185, 186, 193, 194, 195, 196; N RAY 30, 46, 47a; P SHARPE 165, 168, 171; M SHORT 80; A SOUTER 8a, 67; R SURMAN 172; A TRYNOR 117, 120, 133; W VOYSEY 27a, 28, 34, 35a, 35b, 45, 53, 60, 75, 76, 89; R WEIR 188; J WELSH 87a, 88, 105, 107, 108, 135a, 136; L WHITWAM 115b, 119b; H WILLIAMS 21, 33, 49, 50, 51, 65, 83, 135b